RACING TRANSLINGUALISM IN COMPOSITION

RACING TRANSLINGUALISM IN COMPOSITION

Toward a Race-Conscious Translingualism

EDITED BY
TOM DO AND KAREN ROWAN

UTAH STATE UNIVERSITY PRESS
Logan

© 2022 by University Press of Colorado

Published by Utah State University Press
An imprint of University Press of Colorado
245 Century Circle, Suite 202
Louisville, Colorado 80027

All rights reserved

 The University Press of Colorado is a proud member of the Association of University Presses.

The University Press of Colorado is a cooperative publishing enterprise supported, in part, by Adams State University, Colorado State University, Fort Lewis College, Metropolitan State University of Denver, University of Alaska Fairbanks, University of Colorado, University of Denver, University of Northern Colorado, University of Wyoming, Utah State University, and Western Colorado University.

ISBN: 978-1-64642-209-8 (paperback)
ISBN: 978-1-64642-210-4 (ebook)
https://doi.org/10.7330/9781646422104

Library of Congress Cataloging-in-Publication Data

Names: Do, Tom, editor. | Rowan, Karen, editor.
Title: Racing translingualism in composition : toward a race-conscious translingualism / edited by Tom Do and Karen Rowan.
Description: Logan : Utah State University Press, [2022] | Includes bibliographical references and index.
Identifiers: LCCN 2022017918 (print) | LCCN 2022017919 (ebook) | ISBN 9781646422098 (paperback) | ISBN 9781646422104 (ebook)
Subjects: LCSH: English language—Rhetoric—Study and teaching (Higher)—United States. | English language—Composition and exercises—Study and teaching (Higher)—United States. | Multilingual education—United States. | Multilingualism—Study and teaching (Higher) | Anti-racism—Study and teaching (Higher) | Critical race theory. | Critical pedagogy. | Academic writing. | Racism in language. | BISAC: LANGUAGE ARTS & DISCIPLINES / Writing / Composition | SOCIAL SCIENCE / Race & Ethnic Relations
Classification: LCC PE1405.U6 R33 2022 (print) | LCC PE1405.U6 (ebook) | DDC 808.042071173—dc23/eng/20220520
LC record available at https://lccn.loc.gov/2022017918
LC ebook record available at https://lccn.loc.gov/2022017919

Cover illustration © korkeng/Shutterstock.

CONTENTS

Introduction: Racing Translingualism in Composition: Toward a Race-Conscious Translingualism
Tom Do and Karen Rowan 3

PART I: PROBLEMATIZING TRANSLINGUALISM IN COMPOSITION

1 Rearticulating Translingualism: The Translingual Racial Project, Colorblindness, and Race Consciousness
   Karen Rowan 17

2 Averting Colorblind Translingualism
   Rachael Shapiro and Missy Watson 35

3 English as Past and Present Imperialism: A Translingual Narrative on Chicanx Language and Identity in the US-Mexico Borderlands
   Aja Martinez 56

4 Embodying Culture and Identities in Social Practices: Toward a Race-Conscious Translingual Approach
   Tom Do 67

5 Perpetually Foreign, Perpetually Deficient, and Perpetually Privileged: Exposing Microaggressions and Challenging Whiteness
   Bethany Davila 86

PART II: TOWARD A RACE-CONSCIOUS, ANTI-RACIST TRANSLINGUALISM

6 "We Will Know Our Heroes and Our Culture": Revisiting the Five Demands at the City University of New York toward Building Critical Transliteracies Ecologies
   Lindsey Albracht 105

7   Toward a Decolonial Translingual Pedagogy for
    Black Immigrant Students
    Esther Milu   123

8   Multilingual Speaker-Writers' Co-stories as Part of a Race-
    Conscious Translingual Practice
    Yasmine Romero   143

9   "The Alternative Is Sort of an Endless Multiplicity":
    Narrative and Negotiating the Translingual
    Stephanie Mosher   169

10 Segregated Space and Translingual Pedagogy
    Jaclyn Hilberg   196

11 The Raciolinguistics of Translingual Literacies
    Steven Alvarez   213

12 Participatory Research, Home Language, and
    Race-Conscious Translingualism
    Shawanda Stewart and Brian Stone   226

PART III: RESPONSES

Afterword: Rewriting Racing Translingualism:
Difference, Labor, Opacity
    Bruce Horner   245

An Afterword: Some Thoughts
    Victor Villanueva   254

Index   261
About the Contributors   267

RACING TRANSLINGUALISM IN COMPOSITION

Introduction
RACING TRANSLINGUALISM IN COMPOSITION
Toward a Race-Conscious Translingualism

Tom Do and Karen Rowan

In 2020, the United States experienced unprecedented changes and sociopolitical upheavals. In the midst of a global pandemic, scores of protesters throughout the US marched to the streets to demand racial justice and an end to the perpetual racism, violence, and murder of Black bodies. The murders of George Floyd, Breonna Taylor, Ahmaud Arbery, Tony McDade, and countless others prompted the late John Lewis (2020) to note in a *New York Times* opinion essay that "Emmitt Till was my George Floyd. He was my Rayshard Brooks, Sandra Bland and Breonna Taylor." The parallels Lewis drew between Emmitt Till and George Floyd as unabashed displays of White racism underscore the underlying racism of these murders, which rocked the nation—albeit momentarily—of its colorblindness and revealed the systemic racism that continues to plague all levels of our institutions. The sociopolitical upheavals were also a response to a White House administration that not only failed dismally to address racial injustice but was in fact the purveyor and instigator that sowed racial division.

Amid upheaval and calls for racial justice, our field has looked inwardly to reflect on the ways our theories and practices continue to inflict linguistic racism by insisting upon, centering, and perpetuating Standard English as the universal norm. At the start of this decade, April Baker-Bell, Bonnie J. Williams-Farrier, Davena Jackson, Lamar Johnson, Carmen Kynard, and Teaira McMurty (2020) issued a list of demands that call for Black linguistic justice. Broadly speaking, the list de-centers White linguistic supremacy and centers Black English. The list of demands for centering Black English, Black linguistic consciousness, and Black scholars is timely and necessary because many in the field continue to feel threatened by language diversity. For example, just two years earlier, Vershawn Ashanti Young's (2018) use of Black English in the Conference on College Composition and Communication's (CCCC's) 2019 Call for Proposal (CFP) was criticized on a widely read thread on the now-defunct writing program administrators' listserv (WPA-L) as an affected style, inappropriate, and ideologically driven. While some listserv members defended Young's CFP and language, the thread as a whole highlighted persistent tensions between official support for language diversity and linguistic justice and less visible but still prevalent resistance to language diversity in both professional and pedagogical contexts.

As our nation confronts systemic racism—reluctantly, in partial measures—there is an ever-growing need for anti-racist work and scholarship. This need is reflected in the spike in interest in books that address anti-racism, for both academic and non-academic audiences. *Racing Translingualism in Composition: Toward a Race-Conscious Translingualism* contributes to our national and scholarly conversations by confronting the ways racism continues to shape and inform our theories, pedagogical practices, and language policies and strives to develop anti-racist orientations to language and literacy pedagogies. Translingual theory and pedagogy have emerged as one of the most recent manifestations of composition's professed commitment to language diversity. We, too, believe that the translingual movement makes important contributions to our collective efforts to theorize, research, and teach in ways that support language diversity. And yet, for all the progress our field has made in challenging regressive language ideologies and advocating for progressive writing pedagogies, much work remains to effect widespread change in the field. In *Racing Translingualism in Composition*, we take up this work to help move the field forward by directly attending to the links among language, race, and racism and making the case for race-conscious, rather than colorblind,[1] theories and pedagogies.

To situate our work within a larger disciplinary conversation, we offer a brief historical review of the evolution of these conversations, from "Students' Right to Their Own Language" (1974) to translingualism. We then review key themes and movements in translingual scholarship, working to articulate both our orientation to translingualism in this project and the need for focused work on the role of race, racism, and anti-racism in translingual theory and practice. Finally, we offer an overview of contributions to *Racing Translingualism in Composition*.

LANGUAGE DIVERSITY IN COMPOSITION:
HISTORICAL CONTEXT, CURRENT RELEVANCE

In the years following the publication of CCCC's "Students' Right to Their Own Language" (SRTOL) (1974), composition studies engaged in vigorous debate about the relationships among language diversity, writing, writing pedagogy, and racial and social justice. As Geneva Smitherman (2015, 69–71) recounts, some members of the field vocally supported the statement and worked actively to implement its pedagogical vision while others vociferously opposed it, rejecting the claim that students have a right to their own language and arguing that teaching anything other than Standard American English (SAE) is irresponsible. Following these initial responses, efforts to enact SRTOL were hampered in part by confusion about how the theory underwriting the statement might be translated to practice. Unfortunately, the conservative climate that emerged in the late 1970s undermined progressive initiatives like SRTOL, and continued direct attacks on the statement and on language diversity more broadly eroded commitment to the pedagogical project of language diversity (72). To be sure, some teachers in the field continued to develop and implement SRTOL-aligned pedagogies; but sustained, public, scholarly attention to STROL waned. This vacuum created a context in which many in the field supported SRTOL in theory but not in practice, taking the stance that non-SAE languages are good for family and social contexts but not for academic or professional contexts. This "enactment" of SRTOL was perhaps most explicitly articulated by Rebecca S. Wheeler and Rachel Swords (2006), whose conservative approach to code switching is rooted in the separation of languages and valorization of SAE as *the* language for academic writing (see Young 2013).

In recent years, composition studies has seen a (re)turn to language, driven in part by a revitalized interest in SRTOL as well as attention to second language writing (Matsuda 2013). That interest has come both in the form of scholarship that reexamines the history of SRTOL (e.g., Parks 2013; Kynard 2007; Lamos 2011; and others) and in scholarship that articulates the continued pedagogical relevance of STROL, particularly with respect to African American students and language (e.g., Perryman-Clark 2009; Kinloch 2006). Notably, recent historical research, such as the work of Parks and Kynard, highlights the relationship between the SRTOL movement and the activist and radical political movements of the late 1960s and 1970s, though Kynard is more explicit in her efforts to recover the ties among SRTOL, Black Power, and radical

Black politics. In so doing, she calls attention not only to the statement's activist roots but also to the ongoing relevance of radical responses to racism in writing pedagogies.

We call attention to the responses to SRTOL to contrast the statement's reception to the field's responses to translingualism. While many in the field rejected STROL, the emergence of translingual theory has been met with widespread enthusiasm. To be sure, some of the response to translingualism has manifested as critique, and rightly so; but the critiques of translingualism can, by and large, be characterized as generative critique that is meant to move the work of translingualism forward, not to dismiss it entirely. The differences in responses to SRTOL and translingualism are not coincidental. Rather, we believe translingualism's failure to center the intersections of race, language, and writing is consequential and has permitted its enthusiastic uptake. In short, language diversity is far more palatable when distanced from race because it appears safer to evaluate students' writing (Inoue 2015, 26). This absence, we contend, signals a need for critical intervention in translingual theory and practice, one that foregrounds issues of race and racism.

As *Racing Translingualism in Composition* argues, the different responses to SRTOL and translingualism are racialized, and these racialized responses are informed by the different racial projects of these two movements. Likewise, the consequences of those differing responses are significant, leading the field to take up distinctly different stances regarding the racial and social justice work of writing and writing pedagogy. To more fully explicate this argument, we now trace the trajectory of translingual theory and practice in composition studies.

TRANSLINGUAL THEORY AND PRACTICE AS A CHALLENGE TO ENGLISH MONOLINGUALISM

Translingualism, introduced to composition studies by Bruce Horner, Min-Zhan Lu, Jacqueline Jones Royster, and John Trimbur's (2011) manifesto "Language Difference in Writing: Toward a Translingual Approach," is one of the most recent manifestations of the field's commitment to language diversity in writing pedagogy. Here, we offer a broad accounting of translingualism and, importantly, make the case for why we believe it is necessary for translingual theory and practice to engage deeply, explicitly, and consistently with race and racism. We do not aim to provide a comprehensive account of translingualism, either its theory or applications across global contexts; such a goal is beyond the scope of this project, and any attempt to offer a definitive account of translingualism would arguably be antithetical to the central tenets of translingualism itself. Rather, our aim is to hone in on the elements of translingualism that speak to its anti-racist potential and therefore require sustained engagement with race and racism.

While many scholars have outlined the scope and nuances of translingual theory, we find Paul Kei Matsuda's (2014, 479) articulation of translingualism's key assumptions a useful starting point:

- English monolingualism is prevalent and problematic.
- The presence of language differences is normal and desirable.
- Languages are neither discrete nor stable; they are dynamic and negotiated.
- Practicing translingual writing involves the negotiation of language differences.

We further find it valuable to extend these assumptions to begin to articulate how they intersect with issues of race and racism. To that end, we contend:

- English monolingualism is prevalent and problematic . . . largely because it is inextricably woven together with racism.
- The presence of language differences is normal and desirable . . . but some forms of language differences are more normal and desirable than others, and the variability in the ways language differences are valued is linked in large part to race and ethnicity.
- Languages are neither discrete nor stable; they are dynamic and negotiated . . . but some language negotiations are taken up more or less enthusiastically due to the racialization of languages.
- Practicing translingual writing involves the negotiation of language differences . . . but some writers must do more and different kinds of negotiating due to the ways they, as people and writers, are racialized.

Here, we are working to illustrate some of the ways we understand translingualism to be always already linked to issues of race and racism. While we endorse the fundamental tenets underlying translingual praxis, we also offer an important caveat that any theory of language must attend to race and racism to recognize the role language has in reproducing race and racialized language differences. *Racing Translingualism* seeks to highlight the roles race and racism play in how language differences are practiced, negotiated, and recognized.

While the growing body of translingual scholarship in composition has centered questions of language differences and negotiations, it has simultaneously de-centered race and racism in writing and writing instruction. On this point, Keith Gilyard (2016, 285) critiques translingual scholarship for eliding issues of race and racism in its construction of the "linguistic everyperson"—a construct that flattens linguistic difference, overlooks the material and political consequences of linguistic differences, and ignores the struggles for linguistic legitimacy of racialized minorities. One consequence of this flattening is that when the linguistic diversity of monolingual and/or White, middle-class students is addressed (as it should be in translingual pedagogies), it is often attended to in ways that elide the differences in how majority/mainstream and minoritized students experience and negotiate language differences.

The translingual orientation is, indeed, an ideological position meant to challenge monolingual assumptions of standardness that many students (and teachers) entering composition classrooms hold. Much of translingual scholarship has articulated a paradigm that largely revolves around issues of linguistic inclusion, ideology, theory, and pedagogy that seek to challenge discriminatory policies and practices that are viewed as inherent in English monolingualism and SAE. However, as Asao Inoue (2015, 26) observes, translingual pedagogies "often assume racial structures that support and are associated with the linguistic and language competencies of all students" because "the people who most often form multilingual English students or linguistic difference from the dominant academic discourse are racialized in conventional ways." In this and other ways, translingualism gestures toward linguistic inclusiveness and celebrates differences while ignoring the racialized structures that make linguistic difference visible in the first place. Thus, we contend, along with contributors to this collection, that translingualism must attend to institutional contexts, policies, and practices (and how race and racism shape those contexts, policies, and practices) if it is to effectively counter monolingualism.

Fundamentally, we contend that language differences are always already perceived, marked, judged, and racialized in communicative interactions. While "race" is widely understood as a social construct, racism and the racialization of people, their bodies, and their languages have real, material consequences and thus cannot be set aside. Despite its instability, contradictions, and slippages, race functions as a "master category" that structures all facets of our social lives that have real social consequences (Omi and Winant 2015, 106). That is, race functions as a master category precisely because of its resilience to defy absolutes and fixed notions of itself. Accordingly, *Racing Translingualism* aims to critically examine how race is always and already sewn into the fabric of our theories and practices of language, and this collection explicitly grounds the politics of race in dialogue with translingual approaches while recognizing the fluid nature of both race and translingualism as negotiated terms.

Racing Translingualism in Composition is a racial project that signifies a shift in the scholarly conversations in translingualism by examining these intersections. In doing so, this edited collection moves beyond critique to rhetorically refine and thereby extend existing scholarship on translingual praxis by keeping the intersections of race, racism, anti-racism, and translingualism at its center. As we describe below, contributors to *Racing Translingualism in Composition* extend the larger project of interrogating intersections of race, racism, language, and translingualism; but they do so in ways that resist fixed or absolute definitions of these concepts. In this way, we hope this book, much like the concerns articulated in "This Ain't Another Statement! This is a DEMAND for Black Linguistic Justice," interrogates both the means of production and the various institutions that control the means of producing racialized language differences and inequality to create more linguistically and racially just writing theories and pedagogies.

RACING TRANSLINGUALISM IN COMPOSITION: AN OVERVIEW

As the response to Young's (2018) CCCC CFP illustrates, while many in the field accept that there are important intersections among race and racism, language ideologies, and writing and writing pedagogy, there is not widespread agreement on or acceptance of these intersections for either our scholarship and research or our pedagogical practices. Therefore, the chapters in part I collectively bridge the gap between theory and practice by articulating the nuances of those intersections—moving from theoretical analyses to empirical studies of instructors and students—and argue that the field must attend to them in substantive and sustained ways.

The first two chapters focus on the relationships between colorblind racism and language ideologies. Karen Rowan views translingualism as an anti-racist racial project that challenges monolingualist assumptions and ideologies about language difference. Rowan argues that translingualism's focus on difference in *all* languages for *all* translingual subjects runs the risk of being rearticulated in ways that reflect colorblind racist ideologies. Rachael Shapiro and Missy Watson similarly problematize translingualism for its exclusive focus on language fluidity and argue for an approach that actively resists standard language ideology and its concomitant role in colorblind racism. They advance an overtly racialized translingualism as both a theoretical and a pedagogical approach that not only calls attention to the myth of standard language ideologies but also counters the new racism inherent in such ideologies.

Guarding against colorblind racism in translingual praxis begins by looking closely at language and identity in context, a project taken up in the next two chapters. Aja Martinez speaks to the risks of colorblind translingualism by bringing into focus her experience of linguistic marginalization. Martinez narrativizes her experiences of heritage language loss and identity within the historical context of US colonization, recounts the verbal and physical abuse her parents' generation endured for speaking Spanish, and lays bare the fallout of this abuse on successive generations of Mexican Americans and Chicanx—many of whom are, like Martinez, unable to "pass" as either proficient Spanish or English speakers. In so doing, Martinez extends Sara Alvarez and colleagues' (2017) efforts to explore and trouble the ways ethnic identities, heritage languages, and language and writing practices are simultaneously linked and contested. Tom Do further complicates translingualism's understanding of the relationships between language resources and ethnic identity in his examination of how communities of practice both afford and constrain heritage speakers' participation in communal practices that impact their in-group membership and ethnic identity. In three case studies of Vietnamese heritage language speakers, he focuses on social practices—embodied in material artifacts, ritualized processes, and intra-cultural interactions—and argues that a race-conscious translingual paradigm forefronts race and ethnicity by examining the role communities of practice play in the construction and maintenance of heritage speakers' ethnic identity.

The final chapter in part I turns to examine how racialized attitudes about language play out in instructors' responses to student writing. Bethany Davila's empirical research examines instructors' responses to a student paper, responses that illustrated the ways their perceptions of students' race and ethnicity shaped their perceptions of students' languages and accents. These racialized attitudes exemplify the negative stereotypes that students of color are perpetually foreign and deficient while privileging White students as fully capable of Standard English.

Employing a wide range of methodological approaches—from historical to qualitative research methods—and drawing our attention to students, instructors, and institutional contexts, the chapters in part II collectively conceptualize and articulate a race-conscious translingual praxis.

Responding directly to Gilyard's (2016, 288) call for scholars "to write histories of the translanguagers who organized at City College and other places," Lindsey Albracht rereads the five demands from the Black and Puerto Rican student activists in light of race-conscious translingual praxis. Albracht argues that the activists' transformative blueprint provides a guide for "racing" translingual praxis so as to move beyond granting students' rights to their own languages and toward a more fundamental rethinking of the structures, practices, and unexamined ideologies that stigmatize and racialize language in the first place.

Shifting more explicitly to pedagogy, the following chapters draw on case studies of student experiences to inform calls for race-conscious translingual pedagogies. Using stories of three African students and her own experiences, Esther Milu argues that African immigrant students' unique and diverse language repertoires need to be understood in the context of Africa's complex racialized histories and raciolinguistic experiences. Examining the racialized histories and raciolinguistic experiences of students from Rwanda, Angola, and Kenya, as well as students' experiences of double linguistic marginalization from mainstream White America and Black America, Milu demonstrates how each context shapes students' translingual repertoires and language ideologies. Next, Yasmine Romero centers the experiences of Emma, a student in her intermediate course for multilingual language learners. Two relationships emerge among language, race, and racism in Emma's experiences: how accents shape perceptions of multilingual learners and how racial identity shapes multilingual learners' linguistic and rhetorical choices. Romero's project complements both Davila's analysis of the "perpetually foreign" stereotype and Martinez's narrative of exclusion and identity. Like Milu, Romero underscores the need to develop a race-conscious translingualism that emphasizes students' lived experiences.

The next two chapters explore the professional and institutional contexts that inform translingual possibilities. First, Stephanie Mosher explores the challenges and possibilities of inculcating instructor engagement with race consciousness and translingualism. In her interview-based study, Mosher analyzes how each participant uses narrative-in-conversation to put new translingual discourses into productive dialogue with their preexisting beliefs about language correctness and appropriateness; and she identifies several types of narratives of engagement, including resistance, anger, confusion, and conscious efforts to incorporate the new ideas into participants' pedagogies and theories. Shifting the focus to the spaces of teaching and learning, Jaclyn Hilberg argues that translingual pedagogies can avoid flattening racial difference by explicitly framing composition classrooms as racially segregated spaces. Hilberg situates translingualism within a broad disciplinary trend of imagining classrooms as spaces for linguistic contact and suggests that composition instructors complicate contact-oriented notions of classroom space by considering the ways racial and socioeconomic segregation structures literacy education. As an intervention, she proposes that composition instructors frame their classrooms as complex spaces of both contact and de facto segregation and offers multiple framings of classroom space to illustrate how translingual pedagogies might more explicitly account for linguistic exclusion alongside the typical focus on inclusion.

The final two chapters in part II explore research methods as pedagogical interventions for cultivating translingual insight and practice. Drawing on a raciolinguistic framework, Steven Alvarez argues for critical translingual pedagogies that demystify raciolinguistic structures and openly examine and name students' lived experiences with English-only ideologies grounded in White supremacy. Alvarez is particularly interested in reading the ways the practice of policing languages masks the linguistic racism that underlies standard language norms. He proposes ethnographic methodologies as a pedagogical tool for cultivating critical translingual literacies, using his reading of an instance in which both the language practices and people from minoritized groups are publicly policed and shamed as an illustrative example. Shawanda Stewart and Brian Stone likewise propose a research-based approach to developing a race-conscious translingual pedagogy, this time taking up the traditions of participatory action research and Hip-Hop pedagogy as starting points. They attend to the close links between racial identity and language identity and draw on critical race theory to make a case for participatory action research as one way to enact a race-conscious translingualism in the composition classroom.

In part III, Bruce Horner's chapter complicates efforts to race translingualism, pointing to the emergent character of both translinguality and race. In response, he foregrounds translingualism's insistence on opacity as a means for resisting monolingualism's impulse to make people and languages transparent and for highlighting labor as an essential element in all communicative interactions. In his chapter, Victor Villanueva maintains that the coloniality of power, and the racism that follows from it, is manifested in our cultural systems, including rhetoric and composition studies. Racism thus pervades all facets of our lives, and we are all complicit in it. To fully engage in translingualism and its beliefs in linguistic diversity, he argues, we must be "translingual first" by de-linking ourselves from the colonial matrix of power. Taken together, these two response chapters speak to the tensions that both gave rise to this collection and help to frame the continued inquiry that follows from it.

The chapters in this edited collection advance current iterations of translingualism by centering race and racism in reconceptualizing and theorizing a race-conscious translingual praxis. Foregrounding race explicitly this way moves translingualism toward a sustained interrogation of the ways racialized language ideologies and practices continue to disenfranchise our most vulnerable students and confronts both the challenge and the necessity of cultivating a race-conscious and antiracist translingualism.

NOTE

1. Since the inception of this book, the term *colorblind* has been called into question. We use the term *colorblind* figuratively to indicate how the intentional or unintentional refusal to acknowledge racial differences ignores the consequences of racism. Some of our contributors have opted to use different terms, such as *color evasive*, to arrive at a similar concept or idea.

REFERENCES

Alvarez, Sara, Suresh Canagarajah, Eunjeong Lee, Jerry Won Lee, and Shakil Rabbi. 2017. "Translingual Practice, Ethnic Identities, and Voice in Writing." In *Crossing Divides: Exploring Translingual Writing Pedagogies and Programs*, ed. Bruce Horner and Laura Tetrault, 31–47. Logan: Utah State University Press.

Baker-Bell, April, Bonnie J. Williams-Farrier, Davena Jackson, Lamar Johnson, Carmen Kynard, and Teaira McMurtry. 2020. "This Ain't Another Statement! This Is a DEMAND for Black Linguistic Justice!" Conference on College Composition and Communication. https://cccc.ncte.org/cccc/demand-for-black-linguistic-justice. Accessed March 5, 2021.

Gilyard, Keith. 2016. "The Rhetoric of Translingualism." *College English* 78 (3): 284–89.

Horner, Bruce, Min-Zhan Lu, Jacqueline Jones Royster, and John Trimbur. 2011. "Language Difference in Writing: Toward a Translingual Approach." *College English* 73 (3): 303–21.

Inoue, Asao. 2015. *Antiracist Writing Assessment Ecologies: Teaching and Assessing Writing for a Socially Just Future*. Fort Collins, CO, and Anderson, SC: WAC Clearinghouse and Parlor Press.

Kinloch, Valerie. 2006. "Revisiting the Promise of *Students' Right to Their Own Language*: Pedagogical Strategies." *College Composition and Communication* 57 (1): 83–113.

Kynard, Carmen. 2007. "'I Want to Be African': In Search of a Black Radical Tradition/African-American–Vernacularized Paradigm for 'Students' Right to Their Own Language,' Critical Literacy, and 'Class Politics.'" *College English* 69 (4): 360–90.

Lamos, Steve. 2011. *Interests and Opportunities: Race, Racism, and the University Writing Instruction in the Post–Civil Rights Era*. Pittsburgh: University of Pittsburgh Press.

Lewis, John. 2020. "Together, You Can Redeem the Soul of Our Nation." *New York Times*, July 30.

Matsuda, Paul Kei. 2013. "It's the Wild West Out There: A New Linguistic Frontier in U.S. College Composition." In *Literacy as Translingual Practice: Between Communities and Classrooms*, ed. A. Suresh Canagarajah, 128–38. New York: Routledge.

Matsuda, Paul Kei. 2014. "The Lure of Translingual Writing." *PMLA* 129 (3): 478–83.

Omi, Michael, and Howard Winant. 2015. *Racial Formation in the United States.* 3rd ed. New York: Routledge.

Parks, Stephen. 2013. *Class Politics: The Movement for the Students' Right to Their Own Language.* 2nd ed. Anderson, SC: Parlor Press.

Perryman-Clark, Staci M. 2009. "Writing, Rhetoric, and American Cultures (WRA) 125—Writing: The Ethnic and Racial Experience." *Composition Studies* 37: 115–34.

Smitherman, Geneva. 2015. "CCCC's Role in the Struggle for Language Rights." In *Students' Right to Their Own Language: A Critical Sourcebook*, ed. Staci Perryman-Clark, David E. Kirkland, and Austin Jackson, 58–82. Boston: Bedford/St. Martin's.

"Students' Right to Their Own Language." 1974. *College Composition and Communication* 25 (3): 1–18.

Wheeler, Rebecca S., and Rachel Swords. 2006. *Code-Switching: Teaching Standard English in Urban Classrooms.* Urbana, IL: NCTE.

Young, Vershawn Ashanti. 2013. "Keep Code-Meshing." In *Literacy as Translingual Practice: Between Communities and Classrooms*, ed. A. Suresh Canagarajah, 139–46. New York: Routledge.

Young, Vershawn Ashanti. 2018. "Performance-Rhetoric, Performance-Composition." Conference on College Composition and Communication. https://cccc.ncte.org/cccc/conv/call-2019. Accessed November 5, 2019.

PART I

Problematizing Translingualism in Composition

1
REARTICULATING TRANSLINGUALISM
The Translingual Racial Project, Colorblindness, and Race Consciousness

Karen Rowan

In "The Rhetoric of Translingualism," Keith Gilyard (2016) highlights the subtle but consequential differences between the Students' Right to Their Own Language (SRTOL) movement and the current translingual movement in composition. Though early advocates for translingualism have affirmed their alignment in principle with SRTOL (Horner et al. 2011, 304), translingual scholarship has, by and large, not attended closely to the ways these movements align and diverge. For his part, Gilyard contends that for the SRTOL movement, "the language rights of ethnic assemblages, most prominently African Americans, were the issue and not the language rights of students conceived as individuals" (285). He continues, arguing that translingual scholarship foregrounds individuals rather than groups and that the "translanguaging subject" functions as a "linguistic everyperson," a flattening that, in turn, runs the risk of obscuring the material and political consequences of linguistic difference for different groups (285).

Though Gilyard (2016, 289) offers a substantive and multifaceted critique, he nevertheless writes that "the translingualist project will not be denied. It needs rhetorical refinement . . . But its rejection of the monolingual paradigm is certainly the way forward." My project takes up the spirit of Gilyard's analysis and seeks to offer some of the rhetorical refinement that will support and sustain translingualism's challenge to monolingualism. Specifically, I argue that translingualism is at risk of being rearticulated and contained by colorblind racism and that if we are to realize translingualism's radical potential, we must work to develop a race-conscious, anti-racist translingualism. Like Gilyard, I recognize that translingual advocates are committed to countering linguistic discrimination and that they do not endorse a rhetoric or ideology of

https://doi.org/10.7330/9781646422104.c001

colorblind racism. And yet, I am also mindful of the "spaces of surplus meaning beyond explicit statement" (286) and of the ways unintended alignments between colorblind racism and translingualism can, if left unchallenged, undermine translingualism's radical potential. A. Suresh Canagarajah (2013a, 9) notes that we must be attentive to "traveling theories being taken up in new ways in different communities and disciplines"; as translingualism continues to travel across composition studies and its sister disciplines, so, too, must we attend to how it is taken up and the consequences of the resonances that accrue to it.

To make this case, I first draw on the concept of racial projects to highlight the different work SRTOL and translingualism do in composition studies with regard to language difference, language ideologies, and race and racism. Next, I draw on Michael Omi and Howard Winant (2015) and Eduardo Bonilla-Silva (2014) to highlight how rearticulation serves as a strategy to forward both racist and anti-racist movements, which sets the stage for my argument that rearticulation serves as a strategy to forward both the rise and the containment of the translingual movement. Specifically, I explicate the "ideological themes and interests" (Omi and Winant 2015, 165) of the translingual movement to explore how scholars use rearticulation as a strategy to facilitate translingualism's rise and how these emerging themes and interests might, in turn, be vulnerable to colorblind containment. Given the risks posed by colorblind containment, I conclude by arguing that we can mitigate this risk by developing a translingualism that is both race conscious and anti-racist.

TRANSLINGUALISM AS A RACIAL PROJECT IN COMPOSITION STUDIES

To develop a race-conscious, anti-racist translingualism, we must first understand translingualism as a racial project or, more accurately, as racial projects, since translingualism is certainly not monolithic or unified. In invoking the concept of racial projects, I am calling on the work of Omi and Winant (2015, 13), who examine how racial projects "shape the ways in which human identities and social structures are racially signified, and the reciprocal ways that racial meaning becomes embedded in social structures." Racial projects take place "whenever race is being invoked or signified, wherever social structures are being organized along racial lines" (13), though they do not all work to the same ends. Rather, "every racial project attempts to reproduce, extend, subvert, or directly challenge that system" (125) and, in this way, can be either racist or anti-racist (128–29). Thus, examples of racial projects range from restrictive voting rights laws and mass incarceration to organizing for immigrants' rights and protesting against police brutality (125). Finally, racial projects both "travel" across contexts (126) and are, as I discuss below, subject to rearticulation or co-optation.

Composition, from the start, has been shaped by and has carried out racial projects. Indeed, I would argue that given the historical links among literacy, education, and racism, writing and rhetorical education is always a racial project. Some examples of racial projects in writing and rhetorical education include Citizenship Schools (e.g., Lathan 2015); the implicit English-only, monolingual orientation in composition studies (e.g., Horner 2001; Matsuda 2006; and others); the Open Admissions movement and its impact on basic writing programs (e.g., Lamos 2011); the Students' Right to Their Own Language statement and movement (e.g., Smitherman 2003); and writing assessment (e.g., Inoue 2015). While readers could supply many other examples here, including those that play out on much smaller and more localized scales, these examples illustrate how composition studies—from the start of our discipline to the current moment—has been doing and continues to do racial work. These examples also illustrate that our racial projects range from those that reinforce and reproduce the racial and social status quo to those that subvert or challenge dominant racial structures. Further, because of the ways language and language difference serve as proxies for race in both spoken and written language, language is central to the ways such racial projects are carried out and do their work in composition studies (e.g., Alim, Rickford, and Ball 2016; Flores and Rosa 2015; Greenfield 2011; Young 2011; and others). In short, we are never not doing racial work in writing and rhetorical education. The question, then, is not whether we are doing racial work but rather what kinds of racial work we are doing and to what ends.

This question of the ends of our racial work is embedded in Gilyard's (2016) comparison of SRTOL and translingualism. As Gilyard notes, SRTOL was conceptualized as a race-conscious and anti-racist framework for educating particular groups of students in ways that challenged the racial and racist status quo (285). Further, SRTOL is grounded in and emerges from a long tradition of Black rhetorical education that similarly has attended to and challenged racism and racist structures (e.g., Freedom Schools, Citizenship Schools, Historically Black Colleges and Universities and other minority-serving institutions, and civic education). By contrast, while translingual advocates have articulated a shared concern for challenging racist linguistic ideologies and writing pedagogies grounded in those ideological frameworks (e.g., Lu and Horner 2013; and others), the scholarship on translingualism since Bruce Horner and colleagues' (2011) "Language Difference in Writing: Toward a Translingual Approach" has not consistently attended to the links among language, racism, and writing pedagogies. For example, contributors to two prominent collections on translingual practice and pedagogy (*Literacy as Translingual Practice*, edited by Canagarajah [2013b], and *Crossing Divides: Exploring Translingual Writing Pedagogies and Programs*, edited by Horner and Tetrault [2017]) make implicit references to the links among language, racism, and writing pedagogies; but terms such as *race, racism,* and *anti-racism* appear in the indexes infrequently, if at all, in these collections. This is by no means an exhaustive review of the full body of translingual scholarship, but it does suggest an emerging trend: a lack of explicit and sustained discussion of how race and racism intersect with translingual theory, practice, and pedagogy to date. In highlighting this trend, I seek to extend Gilyard's (2016) call for consideration of how these concerns have dropped out of our explicit conversation and, in turn, how the lack of race-conscious and anti-racist engagement with translingualism creates the conditions for translingualism to be rearticulated by colorblind racism.

To be sure, translingualism is a racial project and, by working to challenge monolingualist ideologies and pedagogies in composition, it implicitly forwards an anti-racist racial project. Further, translingualism's reframing of difference as the norm in all language challenges the monolingualist framing of some languages as the "norm" and others as "different," and it is this inclusiveness and scope that likely appeals to many in composition studies who wish to forward anti-racist writing pedagogies. This inclusivity is also part of the pedagogical appeal of translingualism, in that it offers an ideological and theoretical framework that can be fruitfully adopted in all composition classrooms, with all students, by all teachers. Indeed, my own engagement with translingualism is informed by the fact that my students come from a range of linguistic, racial, ethnic, and national backgrounds; and translingualism, precisely because it is not linked to a specific racial and linguistic group, offers both a clear ideological framework and a flexible pedagogical approach that can be taken up by all students, whether monolingual or multilingual—albeit in different ways and to different ends. While it might be argued that translingualism's rearticulation of language difference as the norm is, at its root, anti-racist even when our scholarship and pedagogy do not explicitly attend to race and racism, I argue that not attending to race and racism puts translingualism's radical potential at risk of being rearticulated by colorblind racism. It is that possibility of rearticulation that I explicate in the next section.

COLORBLIND RACISM, REARTICULATION, AND TRANSLINGUALISM

My caution about the risks of rearticulation is informed by analyses of colorblind racism and racial formation forwarded by Bonilla-Silva (2014) as well as Omi and Winant (2015). Omi and Winant, drawing on Gramsci, "define rearticulation as a practice of discursive reorganization or reinterpretation of ideological themes and interests already present in subjects' consciousness, such that those elements obtain new meanings or coherence" (165). They argue that colorblindness itself was once "a radical, movement ideal" before it was appropriated by the racial reaction and rearticulated "into a cheap simulacrum of the movement's ideal, a parody of the 'dream,' something that ratified instead of challenged the racial status quo" (264). Similarly, in his analysis of "racism without racists," Bonilla-Silva (2014, 7) describes the ways colorblind racism has used rearticulation as a strategy to draw on values central to traditional liberalism—values such as "work ethic, rewards by merit, equal opportunity, individualism," and so on—to realize "racially illiberal goals." For example, Bonilla-Silva points to the ways his study participants rely on "neutral" appeals to rewards by merit to challenge race-conscious programs that emerged from the Civil Rights movement. Instead of such programs being recognized as challenges to institutionalized racism, they are rearticulated as an affront to the liberal ideal of meritocracy (80) and recast as "reverse racism."

Bonilla-Silva (2014) further identifies several frames through which the logic of colorblind racism is articulated and perpetuated, two of which are abstract liberalism and naturalization. Abstract liberalism, as Bonilla-Silva writes, is the practice of "using ideas associated with political . . . and economic liberalism in an abstract manner to explain racial matters" (76). For example, abstract liberalism allows people to regard "each person as an 'individual' with 'choices'" (76) and to use this framework to explain away structural and institutionalized racism. The second frame, naturalization, "allows whites to explain away racial phenomena by suggesting that they are natural occurrences" (76). We see these frames in play, for example, in the way the logic of colorblind racism accounts for residential segregation. Through the frame of abstract liberalism, residential segregation is regarded as simply individual choices about where to live; through the frame of naturalization, segregation is the inevitable consequence of people's tendency to "gravitate toward likeness" (76). Both frames obscure the impact of institutional racism and how practices such as redlining and racial covenants sustain de facto segregation (and, following Hilberg, chapter 10, this volume, how such practices shape students' access to educational institutions).

Colorblind frames not only explain racism away, they also inoculate speakers against charges of bias. For example, as Bonilla-Silva (2014) contends, abstract liberalism allows Whites to simultaneously appear "reasonable" and "moral," even as they resist "almost all practical approaches to deal with de facto racial inequality" (76). Naturalization, on the other hand, might seem to violate colorblind logic because it identifies race as a significant factor in people's preferences about who to associate with and have as neighbors; but, on another level, such explanations nevertheless sustain colorblind racism because the "logic" here is that "everyone does it"—this is a natural process that is not specific to any race, so therefore race is not a factor.

Finally, Bonilla-Silva (2014) notes that the primary frames of colorblind racism are rarely deployed in isolation (95); in fact, they are often combined in ways that are both contradictory (such as when the individual choice of abstract liberalism is reinforced by the "just the way things are" logic of naturalization) and complementary. In this way, if one element of the logic is challenged, another angle can be deployed, thus ensuring that colorblind racism is sustained.

Bonilla-Silva's (2014) frames highlight how racialized phenomena, structures, and experiences are rearticulated by colorblind racism, re-explained as individual choice (abstract liberalism), just the way things are (naturalization), essentialized characteristics (cultural racism), or just not all that bad anymore (minimization). Though rearticulation is often used toward hegemonic ends to incorporate opposition (Omi and Winant 2015, 264), it is equally useful to recognize that while the process of rearticulation is ideologically driven, the strategy itself is ideologically flexible. That is, the work of rearticulation is inherently ideological, but the specific ends of rearticulation are not fixed. Just as the right can use rearticulation to undermine progressive projects, so can the left make use of rearticulation to reframe the oppressive status quo. Indeed, Omi and Winant argue that the Civil Rights movement relied heavily on rearticulation strategies to redefine Black collective subjectivity in an effort to cultivate "a new black politics," reframe "established cultural norms" of responding to racial oppression, and gain support within many Black communities for direct action strategies (165–66). More broadly, they argue, the movement had to rearticulate how we understood racial identity and race so as to make national conversations about race and challenges to racism possible within the realm of "normal politics" (165).

Just as rearticulation served as a critical strategy in the Civil Rights movement, it has been central to the emergence, rise, and primary goals of translingualism. Translingualism is built in part on a reinterpretation of key ideological themes and interests related to language difference in composition studies, "such that [language differences] obtain new meanings or coherence" (Omi and Winant 2015, 165) in writing and writing pedagogy. Specifically, translingual advocates have sought to reinterpret composition's ideological themes and interests regarding language difference, seeking to "obtain new meanings or coherence." To be sure, language difference has long been a primary interest in the field, especially given the ways language difference serves as a proxy for race and is a primary vehicle for composition's racial projects, both progressive and conservative. In conservative traditions, language difference is understood as difference from the norm, a deficit, something to be eradicated; pedagogies in this tradition seek to teach all students how to write using "Standard English"—posited as a colorblind universal language variety—and, in so doing, to preserve the racial status quo by teaching all students to conform to the norm. More progressive traditions such as the SRTOL movement, World Englishes, and codemeshing pedagogies have argued that writers have the right and/or the ability to draw on and use their full range of linguistic resources despite (and/or because of) their differences from "Standard English." Though this is a blunt and therefore reductive representation of approaches to language diversity, my goal here is to highlight, however briefly, composition's ideological themes and interests in language diversity, language difference, race, and racism.

The translingual movement has taken up the field's interest in language and sought to reimagine—to rearticulate—how we understand language difference in ways that draw on but reinterpret these existing ideological themes. From the translingual perspective, this reimagining is particularly necessary given the fact that across these divergent approaches to language diversity, both conservative and progressive, "difference in language remains understood as deviation from an assumed norm of language sameness" (Lu and Horner 2013, 584). Indeed, in composition studies, language difference is often understood to mean "language that is different from the Standard Academic English"; thus, "language difference" implies a link to writers who are not White, middle class, and/or native English speakers.

As others have argued, this understanding of "Standard English" as the norm and of "language difference" as deviation from the norm is rooted in monolingualist ideology (Ayash 2016; Matsuda 2006; Shapiro and Watson, chapter 2, this volume; Watson and Shapiro 2018). Nancy Bou Ayash (2016) has succinctly distilled the differences among monolingualism, conventional multilingualism, and translingualism on this point. Monolingual ideology, she writes, "propagates representations of language as fixed, self-standing, having status outside the cultural, political, and economic forces that bring about its practice" (557). While multilingualism counters monolingualism by "legitimizing and accommodating the heterogeneity of language, [it] still reinforces tenets of residual monolingual ideology insofar as it treats Englishes and languages as static, detached entities," thus reifying rather than challenging the boundaries between languages (558). Translingualism, by contrast, "foregrounds complex understandings of languages as in-process, malleable, leaking into and out of one another, and having no existence outside the realm of practice across time and space" (558).

Ayash's 2016 distinction among these ideologies helps highlight the ways monolingualism has implicitly informed both conservative and more progressive approaches to language difference throughout composition history (e.g., Greenfield 2011; Horner 2001; Watson and Shapiro 2018). As Shapiro and Watson argue in chapter 2 (this volume), the pervasiveness of monolingualism in composition studies and its influence on what Ayash (2016) calls conventional multilingualism speaks to the need for a rearticulation of language difference at an ideological level. That is, while recognizing and valuing a diversity of languages and language varieties is important, if we focus on glossodiversity and an enumerative approach to language difference, we are not fundamentally challenging monolingualism (Canagarajah 2013a, 5). That is, privileging glossodiversity orients us to defining language diversity as marked primarily by distinctly different forms of language (i.e., varieties of Englishes and different languages). Further, privileging glossodiversity obscures from notice semiodiversity, the diversity of meaning, a form of language diversity that can be found in any form of language—including those forms commonly regarded as the "norm" by the monolingualist status quo. Indeed, part of translingualism's radical potential lies in its rearticulation of language difference as "differences not as deviation from a norm of 'sameness' but as itself the norm of language use" (Lu and Horner 2013, 584), a rearticulation that calls on us to attend to semiodiversity as much as to glossodiversity in all language use.

As I discuss below, this understanding of difference as the norm has at least two key implications. First, it speaks to the kinds of language diversity we attend to and, second, it speaks to whose languages and language differences we attend to.

The first implication has to do with what kind of language we recognize as shaped by difference. Instead of recognizing language difference only in some forms of language—that is, language "that dominant ideology has marked as different" (Lu and Horner 2013, 585)—we must also recognize difference in "utterances that dominant definitions of language, language relations, and language users would identify as 'standard'" (585). In this way, the translingual approach challenges us to read and write not only with glossodiversity but also semiodiversity in mind. Though glossodiversity is, of course, an important element of language diversity, when our primary or dominant frame for recognizing and valuing language diversity is grounded in differences in form, we fall prey to one of the key limitations of conventional multilingualist ideology—the overemphasis on the boundaries between languages and language varieties (see also Matsuda 2014; Canagarajah 2013a). The emphasis on drawing distinctions between languages and language varieties "projects an enumerative strategy of counting and romanticizing language" and "becomes at best little more than plural monolingualisms" (Ayash 2016, 558). In other words, while conventional multilingualism celebrates language diversity and hybridity, it sees each "different" kind of English or language as a separate, independent system. In this way, we see the pervasive influence of monolingualism on an ideology that seeks to counter it.

By insisting that language diversity and difference are present in and shape even those forms of language that look to be "more of the same" (Lu and Horner 2013, 585), translingual approaches call on us to attend not just to glossodiversity but also to semiodiversity. To that end, we must also focus as much (or more) on the process of translingual practice and the practice of negotiating difference in all our writing, as we focus on the product of translingual practice. For example, Vanessa Kraemer Sohan (2014) draws on translingual approaches to interpreting texts that do not seem to be code-meshed in "typical" ways—that is, texts that do not mesh visibly or recognizably different codes. Instead, Sohan argues for attention to how student texts "employ meshing, not just of codes, but of discourse, genre, convention, or style" (199). In this way, Sohan illustrates the possibilities of a focus on semiodiversity and meshed meanings, to complement our interest in glossodiversity and meshed codes. Further, foregrounding process and practice rather than product encourages us to resist the call to describe and delimit what a "translingual text" looks like or can be, a move that runs contrary to translingualism's central tenets. By focusing on semiodiversity as well as glossodiversity and on process and practice as well as product, we are challenged to understand translingualism not just as a thing we do with and to language but also as "a disposition of openness and inquiry toward language and language differences, not [merely or primarily] as a matter of the number and variety of languages and language varieties one can claim to know" or produce on the page or in our utterances (Lu and Horner 2013, 585; see also Ayash 2016; Lee and Jenks 2016; and others for more on dispositions of openness as translingual practice).

The second implication of understanding difference as the norm is that translingualism has sought to rearticulate whose writing and language we see as shaped by language diversity. Foundational arguments for translingualism diverge from previous movements—notably STROL, World Englishes, and L2 writing—in that they do not identify specific populations or language users as its focus but rather contend that all writers, including White and/or monolingual writers, must contend with language difference. Just as the claim that difference is the norm resists reifying some languages and languages varieties as normal and others as different, translingualism's move to include all language users and writers undercuts the implicit centering of some writers and students (e.g., White, English-speaking, monolingual students) as the norm and others (e.g., students of color, multilingual students, and/or students who speak non-privileged varieties of English) as different. Likewise, this move resists the assumption that only some students need to attend to language difference and language diversity and only some students need or can benefit from writing pedagogies grounded in radical approaches to language diversity.

In my view, translingualism's rearticulation of difference as the norm and subsequent reframing of what kinds of language difference and whose languages, language practices, and language dispositions we attend to is, in many ways, at the heart of translingualism's anti-racist potential. Translingualism's rearticulation of language difference works to challenge monolingualist assumptions about language and opens up new possibilities for transformed dispositions about languages and language practices. Even as I point to this rearticulation as central to translingualism's anti-racist potential, I also contend that the very rearticulations that contribute to and make possible that anti-racist potential also simultaneously put translingualism at risk of being rearticulated by colorblind racism. To make this point, I return to my discussion of what kinds of language difference and whose languages and language practices translingualism calls our attention to, this time with a focus on how translingualism itself might be rearticulated by colorblind racism and thus contained.

First, translingualism's call for us to center difference as the norm in all languages and language varieties poses the risk, as Gilyard (2016) argues, of flattening difference and erasing the material and political consequences of language difference. Indeed, the "translingual everyperson" that Gilyard calls our attention to is emerging as a function of abstract liberalism. That is, rather than attending to ethnic assemblages, translingual scholarship often focuses on individuals and does so in ways that do not consistently address how language differences and translingual practices intersect with and are inflected by race and racism. It is not, to be sure, that translingual scholarship does not include the experiences of writers from a broad range of racial backgrounds and racialized identities. Indeed, recent collections on translingualism and translingual pedagogies such as Canagarajah's (2013b) *Literacy as Translingual Practice* and Horner and Tetrault's 2017 *Crossing Divides*, as well as scholarship published in journals, include contributions that speak to and about writers, writing, and writing pedagogy from contexts as diverse as translingual first-year composition courses in Maine (Dryer and Mitchell 2017), Kenyan Hip-Hop (Milu 2013), and the US-Mexico borderlands (Scenters-Zapico 2013). While some translingual scholars, including many of those cited here, attend to the ways race and racism intersect with language practices and translingualism, it is also often the case that race goes unmarked and the intersections of racism, language ideology, and writing practices are left unexamined. It is this pattern of inattention, rather than any particular scholar's contribution, that I wish to trouble.

Second, and somewhat contradictorily, some strands of scholarship in translingualism are increasingly linking translingual practice and pedagogy with multilingual writers and/or multilingual writing, a move I see as a function of naturalization. Dwight Atkinson and his colleagues (2015) pointed to this conflation in their critique of the collapse of multilingual practice and translingualism. To be sure, multilingual writers and their language practices engage with and deploy translingual practices and dispositions, and faculty and scholars can make use of translingual orientations to teaching and learning with multilingual writers. The problem lies in the conflation of multilingual and translingual, such as when translingual practice and pedagogy imply that multilingual engagement is a precondition of translingual approaches. One result of this conflation is that some attempts to develop translingual pedagogies for primarily monolingual writers entail finding ways to incorporate languages other than English (e.g., through translation activities) or partnerships with multilingual writers (e.g., through cross-institutional courses with international partners). To be sure, these approaches can certainly foster critical and productive engagement with translingualism. However, if we are not mindful of the ways translingualism has come to be conflated with multilingual practice, translingualism is again at risk of being rearticulated by colorblind racism—here, by way of naturalization. In this logic, if naturalization "explain[s] away racial phenomena by suggesting that they are natural occurrences" (Bonilla-Silva 2014, 76) and translingualism is understood as relevant only or primarily to people who speak non-English languages and/or non–"Standard English," then translingualism risks being contained by the idea that only the languages of People of Color, multilingual writers, and international students are of interest to translingualism.

These two possibilities for rearticulation—translingualism's flattening of language difference on one hand and the linking of translingualism to multi-dialectical, multilingual, and/or international writers on the other hand—might at first glance seem to be contradictory moves or moves that counterbalance each other, in that the first move would seem to distance translingualism from specific groups, cultures, and histories as well as material realities whereas the second move would seem to counterbalance that tendency and work to situate linguistic diversity and thus translingualism in the particular experiences of specific groups of students. However, I argue that both of these moves put translingualism at risk of being rearticulated by colorblind racism because they both, in different ways, contribute to the erasure of the language diversity's relationship to racialized and minoritized experiences, histories, and material realities. The first move, rooted as it is in abstract liberalism, individualizes experiences with linguistic diversity, puts all forms of and experiences with linguistic diversity on the same level, and thus—given the ways Whiteness and White experiences are seen as the norm—re-centers White experiences as the norm and the experiences of People of Color as different. The second move, rooted as it is in naturalization, reifies the links between language diversity and multilingual speakers and writers, thus undermining translingualism's central claim that language difference is the norm for all writers, whether monolingual or multilingual, whether White or of color. As Bonilla-Silva (2014) argues, the contradiction between these implications of abstract liberalism and naturalization is not a flaw in colorblind racism's logic and workings but rather a function of it. Indeed, Bonilla-Silva writes, "these frames form an impregnable yet elastic wall" (95); when an argument grounded in one frame is challenged, there is always another argument grounded in a different frame available to sustain racism without appearing racist (96). Thus, the simultaneous but contradictory moves of different frames, here abstract liberalism and naturalization, are part of what allows colorblind racism to persist despite critiques of and challenges to it. In the context of my argument, these contradictory frames are the means by which translingualism can and might be rearticulated by colorblind racism.

TOWARD A RACE-CONSCIOUS, ANTI-RACIST TRANSLINGUALISM

The central aim of this chapter has been to argue that rearticulation is at the heart of what makes translingualism possible and appealing to many in the field, and because rearticulation is an ideologically neutral strategy, it is also what puts translingualism's radical potential at risk of being contained by the racial status quo. In highlighting the centrality of rearticulation to translingualism's rise and possible containment, I argue that those of us who find promise in translingualism must consciously and consistently develop approaches for resisting the colorblind rearticulation of translingualism. While it is beyond the scope of this chapter to fully explicate what those approaches might entail (indeed, that is the work of this collection, writ large), I wish to conclude by suggesting that if we are to prevent a colorblind rearticulation of translingualism, we must do so by cultivating an explicitly race-conscious and anti-racist translingualism.

In making this argument, I am mindful of the ways intersectionality—"a method and a disposition, a heuristic and analytic tool" (Carbado et al. 2013, 303) for attending to intersections of power, oppression, and identity that is rooted in and informed by the experiences and theoretical visioning of Black feminists—has been taken up by a broad range of scholars, practitioners, and activists. To be sure, intersectionality is a flexible theory, one that should not be confined to the experiences of any single group and that should be understood as always generating "necessarily particularized and therefore provisional and incomplete" accounts of power and marginalization (304). However, as Sirma Bilge (2013, 405) argues, intersectionality has also been taken up in ways that depoliticize it, effectively "neutralizing the critical potential of intersectionality for social justice–oriented change." Bilge contends, for example, that neo-liberal rearticulations of intersectionality reframe "all values as market values: identity-based radical politics are often turned into corporatized diversity tools leveraged by dominant groups to attain various ideological and institutional goals . . . ; 'diversity' becomes a feature of neoliberal management . . . ; [and] knowledge of 'diversity' can be presented as marketable expertise in understanding and deploying multiple forms of difference simultaneously" (407). (For a similar analysis related to language diversity, see Flores [2013] on neo-liberal rearticulations of pluralingualism.) Thus, while Devon W. Carbado and his colleagues (2013, 306) resist the argument that "because intersectionality originated in an article on race and gender issues (specifically, the Black female experience), it cannot engage experiences outside of that subjectivity," they endorse Bilge's (2013, 405) call to resist the depoliticization of intersectionality by "reconnecting intersectionality with its initial vision of generating counter-hegemonic and transformative knowledge production, activism, pedagogy, and non-oppressive coalitions."

I call attention to the ways intersectionality has been articulated and rearticulated within both counter-hegemonic and hegemonic orientations to draw a parallel to translingualism, which I understand as "a method and a disposition, a heuristic and analytic tool" (Carbado et al. 2013, 303) for understanding and analyzing the relationships among language(s), identity, power, and marginalization and for articulating and realizing counter-hegemonic change. As with intersectionality (and pluralingualism, in Flores's 2013 analysis), I see the potential for translingualism to be rearticulated by neo-liberalism and the racial status quo in ways that undermine translingualism's radical potential and use translingualism in the service of dominant groups and institutions. Just as Bilge (2013) argues with respect to intersectionality, our field must work to keep the counter-hegemonic, anti-monolingualist, and anti-racist vision centered in our engagement with translingualism.

To that end, translingualism must be explicitly race conscious and anti-racist to counter the logics of colorblind racism that I have argued make translingualism vulnerable to containment. One of the central tenets of translingualism—that all writers must negotiate difference in language—relies on a counter-hegemonic rearticulation of language difference and is also vulnerable to hegemonic rearticulation. To resist colorblind containment of translingualism, we must consistently attend to the ways racial formation and racial projects are at play in the ways we construct language difference, writers, and the relationships among language, writing, identity, power, and oppression. As a field, we must develop a body of translingual scholarship and research that is consistently race conscious and anti-racist.

I argued above that translingualism's rearticulation of difference as the norm calls on us to rearticulate the kinds of language difference we attend to and the people and groups whose languages and language differences we attend to. We must carry these concerns forward into our future scholarship, research, pedagogies, and practices as well. As we sustain our engagement with translingualism in theory and practice, we must resist reducing it to particular languages and writing practices. To be sure, multilingual languaging, translanguaging, code meshing, and other such practices all reflect language practices that can be understood as translingual practice, and it is valuable to continue to study these practices through a translingual frame. However, it is limiting to forward arguments, implicitly or explicitly, that translingualism is only relevant to texts and practices that reflect languages other than "Standard English." To do so suggests that texts and language practices that reflect "Standard English" or any other "standard" language are not also translingual and therefore that translingualism is not relevant to those writers and speakers. Similarly, arguments that conflate particular practices with translingualism misunderstand translingualism's central tenants and undermine its radical potential (see, for example, Gevers [2018] and a response by Schreiber and Watson [2018]) by rearticulating and containing what can be understood as translingual. To argue that translingual practice must entail multilingual code meshing is to imply that monolingual writers do not always already enact translingual practices. Rather, our approach might be to ask, what happens when we understand and engage with both multilingual and multi-dialectical code meshing *and* apparently monolingual writing through a translingual lens? What kinds of engagements with language diversity do we find in both kinds of texts? What are the implications—textual, material, pedagogical, political, and ideological—of those engagements?

Even as we resist linking translingualism to particular kinds of language, we must also collectively resist the idea that translingualism speaks only to and about particular groups of people or writers. When we begin to link translingualism with particular groups of speakers or writers (and in ways that don't articulate race but are racially driven), then we are participating in the rearticulation of translingualism toward a hegemonic colorblind status quo. With this in mind, race-conscious and anti-racist translingual scholarship must consistently attend to the individual and collective identities of the writers we center in our projects, including their race and racialized identities, even when issues of race and racism are not foregrounded in particular projects. Consistently attending to the ways writers identify racially and are racialized serves as a necessary corrective to the tendency to ignore issues of race and racism in scholarship about White monolingual writers and multilingual international writers, to name but two groups of writers who are often not read through race-conscious lenses. Further, we must cultivate a body of scholarship that attends as much to the experiences, writing, and dispositions of monolingual writers of all races, including White monolingual students, as to those of multilingual writers of all races—and to the differences across and within those experiences. Just as Sohan (2014) argues for translingual approaches to reading the texts of monolingual White students, we must also develop approaches to teaching monolingual and/or White students to attend to difference in their language practices and cultivate dispositions of openness to language diversity in their writing. We must also resist the assumption that it is only White and/or monolingual students who need to be convinced of the value of language diversity and the need for open dispositions to language diversity. We must, for example, attend to the language practices and dispositions of White and/or monolingual students within the contexts of White spaces and White habitus, even as we must also attend to the language practices and dispositions of multilingual and/or students of color within the contexts of their communities and spaces.

To do so would push back on the (presumably) unconscious but consequential tendencies to read "monolingual" as "White" and "multilingual" as "of color" and/or "international" or vice versa; further, attention to differences within and across the experiences of writers of all races would mitigate the flattening of difference that Gilyard (2016) points to. For example, in this volume, Aja Martinez (chapter 3) offers a counter-story centered on her experience navigating racist educational systems as a monolingual Chicana; Esther Milu (chapter 7) offers a careful consideration of the intersections of national and racial identities, racialization, racism, and language diversity in the experiences of a group of Black African students in the US; Yasmine Romero (chapter 8) explicates a case study of an Asian American student navigating linguistic racism in the university and the workplace; Tom Do (chapter 4) attends to the ways communities of practice enable and constrain Vietnamese heritage language speakers' language practices, group membership, and ethnic identity. Individually and collectively, these scholars are working to cultivate nuance in our accounting of language difference and translingual practice, but their work must be read as invitations for further research and models for how we might account for and respond to the ways language differences are always already linked to, read through, and shaped by race and racism and other forms of identity and oppression.

Ultimately, if we accept the arguments that language serves as a proxy for race and that judgments about language and language difference likewise serve as a proxy for racism, we cannot attend to language alone without attending to race and racism. To do so is to implicitly endorse and forward a colorblind translingualism, one that will not only not challenge racist monolingualism but will, in fact, re-inscribe monolingualism in practice even as we counter it in principle. We must, collectively and individually, attend to the flattening and erasing of difference in translingual scholarship and practice where we see it and contribute to a more robust, race-conscious, and anti-racist translingualism through both our theory and our practice.

REFERENCES

Alim, H. Samy, John R. Rickford, and Arnetha F. Ball, eds. 2016. *Raciolinguistics: How Language Shapes Our Ideas about Race.* New York: Oxford University Press.

Atkinson, Dwight, Deborah Crusan, Paul Kei Matsuda, Christina Ortmeier-Hooper, Todd Ruecker, Steve Simpson, and Christine Tardy. 2015. "Clarifying the Relationship between L2 Writing and Translingual Writing: An Open Letter to Writing Studies Editors and Organization Leaders." *College English* 77 (4): 383–86.

Ayash, Nancy Bou. 2016. "Conditions of (Im)Possibility: Postmonolingual Language Representations in Academic Literacies." *College English* 78 (6): 555–77.

Bilge, Sirma. 2013. "Intersectionality Undone: Saving Intersectionality from Feminist Intersectionality Studies." *Du Bois Review* 10 (2): 405–24.

Bonilla-Silva, Eduardo. 2014. *Racism without Racists: Color-blind Racism and the Persistence of Racial Inequality in America.* 4th ed. Lanham, MD: Rowman and Littlefield.

Canagarajah, A. Suresh. 2013a. "Introduction." In *Literacy as Translingual Practice: Between Communities and Classrooms,* ed. A. Suresh Canagarajah, 1–10. New York: Routledge.

Canagarajah, A. Suresh, ed. 2013b. *Literacy as Translingual Practice: Between Communities and Classrooms.* New York: Routledge.

Carbado, Devon W., Kimberlé Williams Crenshaw, Vickie M. Mayes, and Barbara Tomlinson. 2013. "Intersectionality: Mapping the Movements of a Theory." *Du Bois Review* 10 (2): 303–12.

Dryer, Dylan B., and Paige Mitchell. 2017. "Seizing an Opportunity for Translingual FYC at the University of Maine: Provocative Complexities, Unexpected Consequences." In *Crossing Divides: Exploring Translingual Writing Pedagogies and Programs,* ed. Bruce Horner and Laura Tetrault, 135–60. Logan: Utah State University Press.

Flores, Nelson. 2013. "The Unexamined Relationship between Neoliberalism and Plurilingualism: A Cautionary Tale." *TESOL Quarterly* 47 (3): 500–520.

Flores, Nelson, and Jonathan Rosa. 2015. "Undoing Appropriateness: Raciolinguistic Ideologies and Language Diversity in Education." *Harvard Education Review* 85 (2): 149–71.

Gevers, Jeroen. 2018. "Translingualism Revisited: Language Difference and Hybridity in L2 Writing." *Journal of Second Language Writing* 40: 73–83.

Gilyard, Keith. 2016. "The Rhetoric of Translingualism." *College English* 78 (3): 284–89.

Greenfield, Laura. 2011. "The 'Standard English' Fairy Tale: A Rhetorical Analysis of Racist Pedagogies and Commonplace Assumptions about Language Diversity." In *Writing Centers and the New Racism: A Call for Sustainable Dialogue and Change,* ed. Laura Greenfield and Karen Rowan, 33–60. Logan: Utah State University Press.

Horner, Bruce. 2001. "'Students' Right,' English Only, and Re-Imagining the Politics of Language." *College English* 63 (6): 741–58.

Horner, Bruce, Min-Zhan Lu, and Paul Kei Matsuda, eds. 2010. *Cross-Language Relations in Composition.* Carbondale: Southern Illinois University Press.

Horner, Bruce, Min-Zhan Lu, Jacqueline Jones Royster, and John Trimbur. 2011. "Language Difference in Writing: Toward a Translingual Approach." *College English* 73 (3): 303–21.

Horner, Bruce, and Laura Tetrault, eds. 2017. *Crossing Divides: Exploring Translingual Writing Pedagogies and Programs*. Logan: Utah State University Press.

Inoue, Asao. 2015. *Antiracist Writing Assessment Ecologies: Teaching and Assessing Writing for a Socially Just Future*. Fort Collins, CO, and Anderson, SC: WAC Clearinghouse and Parlor Press.

Lamos, Steve. 2011. *Interests and Opportunities: Race, Racism, and the University Writing Instruction in the Post–Civil Rights Era*. Pittsburgh: University of Pittsburgh Press.

Lathan, Rhea Estelle. 2015. *Freedom Writing: African American Civil Rights Literacy Activism, 1955–1967*. Urbana, IL: NCTE.

Lee, Jerry Won, and Christopher Jenks. 2016. "Doing Translingual Dispositions." *College Composition and Communication* 68 (2): 317–44.

Lu, Min-Zhan, and Bruce Horner. 2013. "Translingual Literacy, Language Difference, and Matters of Agency." *College English* 75 (6): 582–607.

Matsuda, Paul Kei. 2006. "The Myth of Linguistic Homogeneity in U.S. College Composition." *College English* 68 (6): 637–51.

Matsuda, Paul Kei. 2014. "The Lure of Translingual Writing." *PMLA* 129 (3): 478–83.

Milu, Esther. 2013. "Translingual Practices in Kenyan Hiphop: Pedagogical Implications." In *Literacy as Translingual Practice: Between Communities and Classrooms*, ed. A. Suresh Canagarajah, 104–12. New York: Routledge.

Omi, Michael, and Howard Winant. 2015. *Racial Formation in the United States*. 3rd ed. New York: Routledge.

Scenters-Zapico, John. 2013. "Transnational Translingual Literacy Sponsors and the Gateways on the United States–Mexico Borderlands." In *Literacy as Translingual Practice: Between Communities and Classrooms*, ed. A. Suresh Canagarajah, 182–94. New York: Routledge.

Schreiber, Brooke Ricker, and Missy Watson. 2018. "Translingualism ≠ Code-Meshing: A Response to Gevers' 'Translingualism Revisited.'" *Journal of Second Language Writing* 42: 94–97.

Smitherman, Geneva. 2003. "The Historical Struggle for Language Rights in CCCC." In *Language Diversity in the Classroom: From Intention to Practice*, ed. Geneva Smitherman and Victor Villanueva, 7–39. Carbondale: Southern Illinois University Press.

Sohan, Vanessa Kraemer. 2014. "Relocalized Listening: Responding to All Student Texts from a Translingual Starting Point." In *Reworking English in Rhetoric and Composition: Global Interrogations, Local Interventions*, ed. Bruce Horner and Karen Kopelson, 191–206. Carbondale: Southern Illinois University Press.

Watson, Missy, and Rachael Shapiro. 2018. "Clarifying the Multiple Dimensions of Monolingualism: Keeping Our Sights on Language Politics." *Composition Forum* 38. http://compositionforum.com/issue/38/monolingualism.php. Accessed September 4, 2018.

Young, Vershawn. 2011. "Should Writers Use They Own English?" In *Writing Centers and the New Racism: A Call for Sustainable Dialogue and Change*, ed. Laura Greenfield and Karen Rowan, 61–72. Logan: Utah State University Press.

2
AVERTING COLORBLIND TRANSLINGUALISM

Rachael Shapiro and Missy Watson

The research on translingual approaches helps keep composition studies attentive to the ways language ideologies, practices, and pedagogies serve to maintain social and linguistic hierarchies. But as scholars like Laura Greenfield (2011), Asao Inoue (2015, 2017), Victor Villanueva (2006, 2011), and Vershawn Ashanti Young (2007, 2013) have emphasized, it is racism, not merely language practices and attitudes, that sustains these hierarchies. While the Students' Right to Their Own Language discussion has emphasized specific identities of affected speakers, scholarship in translingualism, as Keith Gilyard (2016, 285) criticizes, may elide race when it portrays students as the "linguistic everyperson," speakers "who are less the repressed indigenous ethnics overdetermined by dialect and more the polyglot products of contemporary global dispersion." Inoue (2015, 26) likewise critiques translingual theories and pedagogies, noting that in their efforts to assign language difference to all writers, some scholars overlook the fact that "the people who most often form multilingual English students or linguistic difference from the dominant academic discourse are racialized in conventional ways, as are their language and writing." When focused myopically on those who work across non-standardized Englishes and other languages, translingualism may problematically suggest that all speakers are equally affected by the forces of idealized language or standardized English. Indeed, a focus on language difference in ways that obscure White language supremacy and the unique costs and opportunities for students of color masks the problem of race and racism that does and should complicate our translingual approaches.

We believe translingualism has the opportunity (and the obligation) to continue the fight for all students, but we agree with Gilyard (2016) and Inoue (2017) that instructors who adopt translingual approaches

https://doi.org/10.7330/9781646422104.c002

must be particularly mindful of immigrants, new learners of English, speakers of non-standardized languages and dialects, working-class folks, and People of Color. To do so, translingual scholars must interrogate the effects of what sociologist Eduardo Bonilla-Silva (2017) termed the "new racism" and "colorblind racism." In what follows, we illustrate the importance of combating monolingualism and standard language ideology to prevent colorblindness in our daily work. Where our translingualism does not work overtly against standard language ideology and the material consequences thereof, we argue, we risk collusion with the new racism in the ways it supports the project of White supremacy through language discrimination. Rather than treat standardized English as merely one among a number of possible language variations from which we may select (as if it were ideologically neutral), we encourage scholars in translingualism to work overtly against standard language ideology and its role in the new racism. We conclude by building from Bonilla-Silva's work to define colorblind translingualism and, accordingly, by rearticulating translingualism. We name some ways colorblindness might manifest in our work, and we highlight the benefits and possibilities of a race-conscious translingualism.

REARTICULATING TRANSLINGUALISM AS CONTESTING ALL FACETS OF MONOLINGUALISM

The concept of *translingualism* has been taken up to describe language practices, an orientation toward language, theory on language, and a pedagogical approach.[1] Research on translingualism in rhetoric and composition centers on several tenets that other scholarly areas—such as education, linguistics, and second language writing—have likewise emphasized: that language and language practices are fluid and evolving (rather than static and stable), that they do and should interact and have bearing on one another (rather than remaining separate), and that linguistic difference is the norm and a resource (rather than an aberration or a deficiency). Many contemporary uptakes or meditations on translingualism focus on code-meshing practices, in which speakers draw from their complex linguistic repertoires—including multiple languages, discourses, and modes—to "shuttle between communities in contextually relevant ways" (Canagarajah 2006, 592–93). While translingualism in rhetoric and composition may certainly encompass code-meshing pedagogy, we understand translingual theory and pedagogy as much more than that (Schreiber and Watson 2018). When treated as an ideology and praxis, we argue, translingualism can more directly identify and oppose what are multiple strands of monolingualism (Watson and Shapiro 2018). Translingualism is, for us, a deeply political and ideological approach to language and literacy wherein practitioners' goal is to contest systems and attitudes that deem language differences as deficits and thus deem users of non-standardized varieties as incompetent or inferior.

Translingualism, in fact, emerges out of a long tradition of radical thinkers who have advocated for People of Color's language varieties (for histories on this tradition, see Trimbur 2016; Do, chapter 4, this volume; Rowan, chapter 1, this volume). Their work calls us to wrest our profession from its complicity with monolingualism and its violences against those with non-standard (read non-White) languages. In the opening of *Talkin and Testifyin*, Geneva Smitherman (1977, 2) writes that in the Civil Rights era, while many Black leaders were calling for pride in Black culture and identity, some educators "were preaching the Gospel that Black English speakers must learn to talk like white English speakers in order to 'make it.'" Arguing that we must honor Black English and understand its essential nature, she offers a definition: "Black Dialect is an Africanized form of English reflecting Black America's linguistic-cultural African heritage and the conditions of servitude, oppression and life in America . . . It has allowed Blacks to create a culture of survival in an alien land, and as a by-product has served to enrich the language of all Americans" (2–3). Setting aside its unique and blended language features, Smitherman's 1977 definition captures the heart of the translingualism we are arguing for herein: Black English reflects an entangling, a hybridization of language, a geopolitical sedimentation—the languages, ways of being, and modes of survival of the subjects of chattel slavery and their descendants in a hostile land. We cannot understand Black English separately from the history of violence and oppression that brought its speakers to the US; we must acknowledge that Black English speakers have *enriched* English, have contributed to its nature and composition. Black English is part of the ongoing story of English, including clashes between enslaved people and enslavers, rhetorics of freedom and assertion of worth, the drafting of civil rights legislation, the sermons of Black churches and their work in community building, the roots of "cool" from the Jazz era to the enduring centrality of Hip-Hop in the US and in the globalization of English, and the hasty hubris of those who in the Obama era were quick to declare ours the "post-racial era." We cannot understand the English language without attending to the history of slavery, colonization, systemic racism, and cultural resistance in the US and beyond. But, of course, the story of racism in the US is not limited to the experiences of African Americans;

the conversation on race must also include the diverse range of populations marked by language difference, including other People of Color, immigrants, and multilingual speakers of non-standardized languages and varieties, as we will discuss further below.

If we are to keep the problem of race central to the work of translingualism, we first must see it as a concept that offers more than a primer on the fluidity and hybridity of language (as an overwrought focus on cross-language practices in our scholarship might suggest). We must clarify to faculty and students alike *why* we're engaging this approach in the first place: because it is a socially just way to acknowledge and confront the many material consequences of linguistic and racial oppression. Translingualism treated solely as non-standardized cross-language practices, we worry, can veer too far away from this politicized and ideological dimension of monolingualism, attending instead to language play and fascination with hybridity and interesting features of apparent divergences from standardized English (see also Horner and Alvarez 2019; Guerra 2016; Lee 2017; Matsuda 2014; Schreiber and Watson 2018). We agree with Gilyard (2016, 289) that despite legitimate criticisms of translingualism, "its rejection of the monolingual paradigm is certainly the way forward." Indeed, translingualism has to be just as ideologically energized to confront monolingualism's racially oppressive consequences—less a textual occurrence or speech act and more a political orientation and rallying cry. As we see it, translingualism was never *just* about inviting, encouraging, or teaching cross-language practices, though such practices could support or extend a translingual approach. Rather, we see "translingualism" as an essential counterpart to "monolingualism." In the context of composition teaching, we understand translingualism to be a theoretical and pedagogical approach to countering monolingualist ideologies (Horner et al. 2011), not just a more accurate label for language practices and processes. This slight but important definitional shift is key to emphasizing the political agenda of translingualism's theoretical and pedagogical turn in composition studies; it is a marked response to our increased awareness of the harmful realities established and perpetuated by monolingualist belief systems.

Should translingualism's focus rest merely on language play or a fascination with the fluid and hybrid nature of language, we may miss an opportunity to serve the racialized populations most targeted under monolingualist ideologies. Monolingualist ideologies, which support and serve "the project of racism" (Winant 2004, 40), result in serious material consequences (see also Inoue 2015; Lippi-Green 2011; Lu 2001; Milroy 2001; Phillipson 1992; Wiley and Lukes 1996). What links "long-term English learners, heritage language learners, and Standard English learners," according to Nelson Flores and Jonathan Rosa (2015, 166–67), "is not their lack of proficiency in objective linguistic practices but their racial positioning in society and how this position affects how their linguistic practices are heard." It's no coincidence that the languages and varieties shunned in a given society belong to already oppressed groups, which are subsequently considered less legitimate, literate, intelligent, and qualified (see Canagarajah 2002, 2013). Such invalid designations set the stage for a range of microaggressions, discrimination, and other social, psychic, and physical violences against targeted communities (Crenshaw 1988; Lorde 1984; Williams 1992). Monolingualist ideologies, in service of racism, exclude groups from communities with social status (e.g., academia, employment, and professional institutions); and they harm speakers' sense of belonging and identity, prevent equal access to opportunities, and sustain (and in many moments rationalize) socioeconomic inequality. In higher education, speakers of non-standardized languages and varieties, including and especially immigrants and students of color, often face additional burdens to succeed in a system that was not designed for, does not account for, and actively maligns their identities and needs. The labor of assimilation under monolingual conditions often translates to more conflict, more gates, more work, more classes, more time, and more costs for these students. They may also miss opportunities to preserve and develop their dialects and languages, perhaps risking relationships with families and cultures (see Watson and Shapiro [2018] for a fuller synthesis of the political and material consequences of monolingualism). While all facets of monolingualist ideology are racist at their core, we consider standard language ideology to be the dimension of monolingualism most strongly tied to racism.

Rosina Lippi-Green (2011, 67) describes standard language ideology as "a bias toward an abstracted, idealized, homogenous spoken language which is imposed and maintained by dominant bloc institutions and which names as its model the written language, but which is drawn primarily from the spoken language of the upper middle class." No perceived standard language, which most closely reflects the language practices of the dominant cultural group, is an organic, natural language code with inherent superiority. Rather, standard languages exist because they are actively *standardized*—because the discursive and linguistic practices of dominant groups are *deemed* correct, proper, clearer, unaccented, and more appropriate, often through authorized agencies that are interested in the preservation of a particular iteration of ethnic and national identity. But these standardized forms are social—and in the case of language deemed Standard English, racist—constructions, not linguistic truths (Greenfield 2011). Unfortunately, understanding standard languages as constructions, as myths, is far from the norm in and beyond the US. As Lippi-Green (2011, 57) explains, "The average person is very willing to describe and define [Standard American English], much in the same way that most people could draw a unicorn . . . even though they know that the thing they are describing is imaginary. That is, your description of a unicorn would be a great deal like everybody else's, because the concept of a unicorn is a part of our shared cultural heritage." We may be able to point to the variety labeled "Standard English" and to draw on it in our communicative encounters, just as we are now. It is not the variety's existence as a set of identifiable (albeit contested and inconsistent) language practices that is a myth; rather, it's the notion that this variety is *standard* that is imagined, constructed, and inaccurate.

Acknowledging, as we must, the myth of standard language doesn't mean we should deny the very real material consequences of standardized English. Similar to the point that "while race is fiction, racism is real," while any standard language is a fiction, standard language ideology and its harmful effects in the world are real and persistent. The constructed nature of the discourse and its racialized material consequences are, in part, what provides the exigence for our current project—our approaches to translingualism and to combating monolingualism must keep racism central. We might thus resist defining and describing standardized English as merely the language of academia or mass media and instead define it as the racially constructed language that it is: the written language variety of English modeled after privileged White groups—a variety deemed standard and superior and which deems all other varieties (and their users) non-standard and inferior. After all, the harms of standard language ideology are not uniform across all groups—People of Color who are subject to the violences of structural racism (not to mention the emboldened return of prejudice and overt racial violence during the Trump era) are more directly at risk for the consequences of monolingualism than are White people.

Avoidance of the role of race is, in part, the essence of colorblind translingualism (defined below) and as such risks complicity with the project of White supremacy. When we treat non-standardized crosslanguage work as a neutral skill that all speakers (White and non-White, native English speakers or otherwise) will have equal access to, orientation toward, and results from, we are sustaining the invisibility of standard language ideology and its material consequences as they have historically manifested (particularly) for People of Color. This is the colorblind translingualism we wish to work against.

DEFINING COLORBLIND TRANSLINGUALISM IN THE NEW RACISM

To meaningfully re-center race in conversations on translingualism, we, like Karen Rowan (chapter 1, this volume), argue that we must subvert colorblindness in our theory, teaching, and practice. In *Racism without Racists: Color-blind Racism and the Persistence of Racial Inequality in America*, Bonilla-Silva (2017, 14) works to update our Jim Crow–era conceptions of racism—rather than overt markings of prejudice, such as slurs, segregation, lynching, and other racial violence, the "new racism" features "covert behaviors" and structural social functions that preserve the long-standing racial dynamic. Whereas most Whites would say they share Martin Luther King Jr.'s dream that skin color should no longer shape social interaction, their ideological dispositions and inherited advantages of racism support the ongoing divide in racial privilege. Colorblind racism describes the rhetorical, symbolic, and strategic ways racism remains cogent and operational, and it supports structural racism—"a network of social relations at social, political, economic, and ideological levels that shapes the life chances of the various races" (32). According to Bonilla-Silva, colorblind racism is characterized by:

1. the increasingly covert nature of racial discourse and racial practices;
2. the avoidance of racial terminology and the ever-growing claim by Whites that they experience "reverse racism";
3. the elaboration of a racial agenda over political matters that eschews direct racial references;
4. the invisibility of most mechanisms to reproduce racial inequality; and, finally,
5. the rearticulation of some racial practices characteristic of the Jim Crow period of race relations. (32)

Through these strategies, the violence of colorblind racism works by denying Black and Brown people access to the tools of power while seemingly avoiding racism by merely erasing racial identity. As Bonilla-Silva describes it, colorblind racism "explains contemporary racial inequality as the outcome of nonracial dynamics" and instead describes "minorities' contemporary status as the product of market dynamics, naturally occurring phenomena, and Blacks' imputed cultural limitations" (14).

Thus, what we understand as *colorblind translingualism* or *translingual scholarship and pedagogy that avoid direct attention to and confrontation with racism and its manifestations in monolingualism* emerges out of the new racism as Bonilla-Silva (2017) has described it. Adapting the five characterizations of colorblind racism to translingualism, we can begin to imagine some of the characterizations of colorblind translingualism. We can initially define colorblind translingualism as emerging when in our translingual teaching and research we, consciously or not:

1. Make or keep covert the impacts of racial discourse and racialized language practices
2. Avoid racial terminology and/or suggest that combating monolingualist ideologies or advocating for cross-language practices will merely "reverse" linguistic hierarchies
3. Remain complicit in the dominance of standardized English, eschewing direct racial references and interventions in discussions of standard discourse under the auspices that its dominance is inevitable and unavoidable
4. Fail to make visible the ways most of our pedagogical and institutional mechanisms, particularly those related to language, reproduce racial inequality; and
5. Condone code switching[2] in ways that rearticulate the segregation practices of Jim Crow–era race relations (see Young 2014).

Of course, these characterizations, while useful starting points, must be extended and further complicated. To begin this work, we should emphasize how the new racism has shaped the contexts of language and literacy, influencing our ideas about what language(s) should be taught, how, and why. While all five characterizations of the new racism may apply to translingualism, the features most pertinent to our definition of colorblind translingualism are "the avoidance of racial terminology," "the elaboration of a racial agenda over political matters that eschews direct racial references," and "the invisibility of most mechanisms to reproduce racial inequality."

For instance, in rhetoric and composition, we might think of "the avoidance of racial terminology" when we discuss language difference and translingualism without explicitly naming linguistic discrimination as a racist enterprise. And we may "fail to make visible the ways most of our pedagogical and institutional mechanisms . . . reproduce racial inequality" when we do not address the disparate impact of difference for White and non-White speakers. Language difference under the new racism signifies deficiency that then becomes the de-racialized cause for racialized consequences, with colorblindness marking these consequences as tied to difference from a raceless standard rather than to racism itself. Translingual approaches that fixate on cross-language practices (e.g., translation, negotiation, and code meshing) fail to unveil and combat the most significant realities affecting speakers' linguistic risks and choices when they do not critically attend to the ways racialization and other forms of power shape communicative contexts. We briefly summarized in the section above some of the many material costs facing groups that speak language varieties other than standardized English, and we highlighted the ways racism plays a major part in systematizing linguistic oppression. When we as translingual scholars avoid discussions of race, we essentially enact Bonilla-Silva's (2017) understanding of colorblind racism; that is, fixating on issues surrounding language use without directly naming race as a signifier therein eschews and thus maintains current structures of racial power. Thus, even when we focus on *linguistic* discrimination against non–Standard English speakers, we're again enacting colorblind translingualism when we do not simultaneously situate our examinations in racial politics.

Because racism works through language, it cannot be extracted from our theory of language (ironic, considering the new racism's avoidance of direct racial terminology). In the new racism, our language is colorblind and yet works to maintain racial hierarchies. Victor Villanueva (2011), in the opening essay of *Writing Centers and the New Racism*, points out that our current experience of racism is based in the rhetorical. He notes that "today's racism, though very clearly having material, economic effects, is again more steeped in the rhetorical, though now containing the sedimentations of the theological, geographical, biological, and the like" (17). Villanueva traces how the epistemological and material character and circumstances of a given time have shaped the projects of race and racism, locating our own era as one in which rhetorical constructions of racism operate in colorblind frames (via Bonilla-Silva 2017). While the character of our current racism is particular to our historical moment, it includes and builds upon those that have been framed by religion, ethnicity, and other historical constructs, whereas today those ideologies of identity and difference get trafficked through (Alexander 2005) our language use and treatment of language difference.

Standard language ideology is one place where such avoidance should be read as an overt structure to maintain White supremacy. Laura Greenfield (2011) explains lucidly how the rejection of some language varieties, despite Lippi-Green (2011) and other linguists' work to demonstrate that all languages are inherently equal in value, reveals that race and racism shape our cultural attitudes toward language difference. She writes that "while many continue to argue that 'Standard English' is a 'neutral' tool that provides access and opportunity to all who use it, evidence continues to suggest that people's prejudices towards certain speakers carry more weight than the speakers' facility with language itself" (Greenfield 2011, 54). Such prejudices are what cause some speakers' language to be perceived as accented, more in accordance with their non-White racial identity than with particular language practices. In Bethany Davila's chapter in this collection (chapter 5), for instance, she finds that White composition instructors were more likely to locate accented language features and score a sample essay lower when they believed the student author was African American. Such attitudes are informed by standard language ideology, a covert vehicle for marking and rejecting difference, especially on the basis of race—which names the speech, rather than the speaker, at fault and in this way avoids overt discussions of race.

We agree with Lisa Delpit's (2006, 29) point that we are supporting "a racial agenda" when we fail to account for the power dynamics of race and standard language. Whereas Delpit concludes that we should therefore help students of color conform to standardized English, our own view is that translingualism should help challenge the monolingualist ideologies that serve racial injustice. But where translingualism fails to directly challenge racism and the ways race is coded into standard language ideology, it lets down Delpit and all who are invested in dismantling systemic violence against People of Color. That said, Delpit's own approach stops short of an anti-racist stance as well where it acknowledges but does not *confront* the racialized underpinnings of the standardization of privileged White English as a racist and historical process. We would, then, echo Elaine Richardson's (2003, 53) argument that encouraging students of color to conform to standardized English does "more to uphold the idea of a monolithic 'correct' English and the system that it supports" than it would "benefit the subordinated, stigmatized, or least preferred social groups." These attitudes, she argues, reinforce and re-inscribe "the societal devaluation of Black people's language and culture" (41). To believe that access to standardized English can solve race-based inequities is to fall into colorblind racism and thus to fundamentally misunderstand (or overlook) the contemporary function of language within systemic racism. Thus, while building translingual dispositions and combating standard language ideology are delicate and challenging endeavors (as Mosher's chapter 9, this volume, demonstrates), they are important paths to a race-conscious translingualism.

In other ways, the new racism colludes with standardized English, as it represents "the invisibility of most mechanisms to reproduce racial inequality." As Inoue (2015) has explained, our disciplinary values and judgment—our execution of power—are often reflected in (racist) classroom-level writing assessment. It is in placement, grading, and pass rates that we can begin to locate the seepage of systemic racism into our day-to-day literacy work, including in standardized examinations, uncritical placement mechanisms, or even "basic writing" as a silo for serving students of color and other linguistically and socially marginalized groups. Our own accountability, once our students and their language variations are in front of us, is in choosing to challenge or maintain the very concept of "Standard English," which is undeniably imbued with race and racism (Greenfield 2011). If we do not directly confront racism in our translingual scholarship, we leave invisible the "mechanisms to reproduce racial inequality." As Inoue (2015, 57) puts it, "Just because we don't call our valuing of a dominant discourse racist doesn't make it not racist." The new racism has undoubtedly affected our efforts for translingualism to combat monolingualism, which again we see as its most important project. When we overlook how monolingualism, particularly in its iteration as standard language ideology, is endemic to systemic racism, we risk a colorblind translingualism that colludes with, rather than confronts, racism.

Further, we would add to the definition above that colorblind translingualism *overlooks racism and English as global constructs while collapsing intersectionality*. For instance, translingual scholarship and teaching cannot treat domestic Black and Latinx speakers as speakers of color while treating new speakers of English as raceless non-native speakers. It would be inaccurate and irresponsible to pretend that the marginalization faced by speakers of other languages and of non-standardized Englishes, including international students, is due solely to their language differences rather than to their racial identity—differences compounded by the "foreignness" associated with their country of origin and its place in the global power arrangement (Kubota and Lin 2009; Motha 2014; Pandey 2015; Shuck 2006; see also Davila, chapter 5, this volume). And it would be inaccurate and irresponsible to pretend that all multilingual English speakers and international students in the university are equally implicated in and affected by racial politics. For instance, White British or Australian English-speaking international students are perceived and received far differently in the US university setting than are non-White students from Asia or the Global South. International students, depending on their national, racial, religious, and socioeconomic identities, will fare differently in universities as well as in daily interactions off campus. When it comes to students' language skills and practices, we have hitherto understood the nature and value of their language resources differently depending on a host of intersectional factors that reflect histories of racism and global struggle: positively valued language difference has more often been associated with White speakers and speakers from predominantly White nations.

As Villanueva (2006, 13) describes in "Blind: Talking about the New Racism," what we once identified as racism connected to "minority" populations has shifted with the political-economic expansion of racism and colonization: "Colonialism is global now . . . and all those from the third world become the colored of the globe." Racism and the global power construct have come to mean in some ways that Whiteness is a power that gets reified through globalization and its accompanying mobilities. Howard Winant (2004) has traced this rearticulation of the racial project in globalization, defining racism as both hegemonic and global (5), as well as micro-social and identity-shaping. He sees globalization as both economic and "racialized social structure," noting the ways institutions like the International Monetary Fund and the World Trade Organization help preserve the cultural hegemony of Whites along the North-South and East-West global axes (135) through "debt peonage" and more (89–91). He recognizes that the increasing mobility under globalization has increased the global diaspora, rendering nationalism and citizenship once again central to racial conflict in local national contexts (145–47). This relationship between racism and global power is just one reason that in our efforts to serve students who are multilingual and who claim nonstandardized varieties, we cannot be colorblind in our translingualism.

Moreover, while racism in micro-contexts means the smallest language acts become entangled with histories of violence against bodies of color, larger-scale circulations tie English to capital in the global economy. As Catherine Prendergast (2008) shows in *Buying into English*, in recent decades, non-dominant nations around the world have seen the falling away of isolationism and the widespread adoption of English as a vehicle for access to global trade and wealth. English's perceived status as the lingua franca serves the global organization of nations and peoples according to historically shaped power arrangements, a move that filters down to affect the bodies and material realities of World English speakers, such as in tongue surgeries to "remove accents" from Asian speakers (as both Prendergast [2008] and Min-Zhan Lu [2006] have written about). While individuals seeking purchase in the global economy by using English in their home nations pay great costs, Prendergast (2008, 4) writes that for them, "entering the global economy was not about mastery of its putative terminology—English—but about negotiating the global order's asymmetries on a daily basis."

These very asymmetries, in which language users representing nondominant identities must take on costs and risks unique to particular subject positions in the matrices of local and global power structures, are precisely the realities that become obscured and erased in colorblind (and, consequently, powerblind) translingualisms. Those of us who subscribe to the tenets of translingual scholarship understand that languages interact with and remake one another; once we recall that no language can be conceived outside of its colonial history and the global matrices of power, we must keep present the problem of race and racism in our work against monolingualism. Averting colorblind translingualism, then, encourages us to remain vigilant against linguistic and racial oppression and to acknowledge the ideological, political, and anti-racist roots and purposes of translingual work.

AVERTING COLORBLIND TRANSLINGUALISM, CONTESTING STANDARD LANGUAGE IDEOLOGY

We have the research; we have the stories in our field that tell us in no subtle detail of the connection between standard language ideology and racism. To avert colorblind translingualism, we must include these invaluable perspectives in translingual work. Often through the power and politics of personal narrative, these scholars have pushed us to consider the academy's violence in its insistence on standardized English for speakers of color. For instance, Villanueva (1993, xiv) describes in *Bootstraps* his successes and struggles as a "portorican" academic, remembering "that for most like him the bootstraps break before the boots are on, that too many have no boots." In his work to find his place in the academy, Villanueva recounts his "struggles with the doctoral dissertation: not trusting in his Latino-literate, ostensibly oral ways, trying to maintain the voice of distance, of objectivity, of the researcher, without race, without a person" (115). Keith Gilyard (1991, 165), in *Voices of the Self*, helps us more deeply understand Black English, Standard English, and racism for those students who "were helped to fail before they could fully develop the sociolinguistic ability necessary to educate themselves." Vershawn Ashanti Young (2007) echoes the problems of race, language, and literacy in education, revealing how pressure to assimilate and perform White (standardized) English "leaves some Black speakers, especially those from the ghetto, at an impasse: either we have to give up our customary ways of speaking and behaving to achieve a measure of mainstream success, risking alienation from family and peers, or we risk remaining in the ghetto" (6). And we can recall

Lyons's (2000, 449) hope for American Indians' rhetorical sovereignty to rectify a history in which the "forced replacement of one identity for another, a cultural violence enabled in part through acts of physical violence, was in so many ways located at the scene of writing." In each of these scholars' depictions of US educational contexts, we see the role of standard language ideology and its disparate impact for People of Color.

Contemporary scholars are continuing the work of uncovering the linkages among racism, standard language ideology, and the classroom and public sphere—conversations that are essential to race-conscious translingualism. Aja Martinez (2009, 593), for instance, reveals how colorblind racism appears in the work of Chicano writers who have internalized the "empire of force," learning to adopt the historically White codes of the academy and to emulate colorblind codes as they "employ what they consciously or unconsciously view as the academic voice in higher education or what could be argued as a 'White voice.'" As a result, she finds, "their narratives are entrenched in color-blind racist ideology." We can turn to Carmen Kynard (2008, 5), who has found that "students who consciously employ rhetorical and intellectual traditions of Black discourses get penalized according to limited notions of academic writing," or to Kevin Browne (2013), who in his reflection on the racist backlash against Rachel Jeantel and her language practices writes that Black English speakers "are forced to make hard choices about how we represent ourselves as language users—these, academic types like myself will corroborate, are examples of complex rhetorical choices that demonstrate the practitioner's awareness of a situation and (often) her conscious response to it."

This is a modest sampling of important voices, but one that helps us recall that in translingual scholarship specifically and in rhetoric and composition more broadly, we have no excuse in adopting what Lu (2001, 59) has called a politics of "linguistic innocence," in which we pretend "that linguistic codes can be taught in isolation from the production of meaning and from the dynamic power struggle within and among diverse discourse." As Lu points out, to do so "enacts a systematic denial of the political context of students' linguistic choices" (65). Indeed, a focus on language difference while obscuring the unique costs and opportunities for students of color masks the problem of race and racism that does and should complicate our translingual approaches. If we are to avoid colorblind translingualism—fueled by colorblind racism and the guise of linguistic innocence in our translingual scholarship and teaching—one concrete path forward is in the confrontation of standard language ideology and its colonizing impact, particularly for People of Color.

Of course, the racialized experiences and perspectives that are possible to explore within translingualism are nuanced, as can be seen in "Translingual Practice, Ethnic Identities, and Voice in Writing," wherein Sara P. Alvarez and her colleagues (2017) respond to the concern that encouraging some forms of translingual practice might destabilize or attack the linguistic traditions of already disenfranchised communities whose identities have sustained amid colonization. The fear here is that where we encourage people to blend their language practices, we are also asking them to blend identities and thereby to sacrifice the traditional identities that some communities have fought hard to preserve (see also Lyons 2009; Cushman 2012). We empathize with this fear of loss, especially for Native Americans and African Americans whose identities and languages have survived inestimable violence through slavery and colonization. Alvarez and colleagues (2017) argue that such a fear is rooted in the idea that languages and identities exist in a pure, static, or previously untouched and uncompromised state that will be tainted once they come into contact with other languages and discourses through translingual practice. The authors respond that translingualism's theory of the natural fluidity, emergence, and blending of languages over time means that no language has resisted contact and change, clarifying that language and ethnicity "influence each other dialectically" (33). For the authors, translingual practice affords us agency in performing our ethnicity through intentional negotiation among discourses, particularly amid others' constructions of our ethnicity and identities.

We agree, but cautiously so. We believe that if translingualism is to make progress in combating monolingualism, its scholarship cannot overlook the violences that target some racial identities more than others. We certainly do not doubt that Alvarez and her coauthors (2017) agree; we wish only to emphasize the importance of highlighting disparate histories. As Lu (2001, 57) writes, "Because different discourses do not enjoy equal political power in current-day America, decisions on how to respond to such dissonance are never politically innocent." Our hope is that more direct attention to histories of race and racism and their structuring impact on language practices will avoid "a systematic denial of the political context" that affects speakers' lives and choices (65). Rather, scholars should move beyond helping speakers enhance their communicability across contexts through rhetorical and linguistic flexibility, aiming further to enhance speaker agency "in combating, linguistically and otherwise, the injustices they encounter along the way" (58). Thus, our work is in honoring the survival labor of new (sometimes forced) speakers of English and speakers of color, attending to the historical and material violences against their bodies and language practices while not mandating a particular linguistic path forward or shaming students of color who seek proficiency in standardized English. Explicit work with students from dominant linguistic backgrounds to confront the costs of the privilege afforded to their own language variety may promote increased sharing of the burden to ameliorate the racist and material harm of standard language ideology. Translingualism that interrupts racism in such ways will prompt further freedoms in language practice through rallying against monolingualisms rather than attempting to impose a particular rhetorical and linguistic course.

Since standard language ideology and its consequences have had the most dramatic impact for students of color, here we urge all who are sympathetic with translingualism's goals to recognize how critical race theories and rhetoric and composition scholars who write about race should inform and guide our work. While we argue that translingualism must attend to the politics of race if it is to interrupt monolingualism, we do not wish to put forth an essentializing caricature of race and language. We recognize the complexity of racial and linguistic identity, and we hope to avoid a seemingly proscriptive depiction of the experiences of speakers of color. We believe in translingualism's potential to confront standard language ideology as we harness its power to change minds, practices, and policies. However, we also understand that people experience race, racism, and linguistic oppression in unique, emergent, and ever-shifting ways across a lifetime. Truly, the interrelated and intersectional natures of language and identity constitute one of the primary sources of translingualism's richness and promise.

TOWARD RACE-CONSCIOUS TRANSLINGUALISM

Colorblind translingualism overlooks the connections between standard language ideology and racism, missing what we see as the best opportunities of the approach. Working against racism by confronting standard language ideology, on the other hand, *is* a translingual project, as it explicitly works against monolingualism and its collusion with the project of White supremacy. In defining colorblind translingualism, we hope to return race as a central concern and keep the material consequences of language politics, standard language ideology, and race tightly linked in ongoing work on translingualism. Translingual scholarship's focus on language difference ought to be a natural opportunity for discussions of race; after all, the language practices of multilingual English speakers and People of Color have been the primary model of and exigence for translingual practice and scholarship, *and* they have been targets of racism in the US since their (sometimes violent and compulsory) arrival to this land. Whereas we fully embrace translingualism's central claim that difference in language is the norm, People of Color have long faced harmful material consequences due to their language variation in connection with skin color in a racist society. White speakers, whose language practices also reflect variation, have not experienced these unique consequences.

To keep colorblind translingualism at bay, we urge scholars to help us tangle with these questions:

- How are we avoiding racial terminology when we address translingualism, language, and language politics in our courses and research?
- How are we perpetuating the dominance of Whiteness in academic discourse while obscuring the fact that it is a distinctly raced discourse?
- How is our instruction or feedback on writing and language responsive to the racialized and racializing forces of standard language ideology?
- How do we overlook the ways the mechanisms of our work—the practices, tools, and materials embedded in our institutions and teaching—sustain racial inequality?
- How can we shape our language and literacy work to acknowledge, honor, and respond to the very different and racially informed experiences of speakers from a variety of subject positions?

We can explore these questions in our own scholarship and research, as well as actively with students in the classroom. Imagine, for instance, the transparency and power that may come with acknowledging in our first-year composition courses that the variety of English we have long expected them to master can be referred to not only as standardized English (emphasizing the -ized) but also as White English.[3] Suppose we said directly to students, "in academia and in composition courses, we have historically expected and taught White English, calling it standard." Admitting this connection outright could jumpstart our in-class examinations of the racist roots of academic language practices and could thus initiate our efforts to avert a colorblind approach to the teaching of writing. Such ideological examinations would importantly complement ongoing work that offers students practice in the rhetorical negotiations of language across contexts in translingual pedagogies that take up translation, code meshing, and examinations of etymologies of idioms in border locations (e.g., De Costa et al. 2017; Horner and Tetreault 2016; Kiernan, Meier, and Wang 2016; Lueck and Sharma 2013). Further, we can continue to do work that challenges monolingualisms related to tacit English-only policy, an assumption of linguistic homogeneity, and the myth of linguistic uniformity, stability, and separateness through work that appropriately situates language in histories of racism, colonialism, and oppression. We can do this work by challenging the White gaze in language standardization, as Alvarez describes in his chapter in this collection (chapter 11), or, "even when," as Rowan writes (chapter 1, this volume), "issues of race and racism are not foregrounded in particular projects." Students and researchers can learn even more about the power and function of language when we do so with attention to the hegemonic contexts that shape every occasion for its use. These are merely some of the practical ways we imagine we can challenge the racist foundations of literacy and language in the university.

When translingualism is race conscious, we agree with Ellen Cushman (2016, 237) that "the translingual approach aspires to the proposition that revealing and leveling colonial matrices of power might be possible." This work requires that we continue to interrogate the roots and fruits of our work as perpetually shaped by systemic racism; we must define and practice our decolonial, anti-monolingualist, anti-racist translingualism in direct contestation of our complicity in standard language ideology and systemic racism. We have to be good listeners, learning from those who have long taught us about the connections among racism, standardized English, and monolingualist ideologies that harm all language users. As long as we don't flatten what should be understood as a complex and dynamic topography of language use, identity, and experience by de-racializing our research and teaching, translingualism can be responsive to the particular needs of speakers of color.

NOTES

1. What we refer to here as translingualism should not be conflated with translanguaging, though the two concepts overlap somewhat. Whereas research discussed in this chapter is situated in rhetoric and composition, the concept of translanguaging is conceptualized and studied in the field of bilingual education. Translanguaging research examines speakers' abilities to draw from a full range of their linguistic assets and posits pedagogical responses aimed at tapping into those assets. Likewise, opposing the perception of discrete "named languages," translanguaging research posits that an individual's complex linguistic repertoire features the interaction of languages and reflects the transcendence of any invented "container" for a given named language (García and Kleyn 2016, 10). Translanguaging pedagogies understand the command of language to originate within the speaker rather than in any external authority and seek to cultivate agency and intention regarding which linguistic features the speaker engages across various literacy and communicative contexts. While we would, of course, encourage further cross-talk among researchers in

translingualism and translanguaging, our purpose here is to discuss translingualism in rhetoric and composition.

2. We are aware that Young has been criticized for his use of the term *code meshing*. Matsuda (2013) considers the coining of this term irrelevant since the term *code switching* signifies the same practice. However, we, like Young, find the coining of "code meshing" to necessarily counter the problematic ways teachers and laypeople have wrongly interpreted the concept of "code switching" to suggest that students can and should simply "switch off" their vernaculars upon entering classroom and other public spaces. We believe, with Young, that "meshing" better connotes the blending practices at work when a speaker draws from multiple varieties, languages, or discourses, despite both terms describing this practice (see also Young, Barrett, and Lovejoy 2014; Schreiber and Watson 2018, 95).

3. We wish to thank Marcos Gonsalez, a doctoral student at the CUNY Graduate Center, who in conversation reminded us about the power of using "White English" in place of "Standard English" or even "standardized English" to acknowledge the perpetuation of colorblind racism when "Standard English" is assumed to be raceless and to emphasize, as frequently and honestly as we can, the variety's raced and racist roots.

REFERENCES

Alexander, M. Jacqui. 2005. *Pedagogies of Crossing: Meditations on Feminism, Sexual Politics, Memory, and the Sacred.* Durham, NC: Duke University Press.

Alvarez, Sara, Suresh Canagarajah, Eunjeong Lee, Jerry Won Lee, and Shakil Rabbi. 2017. "Translingual Practice, Ethnic Identities, and Voice in Writing." In *Crossing Divides: Exploring Translingual Writing Pedagogies and Programs*, ed. Bruce Horner and Laura Tetrault, 31–47. Logan: Utah State University Press.

Bonilla-Silva, Eduardo. 2017. *Racism without Racists: Color-blind Racism and the Persistence of Racial Inequality in America.* 5th ed. Lanham, MD: Rowman and Littlefield.

Browne, Kevin. 2013. "Rhetoric and the Stoning of Rachel Jeantel." *Enculturation* 16. http://enculturation.net/rachel-jeantel. Accessed April 1, 2015.

Canagarajah, Suresh. 2002. *A Geopolitics of Academic Writing.* Pittsburgh: University of Pittsburgh Press.

Canagarajah, Suresh. 2006. "The Place of World Englishes in Composition: Pluralization Continued." *College Composition and Communication* 57 (4): 586–619.

Canagarajah, Suresh. 2013. *Translingual Practice: Global Englishes and Cosmopolitan Relations.* New York: Routledge.

De Costa, Peter I., Xiqiao Wang, Jyotsna G. Singh, Steven Fraiberg, Esther Milu, and Suresh Canagarajah. 2017. "Pedagogizing Translingual Practice: Prospects and Possibilities." *Research in the Teaching of English* 51 (4): 464–72.

Crenshaw, Kimberlé. 1988. "Race, Reform and Retrenchment: Transformation and Legitimation in Anti-Discrimination Law." *Harvard Law Review* 101 (7): 1331–87.

Cushman, Ellen. 2012. *The Cherokee Syllabary: Writing the People's Perseverance.* Norman: University of Oklahoma Press.

Cushman, Ellen. 2016. "Translingual and Decolonial Approaches to Meaning Making." *College English* 78 (3): 234–42.

Delpit, Lisa. 2006. *Other People's Children: Cultural Conflict in the Classroom.* New York: New Press.

Flores, Nelson, and Jonathan Rosa. 2015. "Undoing Appropriateness: Raciolinguistic Ideologies and Language Diversity in Education." *Harvard Education Review* 85 (2): 149–71.

García, Ofelia, and Tatyana Kleyn. 2016. *Translanguaging with Multilingual Students: Learning from Classroom Moments.* New York: Routledge.

Gilyard, Keith. 1991. *Voices of the Self: A Study of Language Competence*. Detroit: Wayne State University Press.

Gilyard, Keith. 2016. "The Rhetoric of Translingualism." *College English* 78 (3): 284–89.

Greenfield, Laura. 2011. "The 'Standard English' Fairy Tale: A Rhetorical Analysis of Racist Pedagogies and Commonplace Assumptions about Language Diversity." In *Writing Centers and the New Racism: A Call for Sustainable Dialogue and Change*, ed. Laura Greenfield and Karen Rowan, 33–60. Logan: Utah State University Press.

Guerra, Juan C. 2016. "Cultivating a Rhetorical Sensibility in the Translingual Writing Classroom." *College English* 78 (3): 228–33.

Horner, Bruce, and Sara P. Alvarez. 2019. "Defining Translinguality." *Literacy in Composition Studies* 7 (2): 1–30.

Horner, Bruce, Min-Zhan Lu, Jacqueline Jones Royster, and John Trimbur. 2011. "Language Difference in Writing: Toward a Translingual Approach." *College English* 73 (3): 303–21.

Horner, Bruce, and Laura Tetreault. 2016. "Translation as (Global) Writing." *Composition Studies* 44 (1): 13–30.

Inoue, Asao. 2015. *Antiracist Writing Assessment Ecologies: Teaching and Assessing Writing for a Socially Just Future*. Fort Collins, CO, and Anderson, SC: WAC Clearinghouse and Parlor Press.

Inoue, Asao. 2017. "Writing Assessment as the Conditions for Translingual Approaches." In *Crossing Divides: Exploring Translingual Writing Pedagogies and Programs*, ed. Bruce Horner and Laura Tetreault, 119–34. Logan: Utah State University Press.

Kiernan, Julia, Joyce Meier, and Xiqiao Wang. 2016. "Negotiating Languages and Cultures: Enacting Translingualism through a Translation Assignment." *Composition Studies* 44 (1): 89–107.

Kubota, Ryuko, and Angel Lin. 2009. *Race, Culture, and Identities in Second Language Education: Exploring Critically Engaged Practice*. New York: Routledge.

Kynard, Carmen. 2008. "Writing while Black: The Colour Line, Black Discourses and Assessment in the Institutionalization of Writing Instruction." *English Teaching: Practice and Critique* 7 (2): 4–34.

Lee, Jerry Won. 2017. *The Politics of Translingualism: After Englishes*. New York: Routledge.

Lippi-Green, Rosina. 2011. *English with an Accent: Language, Ideology, and Discrimination in the United States*. 2nd ed. New York: Routledge.

Lorde, Audre. 1984. *Sister Outsider: Essays and Speeches*. Trumansburg, NY: Crossing Press.

Lu, Min-Zhan. 2001. "Redefining the Legacy of Mina Shaughnessy: A Critique of the Politics of Linguistic Innocence." In *Landmark Essays on Basic Writing*, ed. Kay Halasek and Nels Highberg, 57–67. Mahwah, NJ: Hermagoras Press.

Lu, Min-Zhan. 2006. "Living-English Work." *College English* 68 (6): 605–18.

Lueck, Amy, and Shyam Sharma. 2013. "Writing a Translingual Script: Closed Captions in the English Multilingual Hearing Classroom." *Praxis* 17 (3). https://kairos.technorhetoric.net/17.3/praxis/lueck. Accessed April 1, 2015.

Lyons, Scott R. 2000. "Rhetorical Sovereignty: What Do American Indians Want from Writing?" *College Composition and Communication* 51 (3): 447–68.

Lyons, Scott R. 2009. "The Fine Art of Fencing: Nationalism, Hybridity, and the Search for a Native American Writing Pedagogy." *JAC* 29 (1–2): 77–105.

Martinez, Aja. 2009. "'The American Way': Resisting the Empire of Force and Color-Blind Racism." *College English* 71 (6): 584–95.

Matsuda, Paul Kei. 2013. "It's the Wild West Out There: A New Linguistic Frontier in U.S. College Composition." In *Literacy as Translingual Practice: Between Communities and Classrooms*, ed. A. Suresh Canagarajah, 128–38. New York: Routledge.

Matsuda, Paul Kei. 2014. "The Lure of Translingual Writing." *PMLA* 129 (3): 478–83.

Milroy, James. 2001. "Language Ideologies and the Consequences of Standardization." *Journal of Sociolinguistics* 5 (4): 530–55.

Motha, Suhanthie. 2014. *Race, Empire, and English Language Teaching: Creating Responsible and Ethical Anti-racist Practice*. New York: Teachers College Press.

Pandey, Iswari. 2015. *South-Asian in the Mid-South: Migrations of Literacies*. Pittsburgh: University of Pittsburgh Press.

Phillipson, Robert. 1992. *Linguistic Imperialism*. New York: Oxford University Press.

Prendergast, Catherine. 2008. *Buying into English: Language and Investment in the New Capitalist World*. Pittsburgh: University of Pittsburgh Press.

Richardson, Elaine. 2003. "Race, Class(es), Gender, and Age: The Making of Knowledge about Language Diversity." In *Language Diversity in the Classroom: From Intention to Practice*, ed. Geneva Smitherman, Victor Villanueva, and Suresh Canagarajah, 40–66. Carbondale: Southern Illinois University Press.

Schreiber, Brooke Ricker, and Missy Watson. 2018. "Translingualism ≠ Code-Meshing: A Response to Gevers' 'Translingualism Revisited.'" *Journal of Second Language Writing* 42: 94–97.

Shuck, Gail. 2006. "Racializing the Nonnative English Speaker." *Journal of Language, Identity, and Education* 5 (4): 259–76.

Smitherman, Geneva. 1977. *Talkin and Testifyin: The Language of Black America*. Detroit: Wayne State University Press.

Trimbur, John. 2016. "Translingualism and Close Reading." *College English* 78 (3): 219–27.

Villanueva, Victor. 1993. *Bootstraps: From an American Academic of Color*. Urbana, IL: NCTE.

Villanueva, Victor. 2006. "Blind: Talking about the New Racism." *Writing Center Journal* 26 (1): 3–19.

Villanueva, Victor. 2011. "The Rhetorics of Racism: A Historical Sketch." In *Writing Centers and the New Racism: A Call for Sustainable Dialogue and Change*, ed. Laura Greenfield and Karen Rowan, 17–32. Logan: Utah State University Press.

Watson, Missy, and Rachael Shapiro. 2018. "Clarifying the Multiple Dimensions of Monolingualism: Keeping Our Sights on Language Politics." *Composition Forum* 38. http://compositionforum.com/issue/38/monolingualism.php. Accessed January 1, 2019.

Wiley, Terrence G., and Marguerite Lukes. 1996. "English-Only and Standard English Ideologies in the U.S." *TESOL Quarterly* 30 (3): 511–35.

Williams, Patricia. 1992. *The Alchemy of Race and Rights*. Cambridge, MA: Harvard University Press.

Winant, Howard. 2004. *The New Politics of Race: Globalism, Difference, Justice*. Minneapolis: University of Minnesota Press.

Young, Vershawn Ashanti. 2007. *Your Average Nigga: Performing Race, Literacy, and Masculinity*. Detroit: Wayne State University Press.

Young, Vershawn Ashanti. 2014. "Introduction: Are You a Part of the Conversation?" In *Other People's English: Code-Meshing, Code-Switching, and African American Literacy*, by Vershawn Ashanti Young, Rusty Barrett, and Kim Brian Lovejoy, 1–14. New York: Teachers College Press.

Young, Vershawn Ashanti, Rusty Barrett, and Kim Brian Lovejoy. 2014. *Other People's English: Code-Meshing, Code-Switching, and African American Literacy*. New York: Teachers College Press.

3
ENGLISH AS PAST AND PRESENT IMPERIALISM
A Translingual Narrative on Chicanx Language and Identity in the US-Mexico Borderlands

Aja Martinez

> *For a people who cannot entirely identify with either standard (formal, Castilian) Spanish nor standard English, what recourse is left to them but to create their own language?*
>
> —Gloria Anzaldúa

A student once asked if there is ever a point at which we (minoritized folk) will get to stop justifying the methodological choice of telling our stories. I believe we've *all* been telling stories *all* along, but some stories are elevated to the status of theory, scholarship, and literature while, too often, minoritized perspectives are relegated to marginalized or overlooked "cultural rhetorics" genres. While I don't know when or if the academy will arrive at a point of admitting that all work is story, I do know that narrative has always been theoretical, and narratives that center voices from the minoritized are crucial in researching and relating our own experiences.

In "Translingual Practice, Ethnic Identities, and Voice in Writing," Sara Alvarez and her colleagues (2017) present compelling personal narratives that describe and analyze how ethnicity is experienced through translingual practice, especially in relation to writing and teaching. These cultural, racialized, and gendered narratives effectively demonstrate the reality that intersectional identities are impossible to locate in predefined constructs. The narratives of each author add dimension beyond the flattening of language difference, as aptly called for by Keith Gilyard (2016, 284) in his translingualism critique "The Rhetoric of Translingualism." Beyond an abstract discussion of translingualism, Alvarez and her coauthors' (2017, 33) rich narratives emphasize "the complex and often unexpected ways ethnicity and translingual practice,

https://doi.org/10.7330/9781646422104.c003

as performative practices, influence each other dialectically" and how these exchanges play out in everyday lives.

Further, as Gilyard (2016, 286) cautions us concerning translingualism's tendency toward a "sameness-of-difference model," seeing as we are not all translingual in the same ways, Nelson Flores and Jonathan Rosa's (2015) contribution of "raciolinguistic ideologies" provides a framework for discussing language in ways that question assimilationist approaches to language diversity. As Flores and Rosa state, these sameness-of-difference approaches to translingualism can invite "discourses of appropriateness" involving "standardized linguistic practices as objective sets of linguistic forms that are understood to be appropriate for academic settings" (150). Thus, a raciolinguistic ideological approach resists a flattening of racialized linguistic difference in its insistence that "racialized speaking subjects . . . are constructed as linguistically deviant even when engaging in linguistic practices positioned as normative or innovative when produced by privileged white subjects" (150).

Accordingly, Gilyard (2016, 285) imparts that language rights of racially discriminated–against groups, not students as individuals or idiosyncratic language users, are what have posed a particular political problem for groups of languagers who are subject to harsh penalizing—students who are "firmly tethered linguistically to an institutionally discredited heritage." Particular to this chapter, Cati V. de los Ríos and Kate Seltzer (2017) illustrate Gilyard's (2016) point in their review of Ofelia García (2009, 111) when she states that the United States has adopted "a policy of debasing and racializing Spanish, linking it to subjugated populations, immigration, poverty, and a lack of education." As a theoretical framework, de los Ríos and Seltzer (2017, 57–58) construct a "border thinking" framework and are primarily concerned with "recognizing the subaltern knowledge production of people living in ongoing colonial or formerly colonized nations . . . with the subjectivities of those who did not physically cross borders, but rather had borders cross them." Because power-laden raciolinguistic hierarchies affect the daily lived realities of Latinx people in the US, I offer the following narrative as illustration of a translingual lived experience—particularly through schooling—in which my race, my ethnicity, my culture, and my languages have been surveilled through restrictive policies (de los Ríos and Seltzer 2017, 55–56). Gilyard (2016) describes "a linguistic everyperson," which I am not, and my narrative concerning Chicanx language and identity in the US-Mexico borderlands adds dimension beyond any translingual linguistic flattening. We don't all differ in the same way. This is how I differ.

MY DILEMMA

As a subject of the US-Mexico borderlands, I yearn for the knowledge and practice of a language that has been denied me. My parents suffered and endured physical pain and punishment because they spoke Spanish. They did not want that life for me. Like Gloria Anzaldúa (1999, 77), I view language as a specific aspect of my identity and Chicanx English as the tongue of the Arizona borderlands in which I've grown up. However, like Anzaldúa, I continue to ask, "Who am I with regard to language? How does my relationship with Spanish *and* English—two tongues of the colonizer—affect affirmation of my existence in education, in American society, in life" (79).

In 1848 the Treaty of Guadalupe-Hidalgo was signed, concluding the Mexican-American War. This treaty ended the North American invasion of Mexico and forcibly annexed half of Mexican territory to the United States. Ever heard the saying "the border crossed us?" The border crossed my family. This treaty claimed to guarantee the linguistic, cultural, and educational rights of Mexican people who, like my maternal great-great-grandmother, found themselves in conquered territory (Villenas and Deyhle 1999, 418). Spanish would be retained as a primary language of my now Mexican American ancestors, even after US colonization. However, we know from evidence (the best/worst example is what the US has done to Native Americans) that complete colonization goes much further than just conquering a people through force of arms. Imperialism and domination are most effective when the mind is conquered, when a people's worldview and way of life are crushed and essentially obliterated (417). This domination, as many Mexican Americans and other Chicanxs[1] of my parents' generation can affirm, was enforced through their formal primary and secondary educations in the US Southwest. My mother recalls the "standard rule" of not being allowed to speak Spanish at school and being punished (e.g., being put in the corner or hit with a ruler) if she was caught speaking the language. My father will not discuss this period in his life; he refuses to remember. When faced with the decision of how to raise their children, the next generation of Chicanxs, they subconsciously[2] decided it would be in my brother's and my best interests to learn English only. It was at this point for me, through no decision of my own, that American colonization took root: domination of my mind.

Fortunately, I did get some Spanish out of my parents through the Chicanx English/Spanish spoken at home, "*Mija dame a huevo* from the fridge*,*" but language purists in both American and Mexican contexts would deem it a bastard language, not really English or Spanish (Anzaldúa 1999, 80). I thought I knew how to speak a solid and passable version of English, but I did not realize at the time that I was learning what would be my primary language from parents who are second language English speakers. My Spanish was bad, broken, and wrong. I was surrounded by grandparents and other family members who spoke perfect Spanish (one grandparent spoke Spanish only), and my parents, when they chose, could speak what I perceived was perfect Spanish as well. However, I could never acquire a solid grasp of Spanish, as if it were evading me, wisp-like. So family members would speak to me in Spanish, and I would answer in English, and we understood each other.

In the second grade I was placed in a bilingual education class to "encourage" and "set an example" for the Spanish-speaking students. I guess my placement in this class meant that I was Brown but that I spoke, by comparison, good English and very bad Spanish. I was a good example of what assimilation can be. I remember being scolded on the city bus by an elderly Mexican woman who wanted me to speak to her in Spanish. "What's wrong with you?" she asked (in Spanish). "Didn't your parents teach you Spanish?" I tried to explain that I understood, but I just couldn't speak, but she was done with me, as she saw the kind of Mexican *I* was. So I started watching *telenovelas*[3] on Spanish-language TV in hopes that my broken Spanish would mend itself. My comprehension improved, but my spoken attempts are still not good enough; I'm still not *really* Mexican. I'm more a Mexi*can't* than a Mexi*can*.

Yet my English apparently isn't good enough either. I was embarrassed and confused when an English professor said my writing suffered because of my background in ESL (English as a Second Language). ESL? That was why he was convinced that I wrote like a B student, yet I was too ashamed to correct him. I was too embarrassed to tell him that I was never an ESL student and that I suffer identity insecurities because I never had the honor of claiming Spanish as my primary tongue. I let this professor believe I was the Mexican that I wish I was. I couldn't let him know I have two broken languages. I couldn't face it myself.

So now, after a life's worth of struggles with Spanish, I have to think about how this bastardized Spanish has affected the other language my parents intended me to master—English. Even though US imperialism denied me Spanish, society will never permit me to be a person who can truly claim Standard American English. I'll never be White, I am not middle-class White. I am not the standard; American standards do not apply to me.

My Mexican and American selves comprise an identity that relates directly to my language. As Anzaldúa (1999, 81) asserts, "If you want to hurt me, talk badly about my language. Ethnic identity is twin skin to linguistic identity—I am my language." Thus, I struggle. I struggle because I am embarrassed when I go to Mexico and am accused of being a *gringa*[4] due to my funny pronunciations and my Spanish that is perceived as borderlands slang. I am ashamed when the real gringas here in the US can speak "proper" Spanish better than I can. I mourn the loss of the indigenous tongues I never knew due to my mestiza ancestry that involves a Spanish colonizer of the past. I am angry when I face the reality that my English is not perfect, not the standard, not the norm. Like Anzaldúa (1999, 81) once said, "Until I can take pride in my language, I cannot take pride in myself." Thus, I have turned to what I view is my only viable option: a Chicanx identity and a mestiza consciousness. Instead of forcing myself to choose one identity over another and one language over another, I refuse to choose either/or and will instead seek a both/and mestiza approach.

AFFIRMING OUR LANGUAGE

When I was in graduate school, all students were required to demonstrate proficiency in a "foreign" language. This requirement applied mainly to domestic US students, and proficiency had to be established in a language secondary to English. One assumption behind this requirement is that all domestic students possess Standard American English as their primary tongue. While this assumption may be accurate for the many White students[5] traditionally present in post-baccalaureate programs, the Chicanx student whose primary language is Chicanx English falls under the radar. My graduate program seemingly presumed that the same language standards that were applicable to my White peers also applied to me because I speak the Standard English I have learned to use in academic spaces (Anzaldúa 1999, 78). However, because I can speak this English dialect, the assumption should not be made that it is my primary language; Chicanx English is. But because Chicanx English is not accepted in academic spaces as a "real language," Chicanx students are viewed as not proficient in more than one language and are thus forced (through taking a translation test)[6] to prove their proficiency in formal, Castilian informed Spanish, a language Chicanxs have been historically denied. Predictably, Chicanx students either have difficulty with this translation test or do not pass the test. We are then forced to take a Spanish grammar course for an entire semester, and if we are able to pass the course, the programmatic language requirement is considered satisfied.

What graduate programs like this remain unaware of and unmoved by is the anguish and embarrassment such requirements cause Chicanx students. Anzaldúa (1999, 80) contends that as we've grown up speaking Chicanx Englishes and Spanishes, we "have internalized the belief that we speak poor Spanish," and graduate program language proficiency requirements only serve as an additional reminder of "how our language has been used against us by dominant culture." Instead of being viewed as individuals proficient in several languages (e.g., Chicanx English, Chicanx Spanish, Standard English, working-class English), Chicanxs are made to feel deficient in a language they were systemically denied but are then relegated to a course meant to remedy this ailment. We, in turn, blame ourselves and wish we had tried harder to learn proper Spanish as children, when in fact we never had a choice in the matter.

Ana Castillo (1995, 5) claims that Chicanxs, as People of Color in the US, have been "forced to succumb to white dominant society's rules, are educated in Western culture," and are thus made subject to this country's assimilationist English-only policies. American Dream ideology insists on a melting-pot model that all peoples, no matter their countries of origin or backgrounds, are supposedly invited to join. However, as Castillo contends, this insistence on assimilation into dominant society works mainly "for *white people* regardless of their ethnic background" (2, emphasis added). For Chicanxs, blending into the "infamous" melting pot has not successfully happened for a number of reasons, all of which Castillo lists. Of her given reasons, what I view as the most important is her assertion that Chicanxs are not immigrants. We are not newly arrived or from Europe or other far-off countries. Many European immigrants had only to pay their dues and in time, due to shifting perceptions of Whiteness and other government-created racial projects (see Sacks 1994; Omi and Winant 1986), were eventually admitted into the melting pot that is Whiteness. On the other hand, a large percentage of Chicanxs, like me, have ancestral ties to the US Southwest and only became Americans when the border changed as a result of the Mexican-American War (Castillo 1995, 2–3). We are thus neither wholly Mexican or American; "we are a synergy of two cultures with various degrees of Mexicanness and Angloness . . . When not copping out . . . we call ourselves Mexican . . . [and] *mestiza* when affirming both our Indian and Spanish (but hardly ever Black) ancestry; Chicano when referring to a politically aware people born and/or raised in the U.S." (Anzaldúa 1999, 85). Because we are all these things, we out of necessity created a "language with which we could communicate with ourselves, a secret language" (77). This secret language affirms our identity as a distinct people and is validated when Chicana literature and art, such as La Chrisx's (1993) poem "La Loca de la Raza Cósmica," is taught in an academic course.

CHICANX LITERATURE COURSES AND THE NEW MESTIZA

> *But many of us—starved for affirmation about who we are . . . realize from strenuous research (usually having to go beyond the university classroom and certainly beyond our local bookstore) that we have descended from people with blood ties traceable on these continents for many thousands of years, people who left phenomenal records demonstrating artistic and scientific brilliance.*
>
> —Ana Castillo

Both Castillo (1995) and Anzaldúa (1999) have felt their existence affirmed when reading novels and poetry written by Chicanxs. I too have felt this affirmation, but in line with what Castillo states above, my encounters with Chicanx literature were nonexistent in an academic context until my final semester as a graduate student. In the same way Spanish has been systemically denied, so has any affirmation of my existence through the institutional dismissal of my people's writings. Anzaldúa (1999, 82) recalls that "when I started teaching High School English to Chicano students, I tried to supplement the required texts with works by Chicanos, only to be reprimanded and forbidden to do so by the principal." Similarly, teachers at schools in my hometown of Tucson, Arizona, have been banned by the state legislature from teaching any curriculum involving the histories and literatures of Mexican American people because of its perceived threat to US White supremacist ideology. On May 11, 2010, Arizona governor Jan Brewer signed into law House Bill 2281, the brainchild of then state superintendent of public instruction (former state attorney general) Tom Horne. The bill bans the following from Arizona K–12 public education:

- Promotion to overthrow the United States Government.
- Promotion of resentment toward a race or class of people.
- Courses designed primarily for pupils of a particular ethnic group (with the exception of courses for Native American students, or the instruction of the Holocaust or any other instance of genocide, or the historical oppression of a particular group of people based on ethnicity, race or class).

- Advocating ethnic solidarity instead of the treatment of pupils as individuals. (Martinez 2013, 15)

Effective March 8, 2013, HB 2281 was upheld by US Circuit Court judge Wallace Tashima, so the ban on Mexican American studies remains (Carcamo 2013). The few ethnic studies courses not affected by this ban still face difficulties persuading the school district to approve African American, Native American, and Asian American courses. Although teachers have clearance to teach ethnic history and literature courses, the district designates only elective credit for these courses toward students' high school graduation requirements. If students are to satisfy the required (for college admission) four years of English and history credits, they must take alternate classes in which *real* " 'American' and English literature" and history are taught (Anzaldúa 1999, 82).

I attended the same high school that came under fire during this ethnic studies ban. The school is on the southwest side of Tucson, and upon graduation, my class of 250 consisted of 95 percent students of color, split more or less between Chicanx and African American students. Of the 250, only 11 would go on to attend a four-year university because only 11 of us were granted access to the idea that a college education was an option for us. At my high school, only students in the Honors and Advanced Placement cohort were allowed to meet with the local university's minority student recruitment representative, so the 11 with whom I began and finished my high school career were the only students in my grade who were ever told by the institution "hey, you should go to college." Because I was in this college-bound cohort, the only curriculum we were made to believe was valid was the "real American and English" literature, histories, and ways of knowing taught in Honors and Advanced Placement courses. As Castillo (1995, 5) notes, "Yet, white society insists that only European history and Greco-Roman civilization have intellectual importance and relevance to our society . . . The ignorance of white dominant society about our ways, struggles in society, history, and culture is not an innocent and passive ignorance, it is a systemic and determined ignorance." Thus, I am not surprised that I managed to get through nearly twenty years of a US education without ever being taught a Chicanx novel or poem; it is this "determined ignorance" that makes ethnic studies courses all the more crucial.

Reflecting on my experience in my first ever Mexican American literature course, I realize that because of my Chicanx identity (in terms of language, culture, and history), I occupied a liminal space between White students and the professor. On most days I felt like a witness: an outsider looking in on how the novels, short stories, and poems made radiant the few other Chicanx students in the course. The course materials gave Chicanx students agency over course content and knowledge that in all the years I had attended school, I had seldom experienced. This experience demonstrated to me that "although dominant society has rendered us powerless and silent, it does not naturally equate that we are indeed powerless (inconsequential) and silent (stupid)" (Castillo 1995, 17). Particularly poetry, such as la Chrisx's (1993) "La Loca de la Raza Cósmica," illustrates well the power and *voice* Chicanxs can express through sonic use of the Chicanx English and Spanish many of us know so well, and this power of voice and language was most obvious and powerful when we (as a class) read the poem aloud.

Many characterize "La Loca de la Raza Cósmica" as a feminist response to Corky Gonzales's "I Am Joaquin."[7] While I agree with the feminist reading, I contend that this poem also serves as an illustration of a mestiza consciousness. Chicanx language and identity are represented through la Chrisx's (1993) use of a code-meshed voice (Young and Martinez 2011, 2011), "Soy 'tank you' en vez de thank you / soy 'chooz' en vez de shoes," and her embracing of all contradictory aspects of Chicanx identification: "soy dumping my old man, even though I'm / pregnant with his child" (lines 61–62, 42–43). As Anzaldúa (1999, 101) asserts, the mestiza "has a plural personality, she operates in a pluralistic mode—nothing is thrust out, the good the bad and the ugly, nothing rejected, nothing abandoned. Not only does she sustain contradictions, she turns the ambivalence into something else." Anzaldúa's notion of the mestiza is represented through la Chrisx's (1993) likening her people to "capirotada" (line 6), a dish made essentially of a little bit of everything, both good and bad—even old leftover ingredients whose tastes may contradict one another. The ambivalence Anzaldúa refers to can also apply to *capirotada* because one can have both positive and negative feelings toward the dish; sweet foods and salty foods may be appetizing separately but put together may result in an inedible concoction. However, with a mestiza consciousness we embrace the contradictions and turn ambivalence into a strategy that assists us in coming to terms with our split-selves. Instead of having to choose one identity over another or one language over another, mestizo@s embrace all aspects of our identities and create a new tongue out of multiple and separate languages.

The language/identity dilemma detailed above can only be resolved by sustaining the contradictions and channeling ambivalence into strategy. As a Chicanx, I received mixed messages all my life: "Don't learn Spanish, but hey, why don't you know Spanish?" "Get an education, assimilate, but you'll never *really* be one of *us*," "Do us proud, *mija*, but don't start thinking you're better than us." These contradictions are enough to drive any person insane, but when viewed through the lens of Chicanx literature in a course that actually honors these writings, the mestizx can (re)imagine her-/himself in relation to language and identity, just as la Chrisx's (1993) poem establishes Chicanx English as a real language with rules those outside Chicanx culture do not know. Although theoretical texts can discuss the existence of Chicanx English, this language, as represented through Chicanx literature and art, is brought to life and has the potential to affirm Chicanx language and identity. However, beyond this self-affirmation is the more revolutionary task of convincing programs within institutions and institutions within systems of ideology that Chicanx English is a real language that should be acknowledged and honored. In this sustained era of standardized English-language imperialism, though, this is admittedly and, alas, no easy task.

NOTES

1. Chicanx is used in my work synonymously with Mexican American. I use these terms to refer to women and men of Mexican descent or heritage who live in the United States. According to Yosso (2006), Chicanx "is a political term, referring to a people whose indigenous roots to North America and Mexico date back centuries" (16). Also see Acuña (2010) for more on the history and origins of this term.
2. I have discussed with my parents their decision to primarily speak English in our household, and they deny making a planned, conscious decision not to teach their children Spanish. However, I gather from what they have shared about their schooling experiences and the educational plans they had for my brother and me that English was viewed as the language with which we would have the least trouble navigating through society.
3. Spanish-language soap operas.
4. A White American.
5. I acknowledge that proficiency in Standard American English depends on both race and socioeconomic status. I acknowledge also that some argue that "Standard *Academic* English" is a foreign language to all, something that *all* people in the process of becoming educated must learn. However, I maintain that acquisition of academic English is a raced and classed experience that favors White middle-class backgrounds over others.
6. This test involved translating one written paragraph of English in a paragraph of written Spanish. The practice thus privileges written literacies of Spanish over sonic literacies.
7. http://www.latinamericanstudies.org/latinos/joaquin.htm.

REFERENCES

Acuña, Rudolfo F. 2010. *Occupied America: A History of Chicanos*. 7th ed. New York: Pearson Longman.

Alvarez, Sara, Suresh Canagarajah, Eunjeong Lee, Jerry Won Lee, and Shakil Rabbi. 2017. "Translingual Practice, Ethnic Identities, and Voice in Writing." In *Crossing Divides: Exploring Translingual Writing Pedagogies and Programs*, ed. Bruce Horner and Laura Tetrault, 31–47. Logan: Utah State University Press.

Anzaldúa, Gloria. 1999. *Borderlands/La Frontera: The New Mestiza*. San Francisco: Aunt Lute Books.

Carcamo, Cindy. 2013. "Judge Upholds Arizona Law Banning Ethnic Studies Classes." *Los Angeles Times*, March 12.

Castillo, Ana. 1995. *Massacre of the Dreamers: Essays in Xicanisma*. New York: Plume.

de los Ríos, Cati V., and Kate Seltzer. 2017. "Translanguaging, Coloniality, and English Classrooms: An Exploration of Two Bicoastal Urban Classrooms." *Research in the Teaching of English* 52 (1): 55–76.

Flores, Nelson, and Jonathan Rosa. 2015. "Undoing Appropriateness: Raciolinguistic Ideologies and Language Diversity in Education." *Harvard Education Review* 85 (2): 149–71.

García, Ofelia. 2009. "Racializing the Language Practices of US Latinos: Impact on Their Education." In *How the United States Racializes Latinos: White Hegemony and Its Consequences*, ed. José A. Cobas, Jorge Duany, and Joe R. Feagin, 101–115. New York: Routledge.

Gilyard, Keith. 2016. "The Rhetoric of Translingualism." *College English* 78 (3): 284–89.

La Chrisx. 1993. "La Loca de la Raza Cósmica." In *Infinite Divisions: An Anthology of Chicana Literature*, ed. Tey Diana Rebolledo and Eliana S. Rivero, 84–88. Tucson: University of Arizona Press.

Martinez, Aja Y. 2013. "Critical Race Theory Counterstory as Allegory: A Rhetorical Trope to Raise Awareness about Arizona's Ban on Ethnic Studies." *Across the Disciplines* 10 (3). https://wac.colostate.edu/atd/race/martinez.cfm. Accessed March 18 2018.

Omi, Michael, and Howard Winant. 1986. *Racial Formations in the United States: From the 1960s to the 1980s*. 1st ed. New York: Routledge.

Sacks, Karen Brodkin. 1994. "How Did Jews Become White Folks?" In *Race*, ed. Steven Gregory and Roger Sanjek, 78–102. New Brunswick, NJ: Rutgers University Press.

Villenas, Sofia, and Donna Deyhle. 1999. "Critical Race Theory and Ethnographies Challenging the Stereotypes: Latino Families, Schooling, Resilience and Resistance." *Curriculum Inquiry* 29 (4): 413–45.

Yosso, Tara J. 2006. *Critical Race Counterstories along the Chicana/Chicano Educational Pipeline*. New York: Routledge.

Young, Vershawn Ashanti, and Aja Y. Martinez, eds. 2011. *Code-Meshing as World English: Policy, Pedagogy, and Performance*. Urbana, IL: NCTE.

4
EMBODYING CULTURE AND IDENTITIES IN SOCIAL PRACTICES
Toward a Race-Conscious Translingual Approach

Tom Do

The publication of *Language Difference in Writing: Toward a Translingual Approach* challenges the assumptions of standard language ideologies by advancing translingualism. Unlike conventional assumptions of languages that demarcate linguistic boundaries, the translingual approach views boundaries between and across languages as porous. This perspective works against the codification of language and adopts a perspective that considers the "fluctuating character of each set of language practices" (Horner et al. 2011, 306). Translingualism thus "takes the variety, fluidity, intermingling, and changeability of languages as statistically demonstrable norms" (305). The fluidity of language encourages speakers to use language as a tool for self-fashioning (Lu and Horner 2016) or harboring a particular type of disposition toward language difference (Lee and Jenks 2016). But if every speaker is always already translingual and has the tools to self-fashion an identity through language, the approach runs the risk of flattening the difference it seeks to celebrate by creating what Keith Gilyard (2016) notes as the "linguistic everyperson." This risk posits "a sameness of difference" that could be read as "devaluing the historical and unresolved struggles of groups that have been traditionally underrepresented" (286). While Gilyard's critique is in reference to the historical and unresolved struggles of African Americans for linguistic social justice, this holds true for heritage language speakers who have historically been targeted for linguistic and cultural assimilation. Given these limitations, a more nuanced theory and practice of translingualism need to be conceived to account for the ways translanguagers, such as heritage speakers, experience and embody language differently from, say, Whites who speak Standard English. Differences in language thus entail different embodied experiences and relations to a perceived standard, and we would be remiss to assume that all translinguals differ from "said standard in the same way" (286). However, by centering race, a race-conscious translingualism recognizes how racialized language attitudes perpetuate asymmetrical relations in communicative interactions that consistently disenfranchise racially minoritized groups.

Take, for instance, our educational and political institutions in the US. They have long contributed to the ongoing erosion of heritage languages through explicit policies, such as English only, that sanction English as the official language of school and politics. While modern English-only policies have emerged in the past forty years or so, an implicit iteration of English-only policy, or what Bruce Horner and John Trimbur (2002, 594) describe as a "tacit language policy of unidirectional English monolingualism," has always existed. In every facet of life in the US, English has been designed to linguistically and thereby culturally assimilate the "great unwashed." Not surprisingly, the number of heritage speakers has declined, and a demonstrable trend exists that shows a complete loss of heritage language by the third generation (Tse 2001). This decline comes as little surprise, as children of immigrant parents rapidly assimilate linguistically to the dominant language in the US. The loss of heritage languages comes at a higher cost than a decline in the number of languages spoken. When languages disappear, so too do the ontological status and embedded practices of the culture. The residual impact is visible in the affective responses of heritage language speakers who are plagued by shame, guilt, and embarrassment for their inability to speak and understand their heritage languages.

In rhetoric and writing studies, scholars have examined the impact of linguistic colonization on heritage languages and have argued for their preservation. Native American scholar Scott R. Lyons (2010, 139) seeks to preserve heritage languages against "settler languages . . . not because they are 'authentic' in some essentialist manner but because they are threatened" and because "they do carry cultural knowledge and ways of being—a certain habitus, if you will—that are threatened right along with them." Michelle Hall Kells (2010, 210) echoes Lyons's sentiments and argues that "our historical languages . . . represent cultural maps, social lifelines to the ancients—language guides to ways of knowing and ways of being." For scholars like Lyons and Kells, heritage languages and ethnic identities are not merely ideological constructs, but rather they embody cultural ways of existence within communities of practice that transcend both time and space. These cultural understandings of heritage language and ethnic identity contrast sharply with translingual theory and practice. With its emphasis on the fluidity of languages, the translingual approach can be perceived as threatening the ontological status of both heritage languages and ethnic identities (Alvarez et al. 2017). In response to this potential threat, Sara Alvarez and her colleagues (2017, 33) reaffirm that "ethnic identities and heritage languages are always already translingual. They have emerged out of centuries of language and cultural contact." The "cultural resources" and "communicative practices" that help shape and define the identities of cultural groups are constituted by "language ideology" (33). For Alvarez and coauthors (2017, 33), notions of heritage and identity "are constructed and appropriated in contested ways through individual as well as collective ideologies of heritage and ethnicity." However, centering heritage languages and ethnic identities as ideological constructs is an abstraction that elides the material consequences of heritage language loss and ethnic identity on heritage language speakers, particularly in intra-cultural interactions in communities of practices. Thus far, little research attends to the intersection of heritage languages and translingualism that addresses the embodied experiences of heritage speakers in communities of practice. When heritage speakers engage their heritage communities, their identities are constantly renegotiated in intra-cultural interactions. What little research does exist pays no attention to the ways communities of practice shape ethnic identities.

Thus, this chapter examines how communities of practice both afford and constrain heritage speakers' participation in communal practices that impact their in-group membership and ethnic identity. Communities of practice are dynamic and complex, and they often involve highly asymmetrical relations of power that are inherent in social practices and communicative interactions. Examining these interactions through the lens of a race-conscious translingual framework, I complicate translingualism's insistence on ideology and language resources alone to constitute ethnic identity. I focus instead on social practices—embodied in material artifacts, ritualized processes, and intra-cultural interactions—and argue that a race-conscious translingual paradigm forefronts race and ethnicity by examining how the degree of heritage speakers' engagement in a community's social practices plays an important role in the construction and maintenance of an ethnic identity, both real and imagined. Examining how communities of practice both afford and constrain heritage language speakers' ethnic identity not only interrogates the "sameness of difference" implicit in translingual praxis but also, and more important, reveals a need for a race-conscious approach that promotes an analysis of race, ethnicity, language, and power that is absent in translingual theory.

This chapter begins by investigating the ways communities of practice afford heritage speakers opportunities to participate and engage in social and cultural activities. Participating in social practices shaped the way they understood their ethnic Vietnamese identity. Despite their active engagement, participants experienced intra-ethnic discrimination. In this chapter, I examine how participants experienced linguistic discrimination within their heritage communities. Because they did not speak what is perceived as standard Vietnamese dialect, they were characterized as "Americans" whose claims to an ethnic Vietnamese identity were de-legitimatized. Following this discussion, I examine how participants employed imagination to legitimatize their sense of belonging and affirm their ethnic Vietnamese identity. I conclude this chapter by suggesting that a race-conscious translingual approach that focuses on the embodied experiences of heritage speakers help us complicate and unpack the material impact of language differences within a traditional translingual approach.

THE STUDY

This qualitative study investigates how second-generation, Vietnamese heritage language speakers affiliate and self-identify with members of their ethnic communities. In this research, the designation *heritage language speaker* is used to identify individuals who either speak or have a personal connection to their heritage language (Fishman 2001; Cummins 2005; Wiley 2005; Peyton, Ranard, and McGinnis 2001). The term *second generation* denotes "U.S.-born adolescents with at least one foreign-born parent" (Kim and Chao 2009, 30). This research focuses on the lives of three second-generation heritage language speakers: Kate, Jane, and Henry. At the time the study was conducted, all participants were undergraduate students, two of whom were studying at a large land-grant university in Arizona. One other participant was a student at a large state university in Southern California. Participants ranged in age from eighteen to twenty-five years. They were selected on the basis of three criteria: participants were second-generation Vietnamese Americans; they had to have at least an elementary ability to read, write, speak, or understand Vietnamese; and participants had to be at least eighteen years of age. Once participants were selected, a profile of each individual was created.

The participants were recruited through recruitment flyers that were disseminated to the Vietnamese Student Association (VSA) listserv, as well as through contacts with former students and snowball sampling

(Seidman 1998). After conducting a pilot study, I, as the principal investigator, interviewed the three participants, employing phenomenological interviewing procedures as a method of data collection (Seidman 1998). In doing so, I was able to examine participants' past, present, and imagined future selves. The interviews consisted of three ninety-minute interviews that took one–three weeks to complete. For students in Arizona, all interviews were conducted on campus. For the participant in California, all three interviews were conducted at his place of residence. After the interviews, I sought clarification from two participants regarding their answers. Correspondence was conducted through email. The interviews were tape recorded, transcribed, and coded using MAXQDA 11 software. The data were coded for topics, themes, and categories. As themes began to emerge, a chart was created to cross-compare the data and group them together into broader conceptual categories.

PERIPHERAL PARTICIPATION AS A WAY OF LEARNING

Identities are, in part, shaped by our participation in communities of practice. Jean Lave and Etienne Wenger (1991) view learning as a situated social activity where newcomers participate in the sociocultural practices of a community. They define this process of learning as *legitimate peripheral participation*. Legitimate peripheral participation describes a process whereby "learners inevitably participate in communities of practitioners and . . . the mastery of knowledge and skill requires newcomers to move toward full participation in the sociocultural practices of a community" (29). The conditions for learning and knowledge are thus inseparable from participation in the social practices of a community, shaping not only the learning process but also learners' identities.

The degree to which newcomers are given peripheral access to participate in a community constructs learners' identities. Wenger (1998) discusses the importance of participation and non-participation in shaping identities. He argues that "we not only produce our identities through the practices we engage in, but we also define ourselves through practices we do not engage in. Our identities are constituted not only by what we are but also by what we are not" (164). In this regard, identities are constituted by our non-participation. Wenger defines two distinct forms of non-participation as peripherality and marginality. Peripherality requires some form of non-participation to make full participation possible. When newcomers gain legitimate peripheral access to their communities of practice, a degree of non-participation becomes necessary for them to observe, learn, and understand their relationship to social practices that they will engage in more fully. In this sense, non-participation is "an initial relation that allowed them to become involved" in their communities' practices (166). In contrast, marginality is a form of non-participation that restricts and prevents participation from occurring (165–66). When newcomers are given peripheral access to engage in social practices, their identities are shaped within the immediate context of their communities, as is the vision they have of themselves and their future.

Identities are produced not only by participation and non-participation but also through the creative process of imagination. Individuals see themselves, the world in which they live, and their relationship with others across time and space through the act of imagination, which serves as an important mode of belonging and group membership. As Wenger (1998, 181) states, imagination is a creative process that "involves unconstrained assumptions of relatedness; it can create relations of identity anywhere, throughout history, and in unrestricted numbers." The creative process of imagination thus involves "expanding our self by transcending our time and space and creating new images of the world and ourselves" (176). Although Wenger notes that imagination differs from fantasy, it requires an element of it for us to recognize our experiences in others, establish affinities, reimagine new identities, and create alternative experiences and scenarios that foster a fraternity with others in an imagined community.

DISCUSSION

Participation, Heritage Language Learning, and Identities

In communities of practice, identities are co-constructed through social practices. Participation in communities of practice requires learning how to use and understand cultural artifacts and technologies. Raised in a household that values the maintenance of the Vietnamese language and culture, Jane has always been active in her Vietnamese community. She described her experiences of interacting with other Vietnamese and participating in cultural activities during the annual Tet celebration, popularly known as the Lunar New Year. During the Tet festival, older adults perform the traditional ritual of *mung tuoi* whereby *li xi*, or "lucky money," is given to children on the day of the celebration. This time-honored custom of distributing lucky money in red envelopes is part of a larger constellation of other ritualized practices, such as honoring ancestors and preparing special holiday foods. For Jane, Tet is an important holiday filled with busy activity in the home. In her interview, she recounted her experiences of celebrating Tet and explained how the meaning of the holiday had added significance for her as she became older and was able to participate in it in more complex ways:

> When I was younger, like when I was, you know, four or five, Tet to me was like "oh . . . I just get money in a red envelope. Cool. I get free money for nothing." Just *chuc tet* (new year's greeting) and I get money. And then . . . going through religious education, I started learning more about it. And I started realizing [that] the money isn't just money. It's lucky money. You know, *lay hen*. Tet is . . . not really considered a holiday in America. But like I always "oh . . . yay . . . Tet." Like I'm so excited for it.

As a child, Jane did not understand the significance of the artifacts of her community, in part because they were not made transparent to her. While social scientists who study the learning process have long taken artifacts as a given, Lave and Wenger (1991) take an analytical approach to the artifacts of practice, or what they term the "technology of practice," and its relationship to access and understanding. Artifacts embody a practice's history and heritage; thus, understanding their significance to ongoing practices requires more than learning how they operate but also how they help to "connect with the history of the practice and to participate more directly in its cultural life" (101). For Jane, the money she received in red envelopes held no sociocultural significance other than its extrinsic monetary value; however, her ongoing involvement in religious education made it clear that the money she received in red envelopes during the Tet festival "isn't just money. It's lucky money," which signified luck and prosperity for the entire new year. This newfound understanding of li xi helped her develop "a view of . . . the whole enterprise" of Tet "and what there [was] to be learned" about her culture through the social practices and cultural artifacts with which she engaged (93). These instances of participation and engagement with artifacts connected Jane to time-honored traditions, historical practices, and cultural life that shaped her Vietnamese ethnic identity and membership status in her community.

Henry's involvement in Binh Dinh—a traditional Vietnamese form of martial arts—offered multiple points of entry in learning Vietnamese traditions and enabled him to participate in the social practices of his martial arts community. In his interview, Henry described greeting practices practitioners of Binh Dinh must perform before entering the training facility:

> Your first duty is when you show up, you walk straight to the original grandmaster's photo, and you . . . ummm . . . I don't know the English word is called but *bai to*. Like you . . . ahh . . . you *cho* or you greet the photo. And then you greet the master, and then, it wasn't really necessary, but you

can also greet the other black belts like you would say hi . . . in a formal fashion . . . You have to say "hi" to people; you gotta respect your elders.

Henry observed and enacted the appropriate practices regulating formal methods of social acknowledgment. These formal greeting practices were not merely verbal. They entailed a host of ritualized and embodied practices. When entering his martial arts studio, Henry was expected to "chi," or pay homage to the photo of the grandmaster. Paying respect in this matter included a constellation of other ritualized practices—such as burning incense, bowing, and praying to the photo—that connect Henry to a history that informs his present. Henry then acknowledged the other martial artists who are of higher social ranking in his community. These embodied practices replicate the social hierarchy in Vietnamese culture (Kibria 1993). This social hierarchy is predicated on a number of social and cultural factors, such as age, education, and social and economic status. In practicing formal greetings, Henry indexes his own identity as a peripheral participant who honors the Vietnamese traditional practice of deferring to elders in his community. These practices are directly linked to the ways he constructs his ethnic identity.

I draw attention to the embodied experiences of heritage language speakers to demonstrate how a race-conscious translingual approach informs the ways heritage languages and ethnic identities are enacted in social practices. While heritage languages and identities are constructed through language ideology, a race-conscious translingual approach understands that heritage languages and identities never remain simply at the level of ideology. Rather, they are experienced and embodied. This perspective allows for a greater analysis of the relationships among race, ethnicity, identity, and language because these categories are made real in the lives of heritage speakers in communities of practice. As the lives of Jane and Henry demonstrate, identities are produced in and negotiated through their engagement in social practice. Identities, as translingualism rightfully notes, are not stable but evolving. However, identities evolve over time, not merely through language but also through participants' increased engagement and changing social status in communities of practice. Their ongoing participation entails a more complex sense of who they are over time as they take on different responsibilities and assume old-timer status in their communities. However, as much as communities of practice organize opportunities for members to participate, they also exert power to exclude members from engaging in social practices. In social situations where they were judged for speaking a non-standardized Vietnamese, they were indexed and marginalized as "Americans."

Marginalization, Non-Participation, and Identity

While the mantra "we are always translingual" (Bawarshi 2016; Horner et al. 2011; Alvarez et al. 2017; Canagarajah 2013) implies a uniform and universal experience with regard to language and identity, translingual scholars acknowledge that we all differ from each other with respect to a perceive standard. As Gilyard (2016) points out, the mantra echoes a "sameness of difference" that elides the struggles of those most marginalized by standard language ideology. Standard language ideology, according to Rosina Lippi-Green (1994, 166), is "a bias toward an abstracted, idealized, homogeneous spoken language which is imposed from above, and which takes as its model the written language. The most salient feature is the goal of suppression of variation of all kinds." Imposed from above, language ideology shapes social and cultural institutions by linking languages to "group and personal identity, to aesthetics, to morality, and to epistemology" (Woolard and Schieffelin 1994, 56); as this linkage suggests, standard language ideology exerts a powerful influence on the way people conceptualize their language and its users (Milroy 2001).

Standard language ideology has real and material consequences for heritage speakers who are deemed incompetent speakers by members of their heritage community. Standard language ideologies are used to exclude heritage speakers from full participation in communities of practice by de-legitimatizing their ethnic identity. As an example, Kate was raised by her grandparents, but she had minimal interactions with them, which affected her chances of speaking, reading, or writing in Vietnamese. The little interaction she did have with them was to request food or respond to questions that required her to answer either "yes" or "no." Because the language practices in her home afforded Kate little opportunity to develop her Vietnamese, she was unable to articulate her thoughts fluently. Instead, she gestured and spoke single words to express her ideas. To communicate with her grandparents, especially with her grandmother who did not speak English, she would wave her "arms around . . . [and] point at things." She employed physical gestures to communicate because she recognized that her knowledge of Vietnamese was "really basic stuff, but it just wasn't complete. Like, they weren't complete sentences. They weren't complete thoughts. They were just, like, words shattered." Because Kate perceived her Vietnamese proficiency as "basic" and "shattered," she spoke very little or remained silent in the presence of more fluent Vietnamese speakers. For instance, at an outing, her family's friends attempted to engage her in conversation, but because she did not know how to speak the language, she often responded with the only word she knew that would deflect attention away from her and limit her interaction with them. She would simply answer "yes."

> Like, when we would . . . when we would go back to California . . . ummm . . . we'd go to Little Saigon and then . . . this is, like, when I was in high school, I was more aware of, like, people talking to me so then when people would talk to me, because they knew my grandpa or my mom or my dad and then I really wouldn't be able to reply. I'd just be like "*da*" (yes). So then, I'd feel really guilty about it, and then my grandpa or my mom or my dad would reply for me. So, it was kinda like . . . kinda like I was mute or something. Like I couldn't speak. They'd always had to speak for me or I just had to say it in, like, English with a Vietnamese accent.

The guilt and shame Kate experienced were largely reactions to those who sought to de-legitimatize her Vietnamese identity by evaluating her perceived lack of Vietnamese language proficiency. In this particular instance, Vietnamese speakers publicly denounced her because "she doesn't speak Vietnamese"; thus, they perceived that she has lost the very link that connects her to her ethnic Vietnamese identity. Their public shaming was an effort to de-legitimatize the authenticity of Kate's Vietnamese identity and position her as an assimilated Vietnamese whom they regarded as "so American now" for shifting to the dominant language and losing the ability to speak the heritage language. To Kate, "It was pretty obvious that the comment, 'she's so American now' was negative. It wasn't, like, a positive comment. So, I took that . . . like, in a bad way." That is, she rightfully perceived the micro-aggressive comment negatively because it was designed to make her "feel really guilty" for not speaking her heritage language and losing her ethnic Vietnamese culture. Moreover, they would "have their, like, kid next to them or something and the kid can speak in Vietnamese." The child's public display of his or her heritage language proficiency only reinforced the shame and guilty Kate felt. In these instances, Kate withdrew from participating in social and cultural activities; instead, she remained reticent and at times "mute" because she was not invested in the discriminatory language practices of a community where inequitable relations of power defined the interaction between her and other Vietnamese. In the discriminatory practices of her community, Kate was made to feel so ashamed and guilty about her language skills that she even questioned herself: "Oh. Wow. This is so . . . so . . . so bad. Like, am I really that bad?"

A perceived standard accent that is free of regional variation is also used to discriminate and de-legitimatize heritage language speakers' ethnic identities. Lippi-Green (1994, 164–65) notes that the term *accent* "is used as a loosely defined reference to sets of distinctive differences over geographic or social space, most usually phonological and intonation features." Accent discrimination plays out in our social interaction with others. Henry often experienced accent discrimination for his inability to reproduce the paralinguistic features that would have indexed him as a native Vietnamese speaker. When asked about his experience speaking his heritage language among other Vietnamese speakers, Henry acknowledged that he was ridiculed for not pronouncing words like "natives . . . are saying [them]." Throughout his interview, he mentioned that the Vietnamese "in the community . . . would fix you . . . and laugh. 'Hahaha . . . you're an American kid. Your accent is really bad. But this is how you say it.' " By openly ridiculing Henry for his accent, targeted language speakers were rejecting it and thus rejecting his identity. According to Lippi-Green (165), "When people reject an accent, they also reject the identity of the person speaking: his or her race, ethnic heritage, national origin, regional affiliation, or economic class." Accent discrimination becomes the basis for exclusion because it imposes a mythical, region-free dialect. Despite the ridicule, Henry insisted that he never took offense to it. He stated that he was unaffected by the comments so he could reframe their accent discrimination as a positive corrective to his otherwise Americanized Vietnamese accent. During the interview, he was quick to downplay the reaction of those who ridiculed him by portraying it as a tease meant to merely point out that he spoke like an "American kid." In fact, he portrayed them as beneficent, teaching him the proper ways of articulating Vietnamese words.

Although Henry claimed that he was unperturbed by being Anglicized, he was resentful of his aunt who criticized his Vietnamese pronunciation:

> I mean, ummm . . . she was just picking at me, like "oh . . . you . . . you don't say that. You say this. Oh, you don't say this. You say that. Or, no . . . no . . . no . . . this and this." I'll look at her and go "your kid doesn't speak Vietnamese. Why . . . why you're bothering me so much about this." So that's when I got angry. I mean . . . her son lives with my grandmother. My grandmother calls me to go do errands for her at . . . the house because my cousin can't speak Vietnamese . . . And, yeah, I'm about two miles away from their house and my grandma keeps calling me to do stuff at the house. I'm like, "you know he's here. He can do it, too." [To which his grandmother replied] "Yeah, but he doesn't understand me."

What is particularly striking about this example is that Henry is engaged in traditional Vietnamese practices of fulfilling his filial obligation but is denied a legitimate ethnic Vietnamese identity on the basis on his ability to speak the language proficiently. The traditional Vietnamese household is unlike the nuclear family of Western cultures. For many

Vietnamese, the home includes not only the immediate family but also extended kinships across multiple generations. This experience of home socializes children to practices that emphasize the importance of filial obligation over personal interest and self-fulfillment. Hein Do (1999, 9) explains that the virtue of *hieu*, or filial piety, is taught at a very young age and is reinforced in social institutions. As Do states, this virtue "refers to the idea of love, care, and respect that children give to their parents. This obligation is unconditional, even in the case of a parent who abandons the children or does not fulfill his or her parental duties" (9). For children raised with such practices, maintaining strong obligatory ties to home is a display of loyalty to one's family lineage. This collectivist practice defines not only the traditional Vietnamese home but also the construction of one's identity. Notions of self-hood, particularly for immigrant youths, find their meaning in the daily interaction with other members of the household: "Culture dictates that parent-child obligations should be mutual and lifelong" (Zhou and Bankston 1998, 165).

Henry was indeed fulfilling his filial obligation toward his family, so he was particularly agitated when recounting this interaction with his aunt. Unlike his previous encounters with others who corrected his Vietnamese, he was frustrated with his aunt for denying his Vietnamese identity. His interaction with his aunt is significant because "it depicts clearly that a learner's identity is not only constituted by social interaction, but also constitutive of social interaction" (Norton 2000, 136). In this brief interaction, his aunt sought to position Henry as an incompetent and illegitimate Vietnamese speaker, but because Henry was invested in his identity as his grandmother's caregiver, he angrily resisted his aunt's consistent criticism by pointing out that her son, Henry's cousin, cannot speak Vietnamese at all and is thus unable to assist his grandmother with household responsibilities, despite the fact that he lives with her. In this interaction, Henry resisted his aunt's critical comments on his Vietnamese language skills by pointing out her hypocrisy.

Such instances of discrimination based on standard language ideologies erect artificial boundaries that define some languages as proper and appropriate while vilifying others (Horner et al. 2011; Lu and Horner 2016; Alvarez et al. 2017). Translingualism's rearticulation of language differences as the norm flattens the lived experiences of those whose linguistic differences index them as deviant. While translingualism insists that reading, writing, and speaking exist within an economic, social, cultural, and geopolitical landscape that is defined by asymmetrical relations of power (Lu and Horner 2016), rarely are such instances of embodied experiences of translingual practices described. A race-consciousness translingual approach views these examples of discrimination as inherent in both intercultural and intra-cultural exchanges. In these examples, participants' translingual practices were registered as deviations from Vietnamese standard language practices. The fallout of their perceived language difference is that they were othered as "Americans" whose ethnic identity as Vietnamese was de-legitimatized. Embodying these attitudes, Kate experienced shame and guilt that left her "mute" and withdrawing from social interaction. Henry expressed anger at his aunt, who focused exclusively on his language proficiency rather than recognizing that he was fulfilling a traditional Vietnamese practice. Instead of the discrimination they experienced, they desired a shared cultural community that was constructed from their imagined fraternity across time and space. By imagining this community, they were also imagining themselves and others belonging to a homogeneous cultural heritage (Norton 2000). For these participants, imagination played an important role in shaping how they interacted with members outside their imagined communities by defining and demarcating the boundaries that constitute insiders and outsiders. What follows is a discussion of participants' imagined communities and identities and the role such imagining plays in their ethnic identity and heritage language investment.

Imagined Communities and Identities

When participants imagined their communities, they were also reimagining identities in relation to them. They saw themselves as part of a homogeneous Vietnamese community that transcended both time and space. In reimagining this community across time and space, participants were employing "strategic essentialism" (Lyons 2009). In speaking of tribal people, Lyons argues that strategic essentialism serves to "actively resist the threat of language loss [by] construing the language as nationally, religiously, culturally, or even biologically hardwired into one's tribal identity" (78). Both Kate and Jane employ strategic essentialism in their reimagined communities to legitimatize their identities as stewards of Vietnamese history and culture.

Kate's investment in practicing Vietnamese was structured by her identity as a descendent of Vietnamese royalty. The revelation of her family's history came to light on many occasions when her grandfather related stories of their family's royal lineage:

> I think one time during Tet, we went to my great-grandma's house. And . . . ahhh . . . I realize . . . I found out that we were royal, and I was like, "oh my gosh. We're royal. Like, how come . . . I come . . . I didn't know

this?" so then I was like, "okay . . . I need to learn about my family more." So then he [my grandfather] told me about it. And so, yeah . . . basically we were royal. That's why I, like, their last name is so weird. Not mine but theirs. And . . . umm . . . that's why it's so uncommon, which is like *Ton Nu* and *Ton That*. Yeah, so I was, like, "these are really weird last names." But that finally explained it to me, like, why the last names are so weird. So, because we were royal, I was like, "oh my gosh. Like, I wanna learn more."

The revelation that Kate is a descendent of Vietnamese royalty was a transformative experience that shaped her outlook on the language and culture, and it explained why her family members are important figures in their communities. When she discovered her family's history, Kate came to the realization that "this is, like, my family; this is my culture," and this realization served as an important catalyst for her investment to "really learn Vietnamese. That's when I bought the books from Little Saigon, and then I brought them back to Arizona and we [she and her mother] studied Vietnamese." Although her community in Arizona offered few opportunities for her to speak the language, she relied on books and her immediate family members for support. Kate found renewed interest in learning her heritage language because she wanted to be a part of a culture her family had once been instrumental in shaping. She desperately wanted to learn the language to identify with her family's royal lineage and be a good representative of her background. Not knowing the language, she felt "I'm just a terrible representation" of her family, "so that was another factor as to why I wanted to delve into more Vietnamese culture." Here, Kate essentializes Vietnamese culture strategically, equating language with culture to invest her heritage language learning. Kate eagerly invested her time and energy in learning the language so she could fulfill her desire to represent her family. She saw language as a strong indicator of ethnic identity and acceptance into the Vietnamese community.

Furthermore, her identity as a descendent of Vietnamese royalty helped her resist linguistic discrimination and enabled her to speak for herself. Whereas she once remained "mute" in the presence of other Vietnamese speakers out of guilt and shame, she was now confident in practicing her Vietnamese in public spaces:

> Now I order by myself in Vietnamese even though I still mess up. I don't get as embarrassed because I'm learning and trying. There's nothing bad about learning and trying. I see my older sister ordering in English even though she's better than me at speaking Vietnamese, and I don't know why. Now that I'm a young adult, I don't see myself as a dependent kid anymore, so I don't depend on my family to order/speak for me.

Although recognizing that she frequently made mistakes, she did not "get as embarrassed because I'm learning and trying." Kate's imagined identity contributed positively to her confidence and independence, allowing her to reframe the relationship between herself and other Vietnamese speakers and to see discriminatory language contexts as opportunities to practice Vietnamese. She refused to stay "mute" and practiced her heritage language, in spite of the linguistic discrimination and criticism she faced. In this regard, she no longer saw herself through "borrowed eyes" of other speakers (Tse 1998); instead, she positioned herself as a language learner who is "learning and trying."

Jane's imagined community is predicated on an imagined past where the use of cultural artifacts is re-interpreted symbolically to resist cultural assimilation and reassert traditional Vietnamese values and practices. As a member who has gained old-timer status, Jane has sought to resist assimilation, both within herself and especially in her younger sisters, by enforcing the use of traditional Vietnamese dresses, *ao dai*, to ensure that her sisters continue to engage in the social practices of their community: "I tell them 'oh . . . go put on your *ao dai* (traditional Vietnamese dress) for church.' They'll be, like, 'eww . . . no . . . I can wear shorts and a T-shirt.' And I'm just, like, 'GO PUT ON YOUR *AO DAI*.' And they'll be, like, 'no,' so then I'll have to yell so loud to the extent that they know I'm being serious."

Jane believed she acquired old-timer status because she saw herself as a custodian of traditional Vietnamese practices. The impact of assimilation becomes especially pronounced among adolescent immigrants who seek acceptance from mainstream culture. In her study of the changing social, economic, and cultural lives of Vietnamese immigrants, Nazli Kibria (1993, 146) argues that "both young and old conceded, younger Vietnamese Americans were becoming more American in many ways, ranging from . . . modes of dress . . . to their increasingly individualistic orientation toward life." For this reason, the ao dai constitutes an important cultural artifact of group membership that contributes to Jane's sisters' Vietnamese identity. In investigating ao dai pageantry, Nhi T. Lieu (2000, 135) asserts that a "woman's refusal to wear the ao dai can be interpreted as a lack of effort and allegiance to Vietnamese culture; conversely her willingness to embrace the ao dai becomes a major source of ethnic pride for herself as well as the community at large." The ao dai can be interpreted as an artifact that "symbolically . . . invokes nostalgia and timelessness associated with a gendered image of the homeland for which many Vietnamese people throughout the diaspora yearn"

(128). The ao dai thus invokes an imagined past and community that Vietnamese youths today seek to reclaim.

Her sisters' preference for shorts and T-shirts over the traditional Vietnamese dress thus signified to Jane that they have disavowed their Vietnamese cultural values in favor for American cultural practices. In the context of her interaction with her sisters, Jane positioned them as Americans who refused to participate in the practices of their community by not embodying their Vietnamese identity through dress. Much like Kate, Jane essentializes Vietnamese and American cultures by viewing articles of clothing as a vital part of identity formation. Essentializing culture this way allows Jane to simplify the complexity of culture to position herself as a custodian of Vietnamese heritage. Through clothing, she gains the ethos to reprimand her sisters for being "more American now." In this instance, language alone did not determine the level of social interaction but rather the degree to which members participated in cultural practices that defined in-group membership. The excerpt highlights Jane's evolving identity as an old-timer in the practices of her community. Once a newcomer, she gained legitimate peripheral access to her community that enabled her to learn from old-timers and develop a more profound appreciation for its cultural practices. Now positioned as an old-timer herself, she sought to instill a respect for cultural practices in members of her community.

Participants constructed their identities not only through their direct engagement in communities of practice but also through their imagination. Imagination serves an important mode of belonging that allows individuals to view themselves in relation to members of communities of practice to which they do not belong (Wenger 1998). As Norton (2013, 3) states, imagined communities are "also a community of the imagination, a desired community that offers possibilities for an enhanced range of identity options in the future." In imagining a homogeneous Vietnamese community that transcends both time and space, participants engaged in strategic essentialism to legitimatize their identity as stewards of Vietnamese heritage. Their stewardship played an important role in their heritage language learning and cultural participation.

CONCLUSION

In this chapter, I discussed the embodied experiences of heritage language speakers by examining their relationship to communities of practice. Unlike previous translingual scholarship, I argue that a race-conscious translingual paradigm not only focuses on the ideological construct of heritage language and ethnic identity but also examines how communities of practice afford and constrain opportunities for ethnic identity formation. Examining speakers' lived experiences, I contend, allows for a greater analysis of how race, ethnicity, language, and identity are not only performed (Young 2004) but also embodied and negotiated in communities of practice.

For second-generation Vietnamese Americans, constructing a coherent identity is complicated because they constantly negotiate very different and often conflicting cultural worldviews and practices. Nhi Lieu (2000, 143) posits that the "demands made by the community and by dominant American culture have compelled many Vietnamese Americans to construct new hyphenated ethnic identities." The formerly hyphenated ethnic identities Asian Americans construct entail a foreignness or otherness that is always already non-White. Unlike Asian Americans or any People of Color for that matter, White ethnics are viewed as having an "unracialized identity or location" and are thus perceived as representative of all human experience (DiAngelo 2018). Mia Tuan (1998) explores how Asian Americans negotiate their ethnic identities to exercise "choice regarding the ethnic practices and values they wish to integrate or discard," and she compares their ethnic identity options to those of White ethnics. For White ethnics, transmitting cultural knowledge and values is optional. When they do assert their ethnic identity, it often takes on a "superficial function . . . to be taken up in one's free time" (26–27). Although Tuan argues that these ethnic identity options are available to her Asian American participants, she points out that it is only in their personal lives that they can exercise such discretion. In public spaces, Asian Americans are not afforded such options because "others continue to define them in racialized or ethnic terms" (18). For this reason, Asians are continually perceived with suspicion because of their race, or what Tuan calls an "assumption of foreignness" (18).

By centering race, language, and identities, a race-conscious translingual approach examines the ways hyphenated ethnic identities are racialized or defined in ethnic terms. The approach interrogates how speakers conceptualize and negotiate the different social and cultural practices associated with their hyphenated ethnic identities. Thus, being both Vietnamese and American is constructed ideologically not only as two different cultures but also, and most important, as two different ways of being and existing in the world. While translingualism posits that through language, speakers shuttle in and across different spheres of belonging, I argue that a race-conscious translingual approach looks beyond the features of language to examine how communities of practice exert a powerful influence in affording and constraining access to social practices, which is pivotal to ethnic identity construction.

Not surprisingly, participants like Kate "associate Vietnamese language with it being a collectivist culture and English with individualist principles." She recognizes that language, practice, and identity are intertwined in ways that play a "big part of my growth [in] figuring out how much of each I would like to represent day to day." Jane also acknowledges her hyphenated identity by recognizing that "there is no Vietnamese alone . . . I just feel, you know, I'm both, whether people like it or not. I'm Vietnamese and American because I was born here." By investigating the lived experience of speakers in communities of practice, translingualism will be equipped to adequately address the language differences it celebrates without flattening them. A race-conscious translingual approach examines not only how language shapes heritage language speakers' identities but also the social practices in communities that inform their identities, real and imagined.

REFERENCES

Alvarez, Sara, Suresh Canagarajah, Eunjeong Lee, Jerry Won Lee, and Shakil Rabbi. 2017. "Translingual Practice, Ethnic Identities, and Voice in Writing." In *Crossing Divides: Exploring Translingual Writing Pedagogies and Programs*, ed. Bruce Horner and Laura Tetrault, 31–47. Logan: Utah State University Press.

Bawarshi, Anis. 2016. "Beyond the Genre Fixation: A Translingual Perspective on Genre." *College English* 78 (3): 243–49.

Canagarajah, Suresh. 2013. *Translingual Practice: Global Englishes and Cosmopolitan Relations*. New York: Routledge.

Cummins, Jim. 2005. "A Proposal for Action: Strategies for Recognizing Heritage Language Competence as a Learning Resource within the Mainstream Classroom." *Modern Language Journal* 89 (4): 585–92.

DiAngelo, Robin. 2018. *White Fragility: Why It's So Hard for White People to Talk about Racism*. Boston: Beacon.

Do, Hien. 1999. *The Vietnamese Americans*. Westport, CN: Greenwood.

Fishman, Joshua A. 2001. "300-Plus Years of Heritage Language Education in the United States." In *Heritage Languages in America: Preserving a National Resource*, ed. Joy Kreeft Peyton, Donald. A. Ranard, and Scott McGinnis, 81–98. Washington, DC, and McHenry, IL: Center for Applied Linguistics and Delta Systems.

Gilyard, Keith. 2016. "The Rhetoric of Translingualism." *College English* 78 (3): 284–89.

Horner, Bruce, Min-Zhan Lu, Jacqueline Jones Royster, and John Trimbur. 2011. "Language Difference in Writing: Toward a Translingual Approach." *College English* 73 (3): 303–21.

Horner, Bruce, and John Trimbur. 2002. "English Only and U.S. College Composition." *College Composition and Communication* 53 (4): 594–630.

Kells, Michelle Hall. 2010. "Mapping the Cultural Ecologies of Language and Literacy." In *Cross-Language Relations in Composition*, ed. Bruce Horner, Min-Zhan Lu, and Paul K. Matsuda, 204–13. Carbondale: Southern Illinois University Press.

Kibria, Nazli. 1993. *Family Tightrope: The Changing Lives of Vietnamese Americans.* Princeton, NJ: Princeton University Press.
Kim, Su Yeong, and Ruth K. Chao. 2009. "Heritage Language Fluency, Ethnic Identity, and School Effort of Immigrant Chinese and Mexican Adolescents." *Cultural Diversity and Ethnic Minority Psychology* 15 (1): 27–37. doi:10.1037/a0013052.
Lave, Jean, and Etienne Wenger. 1991. *Situated Learning: Legitimate Peripheral Participation.* New York: Cambridge University Press.
Lee, Jerry Won, and Christopher Jenks. 2016. "Doing Translingual Dispositions." *College Composition and Communication* 68 (2): 317–44.
Lieu, Nhi T. 2000. "The Nation through Pageantry: Femininity and the Politics of Vietnamese Womanhood in the 'Hoa Hau Ao Dai' Contest." *Journal of Women Studies* 21 (1–2): 127–51.
Lippi-Green, Rosina. 1994. "Accent, Standard Language Ideology, and Discriminatory Pretext in the Courts." *Language in Society* 23 (2): 163–98.
Lu, Min-Zhan, and Bruce Horner. 2016. "Introduction: Translingual Work." *College English* 78 (3): 207–18.
Lyons, Scott Richard. 2009. "The Fine Art of Fencing: Nationalism, Hybridity, and the Search for a Native American Writing Pedagogy." *JAC* 29 (1–2): 77–105.
Lyons, Scott Richard. 2010. "There's No Translation for It: The Rhetorical Sovereignty of Indigenous Languages." In *Cross-Language Relations in Composition*, ed. Bruce Horner, Min-Zhan Lu, and Paul K. Matsuda, 127–41. Carbondale: Southern Illinois University Press.
Milroy, James. 2001. "Language Ideologies and the Consequences of Standardization." *Journal of Sociolinguistics* 5 (4): 530–55.
Norton, Bonny. 2000. *Identity and Language Learning: Gender, Ethnicity and Educational Change.* New York: Longman.
Norton, Bonny. 2013. *Identity and Language Learning: Extending the Conversation.* Bristol, UK: Multilingualism Matters.
Peyton, Joy Kreeft, Donald A. Ranard, and Scott McGinnis, eds. 2001. *Heritage Languages in America: Preserving a National Resource.* Washington, DC, and McHenry, IL: Center for Applied Linguistics and Delta Systems.
Seidman, Irving. 1998. *Interviewing as Qualitative Research: A Guide for Researchers in Education and the Social Sciences.* New York: Teachers College Press.
Tse, Lucy. 1998. "Seeing Themselves through Borrowed Eyes: Asian Americans in Ethnic Ambivalence/Evasion." *Multicultural Review* 7 (2): 28–34.
Tse, Lucy. 2001. *Why Don't They Learn English? Separating Fact from Fallacy in the U.S. Language Debate.* New York: Teachers College Press.
Tuan, Mia. 1998. *Forever Foreigners or Honorary Whites? The Asian Ethnic Experience Today.* New Brunswick, NJ: Rutgers University Press.
Wenger, Etienne. 1998. *Communities of Practice: Learning, Meaning, and Identity.* New York: Cambridge University Press.
Wiley, Terrence G. 2005. "The Reemergence of Heritage and Community Language Policy in the U.S. National Spotlight." *Modern Language Journal* 89 (4): 594–601.
Woolard, Kathryn, and Bambi B. Schieffelin. 1994. "Language Ideology." *Annual Review of Anthropology* 23 (1): 55–82.
Young, Vershawn Ashanti. 2004. "Your Average Nigga." *College Composition and Communication* 55 (4): 693–715.
Zhou, Min, and Carl Bankston. 1998. *Growing up American: How Vietnamese Children Adapt to Life in the United States.* New York: Russell Sage Foundation.

5
PERPETUALLY FOREIGN, PERPETUALLY DEFICIENT, AND PERPETUALLY PRIVILEGED
Exposing Microaggressions and Challenging Whiteness

Bethany Davila

According to Bruce Horner, Min-Zhan Lu, Jacqueline Jones Royster, and John Trimbur (2011), a translingual approach acknowledges what linguists and many writing scholars have long known: that language is fluid and always multiple. The authors of this first piece on translingualism describe a translingual approach as one that "sees difference in language . . . as a resource for producing meaning in writing, speaking, reading, and listening" (303). More than just recognizing and using the full repertoire of one's linguistic resources, a translingual approach asks readers to consider difference in language as a sign of authorial agency and an opportunity for meaning making. Jerry Won Lee and Christopher Jenks (2016, 317) further describe this aspect of translingualism in terms of dispositions that center on "openness to plurality and difference in the ways people use language." In asking writers and readers to see difference as purposeful, beneficial, and an opportunity to engage in "fluency across language differences" (Horner et al. 2011, 307), a translingual approach challenges both standardized edited American English (SEAE) as the one and only default language variety and standard language ideologies that allow for a belief in SEAE as the only correct language that is superior to other language varieties. Indeed, many proponents of translingualism highlight the potential of this approach in terms of the space it could create for traditionally othered or stigmatized language practices. As an example, Lee (2016, 178) argues that translingualism is important precisely because it creates opportunities for the valuing of stigmatized (or, in his words "pathologized") languages and language practices. In addition, a more recent publication on translingualism lists among the "tenets for a 'translingual' approach"

https://doi.org/10.7330/9781646422104.c005

the acknowledgment that "communicative practices are not neutral or innocent but informed by and informing economic, geopolitical, social-historical, cultural relations of asymmetrical power" (Lu and Horner 2016, 208). These conceptualizations of language position translingualism in direct contrast to deficit models that understand linguistic difference as something to eradicate for a student to have success in SEAE and draw attention to the social nature of communication and the role of power in the production and reception of text.

However, as the editors of this collection note, translingualism has been critiqued—by Keith Gilyard (2016, 284), among others—for its inattention to race, including the ways it can "flatten" differences among language varieties and ignore power. Gilyard cautions that if everyone is always translingual, we may obscure the very real stigma associated with some kinds of linguistic difference and not others, thereby shifting needed attention away from groups that have been marginalized and penalized for their language use. In other words, translingualism must attend to raciolinguistics—the study of the co-production of language, race, and power (Alim 2016, 27)—to avoid becoming a practice of Whiteness, drawing attention away from race while protecting racist outcomes.

Lee (2016) and Paul Kei Matsuda (2014) offer additional reservations, arguing that translingualism's focus on linguistic difference could work against its goals and create stigma through stereotyping and othering. Matsuda notes that translingualism requires a focus on linguistic differences, which could "mask similarities and might lead to stereotyping" (482). The risk that race might overdetermine expectations and, in the process, enable microaggressions is in some ways the opposite of Gilyard's (2016) concern that we might ignore race—or at least pretend to. Nonetheless, if translingual practices fall into either risk category, they will work to enact Whiteness by preserving privilege among already privileged students.

Because translingualism's potential is accompanied by these serious risks, this chapter works to first further interrogate the risks of race evasiveness and linguistic othering. Specifically, I report on the ways instructors' perceptions of student identities help them make sense of difference in student writing, revealing raciolinguistic ideologies that conflate racialized students with language deviance (Flores and Rosa 2015, 150). I then argue that using raciolinguistics to better understand processes of responding to student writing can help writing teachers and scholars purposefully enact translingualism while attending to race.

SURVEYING INSTRUCTORS

In this IRB-approved research project (UNM IRB, #131165), I adapted a matched guise procedure. This approach is designed to examine language attitudes by holding constant as many factors as possible (Bradac, Cargile, and Hallett 2001). Specifically, in a matched guise procedure, one speaker records a message in multiple dialects to allow researchers to focus only on listeners' responses to the linguistic differences. In this case, I used the same student paper but introduced it as having been written by students of different races and genders (using all of the racial categories from the US Census paired with male and female genders; for example: White female, Asian male, and so on). This kind of approach has also been described as "disguised composition" (Roberts and Cimasko 2008, 133).

After instructors consented to participate in this study, they were directed to the student paper along with a short introduction, including the sentence: "As context, this paper was written by a _____ student for an introductory writing course." The blank was filled in with one of the twelve different race and gender combinations through programming that triggered a new identity profile each time someone consented. The survey was programmed to pull identity combinations beginning at the top of the list, going through the whole list, and then starting again at the top. Then, the survey provided the paper and the survey questions. The survey data were automatically grouped according to which identity profile the reader saw before reading the paper, allowing for comparisons within and across identity categories.

The student paper I used in this project was written by a self-identified White, middle-class female student as she was about to begin her first year at a midwestern university. When writing the paper, which is approximately 800 words long or two pages double-spaced, the student responded to a prompt that instructed her to read an essay and to agree or disagree with the author's argument. The paper came from a pool of student papers I used in previous research projects that inspired this project. I chose the paper out of the larger pool based on the range of identities that were ascribed to it during interviews. The instructors who were interviewed about this paper imagined the student author to be male and female, African American and White, and from various socioeconomic backgrounds. In addition, the paper was assigned grades ranging from B+ to C-, which was the largest grade span in those studies.

The survey asked participants to read the student paper, provide written feedback, assign a grade, and answer questions about their responses to the language in the paper and the student author. I used prior interviews on this topic to guide my survey design. As such, the survey includes open-ended questions such as "what was striking to you in this paper and why?" and "in as much detail as possible, describe the student you pictured as having written this paper." I also wanted to examine the relationship between comprehension and perceived identity/linguistic difference, so I asked participants to rank how well they understood the student's main argument on a scale of 0–100—a common scale in grading student writing—with 100 representing complete understanding. The survey questions are included in appendix 5.A.

To recruit participants, I emailed writing program administrators (WPAs) (identified from institutions' web pages) at nearly 175 public research institutions (according to the Carnegie Mellon classification system). In the email, I asked WPAs to forward my invitation for participation to those who teach writing in their program. To provide an incentive and some level of compensation for participants' time, I offered a ten dollar gift card to everyone who completed the survey as well as an opportunity for participants to enter a drawing for one of five Kindle Fire tablets.

Sixty-nine instructors completed the survey. Forty percent had taught writing for ten+ years, and all had taught at least ten sections of writing; most (70%) were either graduate students or lecturers. The remaining 30 percent were adjunct instructors or tenured/tenure-track professors. Fifty-eight percent of respondents identified their disciplinary background as composition and rhetoric, 32 percent as literature, and 9 percent as creative writing. Most of the respondents came from urban (31) or suburban (19) institutions (others noted rural institutions [4] or were unable to choose from among these categories). Their institutions were situated in the Midwest (23), Northeast (10), South (9), Southwest (9), and Southeast (4). Forty-five of the respondents taught at predominantly White institutions; four respondents taught at Hispanic Serving Institutions (HSIs); one respondent taught at a Historically Black College or University; and 12 could not or chose not to classify their institution in terms of these categories.

Of the respondents who chose to provide information about their gender, 55 percent identified as females and 36 percent identified as males. The vast majority of respondents—89 percent—were White. There were also African American (4%), Latinx (3%), Asian (3%), and Native American (1%) respondents. Sixty-one respondents (of the 66 who responded to this question) speak English as their first language; 2 of those 61 listed two first languages; and 3 respondents listed a language other than English as their first language (Russian, Spanish, and Slovenian).

One limitation to this study is my reliance on the census categories for race, which do not always account for the ways different racial groups self-identify. I also treated gender as a binary and did not allow for a more inclusive representation of gender identities. Both of these choices are flaws in my study design. Another limitation is the number of respondents. For each identity combination I have 5–7 responses; or if I analyze my data according to gender alone, I have about 35 responses per category, and for each race, I have about 12 responses. These numbers do not allow me to generalize my findings, and they limit the claims I am able to make. An additional complication to this study design and my analysis of the data is the fact that not everyone who completed the survey paid attention to the introductory text where I indicated the fictitious race/gender combination of the student author. Certainly, some of the respondents specifically referenced the introductory text, thereby indicating beyond doubt that they read that information. However, other participants did not read the introductory text, as they explicitly stated that they imagined a race and gender different from those I provided. Finally, another group of respondents neither referenced the information I provided nor offered any details about race or gender, which doesn't allow me to evaluate whether they read the identity introduction.

These methodological challenges undoubtedly limit my ability to understand the relationship between race/gender combinations and responses to student texts. However, to account for these different interactions with the provided identity profiles, I analyzed the data in multiple ways. First, I looked for patterns within and across the identity groups I provided—regardless of whether the respondent had or had not read the introduction. Then, I recoded the data according to the identity profiles that participants specifically referenced in their responses—meaning that I omitted responses that didn't explicitly reference race and/or gender. Finally, I also coded data according to perceptions of multilingualism—an emergent theme.

I argue that the issues this study illuminates are valid and compelling, especially when put in conversation with other scholarship. The most significant findings from this survey are related to the relationship between perceived identity and perceived multilingualism. Specifically, the survey suggests that readers might attribute linguistic difference to multilingualism based on the perceived identity of the student. In addition, certain kinds of linguistic difference are scored lower than others.

PERPETUALLY FOREIGN

Within the full data set (sorted in the originally provided identity categories), race and gender influenced whether instructors read a written accent in the student's writing. Instructors often read an accent in the writing when they thought the paper was written by Latino and Asian female students: 4 out of 6 (67%) instructors who were told the paper was written by a Latino student commented on second language (L2) features, and 3 out of 6 (50%) instructors who were told the paper was written by an Asian female noted a written accent. In stark contrast, none of the instructors who were told the paper was written by either a White male or White female student (N = 11) commented on a written accent or L2 features. Moreover, the White racial category is the only one in which instructors did not mention other languages/dialects as apparent in the student's writing. See table 5.1 for perceived multilingualism across race, gender, and race and gender.

When instructors did mention other languages/dialects, they didn't always name them; most often, instructors simply noted that they saw signs of English not being the student's first language or did not think English was the student's first language. In a few instances, instructors specifically referenced markers of African American English (AAE) in student writing, and other times instructors noted that English wasn't the student's first language and made explicit comments about student identity that suggested Spanish or an Asian language as the student's first language. It is worth restating here that all of the instructors read the same paper.

The pattern of imagining racialized student identities as also being L2 writers or as multilingual in contrast with imagining White student identities as monolingual is evidence of raciolinguistic ideologies and maps onto documented microaggressions related to language and accent. Specifically, the pattern of perceiving accents among Latino students and Asian female students likely relates to the perpetual foreigner stereotype, which has been well documented in scholarship from the field of psychology. In several studies involving undergraduate students in California, researchers examined the relationship between ethnic identity and national identity. In one study by Thierry Devos and Mahzarin R. Banaji (2005, 451), students were instructed to "judge three ethnic groups on their degree of Americanness . . . [assuming that] individuals from each group were born in the United States, lived in the United States, and were U.S. citizens." They found that Asian Americans "were clearly seen as less American than both white and African Americans . . .

Table 5.1. Perceived multilingualism by race, gender, and race and gender

Identity Marker	Respondents Noting Multilingualism in Paper
African American total (N = 12)	20% (2/12)
African American female (N = 6)	20% (1/6)
African American male (N = 6)	20% (1/6)
Asian total (N = 12)	33% (4/12)
Asian female (N = 6)	50% (3/6)
Asian male (N = 6)	20% (1/6)
Hawaiian total (N = 11)	27% (3/11)
Hawaiian female (N = 6)	33% (2/6)
Hawaiian male (N = 5)	20% (1/5)
Latinx total (N = 11)	45% (5/11)
Latina (N = 5)	20% (1/5)
Latino (N = 6)	67% (4/6)
Native total (N = 12)	20% (2/12)
Native female (N = 5)	0 (0/5)
Native male (N = 7)	29% (2/7)
White total (N = 11)	0 (0/11)
White female (N = 6)	0 (0/6)
White male (N = 5)	0 (0/5)
Male (N = 35)	26% (9/35)
Female (N = 34)	21% (7/34)

not in rights and liberties but in the degree to which they embody the concept 'American'" (451). In other studies, "Consistently, Latino Americans as a group were conceived of as being less American than Caucasian Americans" (Devos, Gavin, and Quintana 2010, 37).

Bill Ong Hing (2001, 455), a professor of law and Asian American studies, also writes about the perpetual foreigner stereotype and argues that "there are two Americas when it comes to race, ethnic background, and who is American," explaining that one America recognizes its diverse backgrounds and origins (in spite of "exclusionary policies aimed at different groups through its history") and one denies the status of *American* to all but a narrow group: "This second vision is Euro-centric, excluding those of Latin and Asian descent, and as we have seen recently, excluding those of Middle Eastern background." Hing describes practices perpetuated by both individuals and the government that range from internment camps to political cartoons (447–49) to propositions "designed to bar immigrant and citizen children from public schools and other public benefits" (453), all of which "de-Americanize" racial and ethnic groups based on "skin color, *accent*, or garb" (454, emphasis added) and thereby ensure that these groups remain "forever foreign, notwithstanding [their] status as a U.S. citizen" (443).

In addition to examining the relationship between ethnicity and perceived nationality or degree of Americanness, Devos and Banaji (2005, 450) also studied possible markers of foreignness and found that being able to speak English was more a marker of Americanness than having lived in America for most of one's life or having been born in America. This link between language and national identity, according to psychologists Derald Wing Sue and colleagues (2007, 276), manifests in a racial microaggression called "alien in [one's] own land: when Asian Americans and Latino Americans are assumed to be foreign-born" and are assumed to speak other languages to the point that when they display no accent, they are told they speak "good English." Another example of this microaggression occurs when native English speakers are presumed to be ESL based on their skin color or name—as seen in the results of this study and in Aja Martinez's experiences described in chapter 3. Again, these microaggressions and this finding in the survey demonstrate raciolinguistic ideologies that link linguistic deviance with racialized identities (Flores and Rosa 2015, 150) and, conversely, merge unmarked (i.e., "standard") White identities with unmarked (i.e., "standard") language. Moreover, these findings highlight the relationship between standard language ideology and Whiteness, a relationship also explored by Rachael Shapiro and Missy Watson in chapter 2 of this volume.

Once the pattern of reading an accent based on certain identity profiles was apparent, I then examined if and how perceptions of language difference showed up in grades and how well instructors understood the student's argument. For this analysis, I coded the data according to perceptions of multilingualism: whether instructors thought the student was an L2 writer, whether the instructor saw possible signs of AAE in the paper (the only specific dialect mentioned in the data), or whether the writing was unmarked and/or unnamed in terms of non-English languages and non-standardized dialects.

PERPETUALLY DEFICIENT

The participants in this survey awarded the same average grade to students perceived to be L2 writers and students with writing unmarked

Table 5.2. Grade and understanding according to perceived linguistic difference

Linguistic Markers	Grade	Understanding
AAE (N = 3)	D+	42
ESL (N = 8)	C	74
Unmarked (N = 52)	C	67

for other languages. However, the scores for average understanding are higher for the instructors who thought the author was an L2 writer in comparison to those who thought the writing was unmarked in terms of multilingualism. In contrast, the instructors who noted markers of AAE—a much smaller subset—gave a lower average grade and a much lower comprehension score (see table 5.2).

These data suggest that the linking of race/gender and L2 status did not necessarily negatively affect instructors' evaluations of the paper or their understanding of the argument. Instead, the average understanding score for papers that were marked with signs of L2 features (excluding the papers that were marked for features of AAE) was higher than the score for unmarked papers. Research by Michael Janopoulos (1992) and Donald L. Rubin and Melanie Williams-James (1997) suggests that when instructors believe a writer is a non-native speaker, they might award higher evaluations to their writing compared to when they think the writing was produced by a native speaker. In fact, one respondent to this survey specifically noted that they "generally take ESL [English as a Second Language] into account when commenting and grading students." Similarly, in Matsuda and colleagues' (2013, 78) survey of writing instructors, one instructor stated that they "look past the surface errors that [ESL students] may make."

Although the papers perceived to have been written by L2 writers received similar grades to the unmarked papers, some linguistic differences were negatively valued. When the paper was read as having signs of AAE, it received the lowest average grade (D+) and understanding score (42), adding to scholarship that argues that perceptions of student authors' race—more so than the presence of specific textual features—influence readers' responses to and evaluations of texts (Piché, Rubin, and Michlin 1978, 115; Inoue 2016, 140; Greenfield 2011, 38). In addition, AAE is arguably the most visibly and consistently stigmatized language variety in our country. Whenever there have been attempts within education to honor AAE, there have been vicious attacks against the language by media, parents, public figures, and other educators who label it as deficient and in direct conflict with possible future success. The controversy surrounding the 1996 Oakland Ebonics Resolution is perhaps the best example of this practice. As Laura Greenfield (2011) has argued, however, AAE is not attacked because of its linguistic features; it is attacked because it is used by African Americans. In other words, racism is the underlying cause of the stigma associated with AAE (38).

Hing (2001, 443–44)—cited earlier in reference to the perpetual foreigner stereotype—specifically contrasts racism based on foreignness with racism based on inferiority, the latter of which, he states, is commonly leveled against African Americans and Black people. The findings in this study seem to mirror those patterns of racism where Latino and Asian female students might be read as linguistic others, but this othering does not negatively affect their grades and, in fact, might lead to a higher understanding score. In contrast, the papers that were read as having signs of AAE were scored the lowest and were the least understood. Although the numbers are particularly low for this finding, as only three respondents noted markers of AAE, this is perhaps the most dangerous finding to ignore or disregard. We have known for decades that AAE is particularly stigmatized. Here I argue that this continues to be the case, that we must do more as a field to uncover the subconscious bias—the "racism by consequence, not by intention" (Inoue 2016, 135)—leveled at our Black students, and that we must pay particular attention to Gilyard's (2016) concerns regarding translingualism, which runs the risk of shifting our attention from racialized linguistic difference to *all* types of linguistic difference.

PERPETUALLY PRIVILEGED

The flip side of these racial microaggressions is a kind of "stereotype lift" (McGee and Martin 2011, 1348) that allows White students to occupy—explicitly and through contrast—the unmarked position of a monolingual, capable American student. Certainly, the survey results indicate that the mythical monolingual student Matsuda (2006) wrote about is very likely a White student, as the instructors who were told the student was White did not comment on markers of other languages or dialects in the writing or in the students' backgrounds. In addition, when I previously interviewed instructors about student papers, asking them to describe the students they imagined having written the papers, instructors commonly noted that their "default" was White when they didn't see any markers of another language variety or dialect. In other words, unmarked language signaled a White author for the instructors in those interviews. In contrast, instructors only imagined African American students when they saw signs of deficiency in the writing (Davila 2012).

In this survey we see the reverse—that suggestions of identities influenced the ways instructors read the student writing, including the social construction of both written accent and deficiency. According to Greenfield (2011, 43, original emphasis), "Privileged white people—regardless of their actual speech—*always already* speak a language of power." She argues that because Standard English is a myth, what gets treated as standard—as privileged and powerful—is the language spoken by White people in positions of power. She supports this argument with evidence of linguistic features that are stigmatized when used by groups of color and accepted when used by White people. One example she offers is that British spelling conventions are commonly accepted as an alternative in the United States but spelling deviations that reflect stigmatized dialects are not (43–44).

In addition, dictionary definitions of *Standard English* further support Greenfield's (2011) claim, as the definitions themselves often point to the user. Merriam-Webster's definition for *Standard English* includes the claim that it is "well established by usage in the formal and informal speech and writing of the educated," and American Heritage is remarkably honest about this process when it states that *Standard English* serves as a model for the educated, "especially when contrasted with speech varieties that are limited to or characteristic of certain regions or social groups." These definitions acknowledge the social construction of standardness through the process of association with privileged social groups ("the educated") and contrast with stigmatized social groups. When put together, these definitions suggest that, as Greenfield (2011) has argued, standardness and privilege are inextricable from White people, which is why she ultimately calls for a refusal to go along with the myth that Standard English exists. Shapiro and Watson (chapter 2, this volume) similarly imbricate so-called Standard English and White people when they suggest referring to this dialect as White English.

Nelson Flores and Jonathan Rosa (2015, 152) similarly push back against the existence of "Standard" English, arguing that we cannot talk about expectations for standardness without considering raciolinguistic ideologies that always already position racialized students as marked and deviant. However, their argument focuses specifically on foregrounding the role of the listener or, I would add, the reader. They argue that talk of standardness assumes "that individuals can control the . . . perception of their language use" (154) and ignores the possibility for "the white listening subject . . . to hear linguistic markedness and deviancy regardless of how well language-minoritized students model themselves after the white speaking subject" (152). Like Greenfield (2011), they argue that responses to language are more about racialized identities than "any objective characteristic of language use" (Flores and Rosa 2015, 151).

Again, translingualism offers significant potential in advancing efforts to challenge the myth of Standard English and the automatic negative evaluation of othered language practices. In fact, Shapiro and Watson (chapter 2) argue that "translingualism should *primarily* be understood as a theoretical and pedagogical approach to countering monolingualist ideologies," which they link to White privilege. However, this potential can only be realized by also rejecting the impulse to contrast language and social identities. The role of contrast is particularly problematic when it comes to the perpetually privileged microaggression. Because privileged White people's language is always already perceived to be standard, one of the ways students are racialized and marginalized in relation to their language use is through the constant contrast between the White, monolingual "standard" and the racialized, linguistically deviant "other." This claim, of course, is not new. Many scholars have argued that language is racializing and that a key mechanism in racializing language and language users is contrast to the so-called standard. However, this survey also demonstrates the ways perceptions of an author can racialize language, revealing the possibility that when instructors face students of color, they might expect, look for, and even construct nonstandardness or otherness in their writing. In other words, the contrast at play is between social identities, not language features.

This last point seems to be part of Matsuda's (2014) hesitation in relation to the current focus on translingualism. When Matsuda warns of linguistic tourism, he notes that the attribution of linguistic difference to L2 identities exoticizes and others students or perhaps creates perpetual foreigners. This study illustrates that not only might we run the risk of exoticizing L2 writers, but we might linguistically other students from particular racial groups regardless of linguistic features. Indeed, this study indicates that instructors might rely on readily available stereotypes and language attitudes to make sense of and evaluate writing (though, certainly, when we know our students, we are likely less inclined to lean so heavily on social identities). Finally, the findings from this study as well as Matsuda's concerns are evidence of the importance of raciolinguistic frames that study both the racing of language and the languaging of race (Alim 2016, 1). A raciolinguistic approach to translingualism would mean we cannot talk about language, power, and standards (even if to challenge current power structures and notions of standards) without talking about race.

CENTERING RACE, DE-CENTERING WHITE MONOLINGUALISM

Both Lee (2016) and Vershawn Ashanti Young (2007) recommend resisting the idea of rigid borders between either translingualism and monolingualism (Lee 2016, 186) or standard languages and non-standard languages (Young 2007, 97), as these divisions create a perpetual contrast—and ranking. And indeed, translingualism itself asks us to challenge boundaries between and among dialects, registers, languages, genres, and similar factors—thereby challenging the notion of contrast. In fact, in working to challenge standardness, translingualism challenges Whiteness. However, the language surrounding translingualism runs the risk of perpetuating the language of race denial as described by Victor Villanueva (2006) in "Blind: Talking about the New Racism," in which he describes four rhetorical tropes—metaphor, metonymy, irony, and synecdoche—that work to disallow conversations about race and racism. Specifically, allowing our attention on difference to elide race simply pushes us into race evasiveness or race denial, a practice critiqued by Karen Rowan and Shapiro and Watson in this volume (chapters 1 and 2, respectively).

As one effort to resist race evasiveness and ableist language, I argue that we must not use "linguistic diversity" or "difference in language" when we really mean racialized linguistic diversity or racialized differences—in other words, we must treat translingualism as a project of raciolinguistics, one that not only seeks to interrogate and disrupt traditional structures of linguistic power but also considers race as fully imbricated in those structures. Villanueva (2006, 6) warns us that metaphor is one way we avoid talking about race; a word like ethnicity or culture gets used and prevents us from talking about race. In this case, I argue that difference or diversity might also work in the same way—allowing us to avoid talking about race when it comes to our reaction to student language. If what we really mean is racialized linguistic difference, we need to say it and have that conversation. If we don't, the difference gets reduced to the level of the individual—everyone is different—which is another rhetorical trope that allows us to avoid talking about race. This time, the trope is metonymy, or a reduction (6). When we focus on individual differences, we don't acknowledge power difference; we don't acknowledge the systematic differences that are read in particular ways based on the identity they are attached to, the differences that become errors because they are created by presumably foreign or deficient students.

As an example, in an attempt to value the rich language diversity that comes from working at an HSI in a state with a large population of Native American students, our first-year writing program adopted a student learning outcome (SLO) that asks students to "recognize and describe the value of different languages, dialects, and registers in your own and others' texts," which we refer to as our linguistic diversity SLO. Despite efforts to support our instructors in understanding and teaching this SLO, several assessments have revealed that instructors don't recognize the SLO as important to students' success as writers and that students largely interpret this SLO to be about individual style (Davila et al. 2017, 70). Our response to these assessments has been a continued focus on professional development and curricula. However, in light of the results of this survey, I now believe we must incorporate race into the SLO. Our goal in creating the SLO was to honor and institutionally recognize and make space for racialized (and therefore historically stigmatized) languages and dialects. By leaving race out of the SLO, we've allowed our instructors and students to interpret this SLO outside of systemic power relations and racial microaggressions tied to language.

Another concern about the language surrounding translingualism is that of linguistic difference as a resource, or as Lindsey Albracht (chapter 6, this volume) has it, "celebrating student literacies or 'empowering' students to make rhetorical choices." While I don't disagree that being able to use multiple languages and language varieties is an advantage, I find that the language of resources often allows for a sidestepping of issues of power and race. Specifically, in my experience, instructors and students are often quick to determine that the most valuable resource in a school setting is a standardized language variety, making it the appropriate choice or the best rhetorical decision or the most effective at communication. All of these terms—appropriate, rhetorical, effective—lead to the same stopping point, SEAE is the right choice, without considering "how students' 'choices' are informed by structural racism, classism, ableism, and heteronormativity" (Albracht, chapter 6, this volume). In other words, these conversations reify a belief in SEAE and do nothing to challenge Whiteness. Furthermore, if these conversations do not interrogate the role of the White listening/reading subject in determining what is appropriate, rhetorical, and effective, we do nothing to disrupt the idea of an attainable, objective standard. As Flores and Rosa (2015, 167) state, "Antiracist social transformation . . . must . . . work actively to dismantle the hierarchies that produce the white listening subject."

Finally, Stephanie Mosher (chapter 9, this volume) suggests that professionalization that includes readings on translingualism and race could help instructors develop dispositions and practices that enact a raciolinguistics translingualism. Ultimately, challenging Whiteness must be constant and is necessarily uncomfortable. There aren't easy solutions to finding the balance between openly acknowledging the role of race in the production and reception of language without allowing race to overdetermine our understandings of language choices. However, if we avoid these conversations through race evasive language (such as linguistic diversity, difference, appropriateness, rhetorical choices, and efficacy), we certainly won't make progress. Instead, we will continue to perpetuate the irony of having a theoretical and pedagogical approach designed to challenge White monolingualism actually work to reinforce it.

APPENDIX 5.A: SURVEY QUESTIONS

Questions about experiences as teacher and with paper

1. What grade would you give this paper?: A+; A; A-; B+; B; B-; C+; C; C-; D+; D; D-; F
2. On a scale of 0–100, how well did you understand the student's main argument? 0 = not at all and 100 = complete understanding.
3. Optional: provide any comments about your previous answer here.
4. Please type your end comments for the student here: _____
5. What was striking to you in this paper and why? _____
6. On a scale of 0–100, based on your experience, how common is this paper in terms of writing level or ability for a first-year composition student? 0 = not at all common and 100 = very common.
7. Optional: provide any comments about your previous answer here.
8. In as much detail as possible, describe the student you pictured as having written this paper. _____
9. Based on the student's language use, what kind of education do you imagine this student had before beginning college? (check as many as apply) Public; private; well resourced; under resourced; average resources; strong preparation; weak preparation; average preparation
10. Based on the student's language use, where do you imagine the student-author grew up? (check as many as apply): rural; suburban; urban; international; northeast; southeast; midwest; south; southwest; west coast; Pacific northwest; other _____
11. Based on the student's language use, what socio-economic class do you imagine this student comes from?: upper class; upper middle class; middle class; lower middle class; working class

12. Are there any features in the writing and language use that reflect the student's race and/or gender?
13. What features in the paper and/or what from your teaching experience influenced the way you pictured this student or imagined the student's identity?

Background Information
1. Age: 20–29; 30–39; 40–49; 50–59; 60–69; 70 or above
2. Gender?
3. Rank: Full Professor; Associate Professor; Assistant Professor; Lecturer; Graduate Student; Parttime/Adjunct; Retired/Emeritus; Other _____
4. Native Language (check all that apply): English; Other than English _____
5. Race (check all that apply): American Indian/Alaskan Native; Asian; Black; Hawaiian/Pacific Islander; Hispanic; White; Other _____
6. Disciplinary background(s) (check all that apply): Literature; Creative Writing; Composition and Rhetoric; other _____
7. How long have you been teaching writing at the college level? _____ years
8. Characterize your institution in terms of geography (check all that apply): rural, suburban, urban, northwestern, western, southwestern, southern, midwestern, southeastern, eastern, northeastern; Other
9. Characterize your institution in terms of student demographics (check all that apply): HBCU, HSI, PWI (predominantly White institution), Other _____
10. Aside from your current institution, have you taught at (please check all that apply): other research institutions; liberal arts college(s); community college(s); technical/professional college(s); other.

REFERENCES

Alim, H. Samy. 2016. "Introducing Raciolinguistics: Racing Language and Languaging Race in Hyperracial Times." In *Raciolinguistics: How Language Shapes Our Ideas about Race*, ed. H. Samy Alim, John R. Rickford and Arnetha F. Ball, 1–30. New York: Oxford University Press.

Bradac, James J., Aaron Castelan Cargile, and Jennifer S. Hallett. 2001. "Language Attitudes: Retrospect, Conspect, and Prospect." In *The New Handbook of Language and Social Psychology*, ed. W. Peter Robinson and Howard Giles, 137–44. New York: Wiley.

Davila, Bethany. 2012. "Indexicality and 'Standard' Edited American English: Examining the Link between Conceptions of Standardness and Perceived Authorial Identity." *Written Communication* 29 (2): 180–207.

Davila, Bethany, Anna Knutson, Andrew Bourelle, and Tiffany Bourelle. 2017. "Linguistic Diversity in Online Writing Classes." *WPA Journal* 41 (1): 60–81.

Devos, Thierry, and Mahzarin R. Banaji. 2005. "American = White?" *Journal of Personality and Social Psychology* 88 (3): 447–66.

Devos, Thierry, Kelly Gavin, and Francisco J. Quintana. 2010. "Say 'Adios' to the American Dream? The Interplay between Ethnic and National Identity among Latino and Caucasian Americans." *Cultural Diversity and Ethnic Minority Psychology* 16 (1): 37–49.

Flores, Nelson, and Jonathan Rosa. 2015. "Undoing Appropriateness: Raciolinguistic Ideologies and Language Diversity in Education." *Harvard Education Review* 85 (2): 149–71.

Gilyard, Keith. 2016. "The Rhetoric of Translingualism." *College English* 78 (3): 284–89.

Greenfield, Laura. 2011. "The 'Standard English' Fairy Tale: A Rhetorical Analysis of Racist Pedagogies and Commonplace Assumptions about Language Diversity." In *Writing Centers and the New Racism: A Call for Sustainable Dialogue and Change*, ed. Laura Greenfield and Karen Rowan, 33–60. Logan: Utah State University Press.

Hing, Bill Ong. 2001. "Vigilante Racism: The De-Americanization of Immigrant America." *Michigan Journal of Race and Law* 7: 441–56.

Horner, Bruce, Min-Zhan Lu, Jacqueline Jones Royster, and John Trimbur. 2011. "Language Difference in Writing: Toward a Translingual Approach." *College English* 73 (3): 303–21.

Inoue, Asao B. 2016. "Racism in Writing Programs and the CWPA." *WPA: Writing Program Administration* 40 (1): 134–54.

Janopoulos, Michael. 1992. "University Faculty Tolerance of NS and NNS Writing Errors: A Comparison." *Journal of Second Language Writing* 1 (2): 109–21.

Lee, Jerry Won. 2016. "Beyond Translingual Writing." *College English* 79 (2): 174–95.

Lee, Jerry Won, and Christopher Jenks. 2016. "Doing Translingual Dispositions." *College Composition and Communication* 68 (2): 317–44.

Lu, Min-Zhan, and Bruce Horner. 2016. "Introduction: Translingual Work." *College English* 78 (3): 207–18.

Matsuda, Paul Kei. 2006. "The Myth of Linguistic Homogeneity in U.S. College Composition." *College English* 68 (6): 637–51.

Matsuda, Paul Kei. 2014. "The Lure of Translingual Writing." *PMLA* 129 (3): 478–83.

Matusda, Paul Kei, Tanita Saenkhum, and Steven Accardi. 2013. "Writing Teachers' Perceptions of the Presence and Needs of Second Language Writers: An Institutional Case Study." *Journal of Second Language Writing* 22 (1): 68–86.

McGee, Ebony O., and Danny B. Martin. 2011. "'You Would Not Believe What I Have to Go through to Prove My Intellectual Value!' Stereotype Management among Academically Successful Black Mathematics and Engineering Students." *American Educational Research Journal* 48 (6): 1347–89.

Piché, Gene L., Donald L. Rubin, and Michael L. Michlin. 1978. "Teachers' Subjective Evaluations of Standard and Black Nonstandard English Compositions: A Study of Written Language and Attitudes." *Research in the Teaching of English* 12 (2): 107–18.

Roberts, Felicia, and Tony Cimasko. 2008. "Evaluating ESL: Making Sense of University Professors' Responses to Second Language Writing." *Journal of Second Language Writing* 17 (3): 125–43.

Rubin, Donald L., and Melanie Williams-James. 1997. "The Impact of Writer Nationality on Mainstream Teachers' Judgments of Composition Quality." *Journal of Second Language Writing* 6 (2): 139–53.

Sue, Derald Wing, Christina M. Capodilupo, Gina C. Torino, Jennifer M. Bucceri, Aisha M. B. Holder, Kevin L. Nadal, and Marta Esquilin. 2007. "Racial Microaggressions in Everyday Life: Implications for Clinical Practice." *American Psychologist* 62 (4): 271–86.

Villanueva, Victor. 2006. "Blind: Talking about the New Racism." *Writing Center Journal* 26 (1): 3–19.

Young, Vershawn Ashanti. 2007. *Your Average Nigga: Performing Race, Literacy, and Masculinity*. Detroit: Wayne State University Press.

PART II

*Toward a Race-Conscious,
Anti-Racist Translingualism*

6
"WE WILL KNOW OUR HEROES AND OUR CULTURE"
Revisiting the Five Demands at the City University of New York toward Building Critical Transliteracies Ecologies

Lindsey Albracht

In the spring semester of 1969, student activists across the City University of New York (CUNY) system organized negotiation meetings, protests, and campus takeovers that pressured university officials to accelerate and greatly expand a modest, tokenizing proposal to increase access to CUNY for students of color. The fall of 1970 saw the start of the policy of open admissions in which high school graduates of the New York City public school system with a grade point average of B or better were guaranteed (briefly tuition-free) admission at one of CUNY's four-year senior colleges, while all high school graduates were guaranteed admission at a CUNY community college. Bruce Horner (1996), Carmen Kynard (2013), Steve Lamos (2000), Min-Zhan Lu (1991), George Otte and Rebecca Williams Mlynarczyk (2010), and John Trimbur (2016) have all documented this student action, which "essentially remade the CUNY system overnight" (Fabricant and Brier 2016, 32). However, with the exception of Kynard's (2013) work, much of the scholarly conversation within writing studies around open admissions has focused on faculty, writing program administration, and the rhetorics of the field of basic writing that emerged in open admission's aftermath.

Building on Keith Gilyard's (2016, 288) call to "write the histories of the translanguagers" who brought open admissions to CUNY, I examine the protest writing and oral history accounts of student organizers in the Black and Puerto Rican Student Community (BPRSC), the Search for Education, Elevation, and Knowledge (SEEK) program, and a solidarity statement written by White students involved in a local chapter of the national organization Students for a Democratic Society (SDS) at CUNY's founding campus, City College. Demanding that City College build a much more robust infrastructure for the co-interrogation of linguistic marginalization that students would do alongside their teachers and their communities, they envisioned a model for enacting a race and racialization-conscious translingual approach that is built on fostering what I call *critical transliteracies ecologies*. This infrastructure included a more thorough engagement with Harlem, where City College is located; the resources to teach and learn about histories of colonialism, imperialism, anti-Blackness, and other forms of racialization; and remediation of teachers' reception practices. Students also demanded a much more substantial role in governance and in programmatic decision making. In short, activists were not only concerned with celebrating, authorizing, or promoting students' right to their own language. In fact, they weren't always concerned with language at all. In this chapter, I suggest that the students' texts teach us that racing translingualism necessitates a move beyond studying or valuing individual languaging practices and toward a commitment to making more substantial infrastructural changes within our writing programs and our universities.

Since the translingual paradigm is still relatively new to writing studies, before analyzing students' texts, I would like to clarify my use of terminology. The bilingual educator Cen Williams developed the term *translanguaging* to describe the way he encouraged students to utilize their full linguistic repertoire in the composing, speaking, and reading process; he also envisioned translanguaging as a strategy to maximize a bilingual child's full range of linguistic abilities (cited in García and Kleyn 11). By referring to the act of "translanguaging," I'm referring to a linguistic performance in which users of language select linguistic resources from a personal repertoire to negotiate and transform language across a variety of contexts in an effort to achieve mutual understanding (Canagarajah 2013; García and Li 2013; García and Otheguy 1989). A translingual approach, however, refers to an orientation that treats difference in language as an expected norm and a useful resource rather than a problem to manage or assimilate (Horner et al. 2011).

"Translanguager" is not a synonym for "emergent bilingual" or "English language learner (ELL)" or "multilingual." It is critical to keep in mind that when Gilyard (2016) refers to CUNY students as "translanguagers," he is not necessarily referring exclusively to students who speak multiple named languages or who use linguistic resources a habitus speaker might consider adjacent to the dominant language. Instead, he refers to students who have been institutionally marked in a variety of ways: as multilingual, multi-dialectical, *and* monolingual users of language who were organizing across difference. He is referring to *all* users of language, who are always selecting from a (wider or more narrow) possible repertoire of resources.

Making this distinction is important for a few reasons. As Paul Kei Matsuda (2014) and Xiaoye You (2016) have noted, a disciplinary divide that separates "mainstream" writing studies scholarship from the work of L2 writing scholarship has persisted for decades. Commonly, this divide programmatically segregates multilingual students, leading to an outcome in which some students who are institutionally marked as "English as a Second Language (ESL)" or "ELL" or "Generation 1.5" can feel stigmatized (Ortmeir-Hooper 2008). It can also prevent instructors in teaching practica from focusing on linguistic marginalization—particularly in contexts where language minoritized students comprise a relatively small percentage of the total student population. Conflating or replacing "multilingual" with "translingual" further entrenches the historical separation between writing studies and teaching English to speakers of other languages (TESOL) and provides students who are institutionally and culturally constructed as monolingual with an opportunity to abdicate responsibility for developing what Jerry Won Lee and Christopher Jenks (2016) call "translingual dispositions" or what Rebecca Lorimer Leonard (2014) calls "rhetorical attunements." Doing translingual dispositions and developing rhetorical attunements includes reckoning with an existing relationship to dominant linguistic ideologies by moving toward and across difference and multiplicity as an agentive performance. Without all translanguagers engaging in this process, linguistic marginalization is certain to continue.

However, while these enactments are possible (and necessary) for all users of language, Gilyard (2016) warns that foregrounding the constructed, abstracted nature of language or the idea that "everyone translanguages" can encourage some translingualists to adopt a worrying "sameness-as-difference" model in which all translanguaged expressions or experiences of linguistic marginalization are falsely equated. This can produce a flattening effect by deemphasizing the lived consequences of (differently experienced) linguistic marginalization (287). It can also encourage what Matsuda (2014, 482) calls "linguistic tourism": a practice that can foster superficial understanding of differences and similarities between complex linguistic traditions with rich and different histories. Given the colonial and classed connotations of tourism and given the histories of segregation that have specifically impacted institutions of higher education in which legacies of anti-indigeneity, colonialism, and anti-Blackness actively persist, linguistic tourism is particularly fraught for its potential to further harm linguistically and racially minoritized students.

This is why the development of not only translingual dispositions and rhetorical attunements but what I call *critical transliteracies ecologies* is so essential and why studying the communicative strategies of groups of activist students who worked across so many axes of constructed difference can so greatly benefit contemporary race-conscious translingualists. To further unpack this term, I first turn to You's (2016, 137) term *transliteracy*, which he defines as literacy development that assumes and promotes "blurred boundaries between languages, between modalities, between cultures, and between identities" and that subverts the monolingualist assumption that named languages, cultures, identities, and modalities are autonomous systems. You (2016) acknowledges in this construction that transliteracy stretches beyond language and toward other factors that support or interfere with its reception. Building on this, I use the word *transliteracies* to acknowledge the multiplicity of cultural, racial, multimodal, and linguistic literacies a race-conscious translingual classroom must simultaneously foster to signify the inextricability of (multiple) identities and language resources. In "Undoing Appropriateness: Raciolinguistic Ideologies and Language Diversity in Education," Nelson Flores and Jonathan Rosa (2015) speak to this inextricability by arguing that a "white listening subject" continues to understand the language of racialized speaking subjects as "deficient" no matter how closely it aligns to a set of rules about appropriateness. For Flores and Rosa, "appropriateness" is a moving target within a system of White supremacy. Thus, while racial identity and language are fluid and socially constructed, they come to matter and to be conflated inside of audience reception practices.

Examples abound of listening or reading subjects marginalizing speakers or writers for their perceived race, no matter how closely a text supposedly hews to privileged conventions. In a 1992 study, Donald L. Rubin showed half of a group of American undergraduate students a picture of a White male professor as they listened to an audio recorded lecture. The other half of the students saw a picture of an Asian male professor as they listened to exactly the same recording. The students who saw the picture of the Asian professor rated him as less effective and the lecture as less comprehensible, and student participants even scored 20 percent lower on a comprehension test than the students who listened to the lecture while looking at the photo of the White professor. A text, which was exactly the same, was perceived differently because of the assumed race of the speaker. In another study, participants listened to an audio recording without video, watched a video recording without sound, and watched an audio-video recording in English of professors whose first language was either Korean or German. Participants were asked to rate the professors' perceived "accentedness." The study found that while participants assessed (Asian) Korean speakers to have an accent across all three recording types, the perceived accentedness of (White) German speakers fluctuated (Gnevsheva 2018). Candidates with names that are racialized as White are approximately 50 percent more likely to receive an interview callback than candidates with identical qualifications whose names are racialized as Black (Bertrand and Mullainathan 2004). White male participants reviewing resumes are more likely to rate presumably Black applicants as less suitable for jobs than they rate Asian, Hispanic, and White candidates, regardless of credentials (King et al. 2006). Emails sent to potential landlords from names with a high likelihood of association with Black identity receive a lower rate of response when the inquiry is about a property in a neighborhood where the racial composition is changing (Hanson and Hawley 2011).

These examples point to the urgency of *all* users of language developing transliteracies that allow them to confront not only *linguistic* biases but raciolinguistic biases as well and the way language is otherwise racialized. However, as Asao Inoue's (2015, 79) work suggests, the development of rhetorical attunements and doing translingual dispositions can be especially difficult for students whose dominant habitus affords them an "unfair inheritance" that marks their linguistic expression as more proximate to an imagined standard—especially when an institution reflects their own worldview back to them. We need to focus not only on the development of individual behaviors but on what Inoue defines as the development of ecologies: "the interconnectedness of all people and things, which includes environments, without denying or eliding linguistic, cultural, or racial diversity, and the politics inherent in all uneven social formations" (77). To challenge audience perception or to avoid flattening difference or to avoid a situation in which certain linguistic performances are fetishized, exoticized, misunderstood, or tokenized by a dominant group, it is critical to create the ecological conditions from which we can more powerfully recognize and confront habitus. It is critical, in other words, for contemporary racialization-conscious translingualists to robustly theorize the production of the people and things, the environments and geographies, and the cultural and political circumstances under which translingual dispositions thrive or wither and to do this *as* a race-conscious translingual pedagogical praxis.

TOWARD A CRITICAL TRANSLITERACIES ECOLOGY: REVISITING THE FIVE DEMANDS

In the vision of the university that student activists at City College articulated, there is extraordinarily ecological thinking. In this section, I analyze a set of five demands made by the BPRSC at City College, as well as an accompanying statement of solidarity written by a group of White students, to consider how these demands point to some components of a critical transliteracies ecology that theorizes large, networked system of linguistic discrimination rather than, or in addition to, focusing on individual student languaging practices. First, some context. In 1965, with financial support authorized by the New York State legislature, City College began a pilot program called Search for Education, Elevation, and Knowledge: a pre-college initiative that provided financial and scholarly support to low-income students who were interested in eventually entering college. To City College's mostly White, low-income, first- and second-generation immigrant campus, the SEEK program attracted a group primarily of students of color, many of whom lived in the surrounding neighborhood of Harlem. Yet in the ensuing three years, as former SEEK student Khadija DeLoach recounted in an oral history, matriculated City College students and SEEK students still remained fairly segregated on campus. This was also true of matriculated Black students who DeLoach suggests "came from better neighborhoods [than SEEK students] even though they were Black" and who made SEEK students feel as though "there was definitely a distinction between us" (Medina 2014, 9).

This distinction prevented meaningful organizing until the 1968 assassination of Dr. Martin Luther King Jr. While individual students had discussed the need to organize prior to 1968, King's death became a catalyst to form a student organizing group called the Black and Puerto Rican Student Community (Medina 2014, 14). By the fall of 1968, BPRSC had started to petition administrators to greatly expand their own meager proposal that would guarantee admission to a slightly larger percentage of high school graduates over the course of ten years. The students also challenged CUNY's plan for "access," insisting that true college accessibility would necessitate much more than simply opening the doors for a few more students to enter.

After nearly six months of students, sympathetic faculty, and community members petitioning college officials to revise and greatly expand their proposal without much of a robust response, the BPRSC and a group of White students acting in solidarity decided to take more drastic action. Presenting to the public the same list of five demands they had previously discussed with college officials, the students overtook several buildings on City College's campus and refused to leave until CUNY officials entered into negotiations. The demands were:

1. The establishment of a separate school of Black and Puerto Rican studies
2. A first-year orientation for Black and Puerto Rican students
3. A determining voice in setting the guidelines for the Search for Education, Elevation, and Knowledge (SEEK) program: a pre-baccalaureate program designed to provide financial and educational support to low-income students (who were primarily students of color)
4. That the racial composition of the incoming first-year class match the racial composition of the New York City public high schools
5. That education majors be required to take Puerto Rican and Black history classes as well as coursework in Spanish.

From this list, three important goals establish the basis for a critical transliteracies ecology and thus for a more race- and racialization-conscious translingual approach: increased representation and community partnership, identification and interrogation of (ongoing and historic) epistemic violence, and participatory governance. I will next examine each of these demands and their implications for building contemporary critical transliteracies ecologies.

REPRESENTATION AND COMMUNITY PARTNERSHIP

The first key tenet in a critical transliteracies ecology is representation bolstered by community partnership. In analyzing the text of the students' demand, I will explain what I mean by both "representation" and "community":

> This demand is the most important of our demands. At present, Blacks and Puerto Ricans comprise 40% of the high school population. Yet at City College (now renamed Harlem University), there are only 9% Black and Puerto Ricans and 91% whites (Day Session)—even though City College is located in Harlem which is 98% Black and Puerto Rican. Along with these shocking figures comes the fact that 95% of all Black and Puerto Rican people are working class people and pay for all schools including the colleges directly through their taxes. (Black and Puerto Rican Student Community 1969, 1–2)

For the BPRSC, the most important demand is more equitable representation of Black and Puerto Rican students throughout the CUNY system. Notably, representation is inextricably linked to reciprocal community partnership: there is a focus on providing ways to access college not only for traditionally "college-bound" students but also for potential students who had been denied opportunities, including "all people who have graduated [from high school] in the past" who are currently employed in low-wage jobs (2). This community partnership is rhetorically invoked in the renaming of City College as Harlem University, in the reminder to the audience that working-class people were paying for a public good to which they didn't have access, and in an accompanying press release issued by the BPRSC on April 26, 1969, in which students called themselves "representatives of the community," acting on behalf of it from within it (Black and Puerto Rican Student Community 1970, 1–2). However, the university-community partnership stretched beyond words. During the takeover—under the leadership of the BPRSC (with partnership by faculty and student allies from outside the organization)—students fed, provided medical attention, and offered places to stay for "the hungry and sick" of Harlem and also offered free tutoring to anyone in the community (1–2). Taking over the college president's on-campus residence, education major activists established a childcare center for those participating in the struggle (Medina 2014, 22–23).

For contemporary translingualists, this demand is worthy of note because part of the critical transliteracies ecology the BPRSC students imagined is one in which representation comes as part of a reciprocal partnership with people who are not already imagined to be part of the existing college community. While, of course, what "representation" can mean will differ from campus context to campus context, it is critical to ask questions about who already appears on which campuses and who does not as part of a critical transliteracies ecological analysis. A recent study the *New York Times* conducted with data from the National Center for Education Statistics found that in the United States, the gap between college-age Black and Hispanic students nationwide and enrolled college students has widened by six points since 1980 (Ashkenas, Park, and Pierce 2017). Black and Hispanic students continue to be underrepresented at the top five most selective CUNY colleges (Hancock and Kolodner 2015) and on the University of California system's most selective campuses as well (Ashkenas, Park, and Pierce 2017). We also see in the BPRSC's vision the building of a more robust infrastructure of support that stretches beyond the "typical" boundaries of a school. For movement participation, education, and representation to work effectively, it was necessary to build and maintain a much broader ecology of support. While, in a transnational analysis, the idea of "representation" must move beyond racial representation to include an analysis of the underrepresentation of other oppressed, minoritized groups of people as well, thinking of this project and the project of infrastructure building as part of a racing translingualism praxis is key.

Compare the BPRSC's statement and actions with those included in the solidarity statement issued by White students, who overtook and renamed a City College campus building Huey P. Newton Hall for Political Action after the Black Panther co-founder. It is noted that the members of BPRSC "fully endorsed [the] statement as a corollary to [their] demand" ("Newton Hall Statement" 1970, 5). However, the justification for the fourth demand differs significantly:

> The present procedure of selecting students based on examinations and grades is both arbitrary and discriminatory. It is discriminatory in that it is clearly certain ethnic groups which suffer by the standards due to inferior education in ghetto schools . . . And examinations and grades are an arbitrary rather than [a] qualitative measure of a student's ability. They force a student to become more concerned with competition than with education, more concerned with doing well than with learning well. (4).

While White students recognize the harm discriminatory standards do to their Black and Puerto Rican peers, they also argue that competitive metrics (which are designed to advantage them) are a detriment to *everyone's* learning because of what those metrics communicate about the purpose of an education. They do this while simultaneously acknowledging that these standards are *more* of a detriment to their peers. The statement recognizes that laboring toward representation requires a different kind of work for White students, who have faced an entirely different set of historical circumstances but who also recognize how failing to do this work will have direct consequences for their own lives. Solidarity with the Black and Puerto Rican students' goals is constructed in this statement as not simply an act of empathy or altruism but as a necessary action for the future of "every student in the university."

Conceiving of representation and community partnership as a tenet of a critical transliteracies ecology raises important questions for racing translingualism. In what ways do we currently labor toward representation in a given local context *as part of a race-conscious translingual praxis*? How might we see theorizing about and laboring toward representation as a critical transliteracies skill? What are the infrastructures that prevent representation in our scholarly communities, our universities, our departments, our graduate programs, and elsewhere; and how are we addressing those infrastructures as part of what will make racing translingualism possible? Finally, how might these complimentary (and yet different) statements from the BPRSC and White City College students help us consider the examination of a broader positionality—and not simply our linguistic biases—as part of the work of a translingual approach?

IDENTIFICATION AND INTERROGATION OF (ONGOING AND HISTORICAL) EPISTEMIC VIOLENCE

Students' demand for a separate, degree-granting school of Black and Puerto Rican studies and their demand that teachers in training be required to take Spanish-language classes and Black and Puerto Rican history classes were not met. However, we might recognize in these demands a second key tenet of a critical transliteracies ecology: tools and strategies to identify and interrogate ongoing and historical epistemic violence. In the fifth demand, students enact one of these tools as they reverse a common deficit narrative about their own "college readiness" by showing how a lack of historical, cultural, and linguistic competence in *faculty* education has resulted from City College's negligence:

> This demand is designed to deal with the attitudes of teachers toward Black and Puerto Rican children. City College produces 40% of the teachers in New York City. We find that a teacher will be better able to teach and relate to our students if he has some understanding of the social, economic and political oppression under which they live. The demand requires that he take a course in Black history and a course in Puerto Rican history. The demand also requires that teachers take Spanish in order that they be more effective when teaching Puerto Rican children. (Black and Puerto Rican Student Community 1969, 2)

In this demand, students turn the magnifying glass toward New York City teachers—many of whom were educated at City College—and claim that *they* had failed to recognize the literacies, histories, linguistic competencies, and life-worlds that Black and Puerto Rican students especially bring into the classroom. This—rather than a lack of intelligence, motivation, or willpower—was what had led to the condition under which it was possible for 91 percent of City College's student population to be White and which kept, according to the students' account, 84 percent of all Black and Puerto Rican students from graduating from high school (Black and Puerto Rican Student Community 1969, 1). By accusing the college of inadequately preparing a large portion of the city's teachers to meet the needs of the majority of the city's students, students demanded legibility from teachers who inhabit the White listening subject position.

In a contemporary critical transliteracies ecology analysis, we should adopt a similar position when critiques of translingualism's "practical application" arise. Rather than asking how translingualists can prepare students who are imagined to inhabit an L2 subject position to become legible to those in a dominant position, we might counter by asking how we are preparing all people (especially teachers) who are imagined to inhabit a dominant subject position to become more adept linguistic and cultural negotiators. How—especially within the cultural context of the United States, with its ongoing legacy of school, neighborhood, social, and cultural segregation—might we expect these critical transliteracies to develop without robust support and intervention? As we move toward a transliteracies praxis, racialization-conscious translingualists should center an approach that interrogates the cultural, historical, curricular, and institutional structures that have created what the sociologist Charles Mills (1997, 15) calls "white ignorance": a form of epistemic violence that arises from structural dedication to the prevention of knowledge and the preservation of White supremacy.

However, it is important to note that the demand for legibility was not only a demand to offer a corrective for the missing components of the *teachers'* education. It was also a demand for Black and Puerto Rican students to see *themselves* reflected in the curriculum. In the first demand, both the BPRSC and Newton Hall statements require the establishment of a separate school of Black and Puerto Rican studies, which would help to further support building the tools and strategies necessary to identify and interrogate ongoing and historical epistemic violence. The Black and Puerto Rican Student Community (1969, 1) explains this demand this way:

> This school [for Black and Puerto Rican studies] will be controlled by the community, students and faculty. The courses and programs offered at this school will be totally geared to community needs. For the first time we will be able to study our true past history in relation to our present condition. We will know our heroes and our culture which has been denied us by the present racist society. The school will bring about an increased understanding of the political, social and economic force[s] which work to exploit us in this society.

The text of this demand envisions a responsive, community-controlled school for Black and Puerto Rican studies that does more than prepare students for assimilation and middle-class mobility. The school would instead prepare students (and their communities and the future teachers of their children) to fill in the massive gaps of knowledge that were left by colonization, settler-colonialism, imperialism, and White supremacy. In what ways does contemporary translingual praxis prepare students (and teachers) to do the same? I argue that our current praxis does not uniformly emphasize engagement with the structures that allow for the identification and interrogation of epistemic violence but that a racialization-conscious translingual praxis *must* do this. Without political, social, and economic analysis, it becomes too simple to draw damaging equivalencies between (for example) linguistic prescriptivism that is fundamentally anti-Black and persecution that results from having a White American southern accent when, in fact, these positions carry vastly different consequences because they are attached to vastly different histories.

One of the takeaways from these two demands is that the first demand for representation cannot be fully and thoroughly supported without other important shifts. In fostering a critical transliteracies ecology in our own local contexts, it is critical to consider the presence (or absence) of opportunities for what the poet, SEEK instructor, and activist Toni Cade Bambara referred to as "two-way learning" founded on "mutual understanding, mutual respect, dialogue" between students and teachers (146). However, as Linda Brodkey's (2012) study of letters between working-class basic writing students and new instructors of composition shows, structural factors can greatly influence individual teachers' capacities for mutual understanding, respect, and dialogue when they don't share a student's subject position and when they aren't engaged in intentional, additional work to unlearn. This is yet another reason to advocate for epistemic legibility that moves beyond individual student practices and encourages the growth and development of opportunities for negotiated, two-way learning in faculty development. By identifying and interrogating the ecologies that prevent or hinder epistemic legibility in our scholarly communities, our universities, our departments, our graduate programs, and elsewhere as translingual praxis, we might confront those structures as part of a race-conscious translingual approach.

There are already models in our field that might help us to do this work, though these models are not necessarily directly associated with a translingual pedagogy. Juan C. Guerra's (2008) notion of fostering *transcultural citizens* through a writing across the communities model in which students draw on their local community knowledge to create a "permeable curriculum" that is capable of adapting to students' experiences, lives, histories, and knowledges very closely aligns with the BPRSC's vision and would be instructive in thinking through how to build community partnership and legibility inside a critical transliteracies ecology. Drawing on Michelle Hall Kells's (2007) model of writing across communities, Guerra (2008) advocates for a model that moves beyond the ways writing across the curriculum typically privileges academic discourse and toward a model that privileges and centers students' experiences, local community knowledge-making practices, and a reciprocal exchange of knowledge with teachers who may or may not inhabit the communities in which their students live. Student knowledge and community connection is not treated as a liability to overcome or a "step" along the way to full assimilation.

However, how might we build critical transliteracies ecologies that incorporate tools and strategies to interrogate epistemic violence but that are also durable across transnational contexts? K. Wayne Yang's (2017) interrogation of "the trafficked technologies" of White supremacy, settler colonialism, and Indigenous erasure might help. In the book *A Third University Is Possible*, Yang, writing under the pen name la paperson, introduces this concept to describe how experiences of alienation, disempowerment, subjugation, and violence travel across transnational lines. While the individual bodies, histories, and circumstances may change, the technologies of Whiteness, anti-Blackness, and Indigenous erasure proliferate through the use of the "machinery" of land dispossession, slavery, war, caging/incarceration, and genocide (13–14). An analysis of this machinery, rather than the privileging of a particular history or linguistic tradition, allows identity to remain an unstable, context-specific assemblage while rigorously recognizing its effects. Analyzing trafficked technologies also enables marginalized groups to draw lines of solidarity across communities with disparate histories who are impacted to different degrees by similar technologies without flattening individual experiences. This becomes especially important when considering the move from a translingual theoretical analysis to a translingual pedagogy. The emphasis on fluidity and permeability of the boundaries of language in translingual writing present opportunities not only for superficial engagement but also for cultural and linguistic appropriation, for the erasure of important histories and differences, and for a lack of acknowledgment of how linguistic hierarchies unevenly impact language users. When we are racing translingualism in teacher education, we must remain especially vigilant of this: strategies that focus on "celebrating" language difference and on linguistic permeability pose a particular danger. Just because the boundaries of language are permeable doesn't mean all languages (or knowledge traditions) should be equally inhabitable by anyone who wishes to access them. However, we can all study the ways language is subjected to trafficked technologies and our varied complicity in the trafficking.

STUDENT AUTONOMY AND PARTICIPATORY GOVERNANCE

The final tenet of a critical transliteracies ecology is derived from the students' demands for autonomy and participatory governance. In the third demand, students ask for a much more significant determining voice in the decisions that were made on their own behalf in the SEEK program, including a decision in which faculty were hired or fired. While several of the SEEK instructors formed close relationships with students, several others seemed out of touch with students' needs: "Teachers, counselors, and tutors are not really accountable to the Seek students. What the students demand is that they have a determining voice in setting the guidelines for the Seek Program including the hiring and firing of Seek Personnel. For up to now, Seek Personnel has [*sic*] not been accountable to anyone" (Black and Puerto Rican Student Community 1969, 1).

The text from the "Newtown Hall Statement" (1970, 4) adds additional important context: "Student control is especially important in the SEEK program, which is presently under the authority of a White college administration, which cannot truly understand and meet the needs of Black students. The student also deserves to have some voice over budgetary matters since the budget determines the implementation of the very guidelines and priorities which the student himself helps to establish." Influenced by Freirean praxis, the idea of students sharing authority with the professor in the writing classroom or problematizing the ways in which this is possible has a long history in writing studies (Kirsch 1985; Bruffee 1986; Cooper and Selfe 1990; Wright 1991; Bizzell 1991; Shor 1996). However, it's much less common to think of the ways "authority" is constructed through things such as budgetary control or the ability of students (especially undergraduates and especially non-matriculated pre-baccalaureate students) to make hiring and firing decisions. It is also uncommon to consult students in the building of programs, curricula, and orientations for new students (beyond assigning students predetermined labor), which was the subtext of the students' second demand to host a separate orientation for Black and Puerto Rican students that could help connect them to students with similar experiences:

> Since Black and Puerto Rican children are alienated and destroyed in the New York City School System, by the time that those few of us reach College we find that we suffer from many basic problems. For example, because of racist attitudes of the teachers throughout the City, our children turn out graduating from high school without being able to read, write or do simple mathematics. These racist teachers teach our children that they are inferior and not worth educating. (Black and Puerto Rican Student Community 1969, 1)

Why should the demand for student autonomy and participatory governance—especially as it concerns faculty hiring practices, budgetary transparency, curricular decisions, and giving students (compensated) leadership roles in mentoring peers—be considered part of racing translingualism? Because—as students show in the text of this demand—student autonomy in remedial writing programs, income-generating pre-baccalaureate programs such as English language institutes, and non-credit-bearing ESL programs that operate on a model of linguistic containment directly impact students' ability to determine their own outcomes. Giving students a direct role in the development, implementation, revision, and funding of these programs (which differs from measuring their satisfaction with a program that has already been implemented) is a critical part of understanding its effect. As the student activists' texts show, a lack of student autonomy and an inability to participate in important administrative decisions can result in a lack of accountability, contribute to the opaque logics of literacy education, and harm the ability to foster a critical transliteracies ecology.

TOWARD A RACIALIZATION-CONSCIOUS TRANSLINGUALISM

Writing studies scholarship has focused significant attention on the enactment of open admissions. However, activists' demands in (re)envisioning the university's structures deserve more attention, as they can help contemporary translingualist toward the project of racing translingualism. Demanding community engagement, robust infrastructures for interrogating ongoing and historical epistemic violence, cultural and linguistic competency in faculty education, and participatory student government would help us more effectively co-investigate alongside our current students, colleagues, and administrators the ideologies of anti-Blackness, Indigenous erasure, White supremacy, and heteropatriarchy that undergird policies, programmatic structures, curricula, relationships between universities and communities, hiring practices, relationships between universities and students (particularly marginalized students), and the university's role in facilitating social reproduction or social change. The need for many of these shifts has already been articulated in the field of writing studies, just not necessarily *in relation* to a translingual pedagogy, which has focused too much on modeling itself after existing linguistic paradigms. As we move toward racing translingualism, we must be cautious to step away from (primarily) celebrating student literacies or "empowering" students to make rhetorical choices, because this plays into a logic that obscures how students' "choices" are informed by structural racism, classism, ableism, and heteronormativity. Racing translingualism necessitates that we interrogate the systemic production of a listening subject who will not evenly recognize gains in linguistic "competency." It demands that we resist pedagogies which suggest that linguistic marginalization can be mitigated with adequate adherence to linguistic respectability politics.

Building stronger critical transliteracies ecologies is one way to resist common "bootstraps" narratives that suggest that the most marginalized students, faculty, and administrators at universities must simply reclaim the space White supremacy, anti-Blackness, anti-indigeneity, and heteropatriarchy have denied them but that similarly suggest that those who are complicit in forwarding these structures have no work to do. As the example of the open admissions protestors demonstrates, it is important to do this not only through supporting the students in our first-year writing, advanced writing, and graduate practicum classrooms but also in the world outside our classroom and university walls.

REFERENCES

Ashkenas, Jeremy, Haeyoun Park, and Adam Pearce. 2017. "Even with Affirmative Action, Blacks and Hispanics Are More Underrepresented at Top Colleges than 35 Years Ago." *New York Times*, August 24.

Bambara, Toni Cade. 2007. "The Children Who Got Cheated." In *Savoring the Salt: The Legacy of Toni Cade Bambara*, ed. Linda Janet Holmes and Cheryl A. Wall, 145–47. Philadelphia: Temple University Press.

Bertrand, Marianne, and Sendhil Mullainathan. 2004. "Are Emily and Greg More Employable than Lakisha and Jamal? A Field Experiment on Labor Market Discrimination." *American Economic Review* (4): 991–1013.

Bizzell, Patricia. 1991. "Power, Authority, and Critical Pedagogy." *Journal of Basic Writing* 10 (2): 54–70.

Black and Puerto Rican Student Community. 1969. "Five Demands." *CUNY Digital History Archive*. https://cdha.cuny.edu/items/show/6952. Accessed September 2, 2017.

Black and Puerto Rican Student Community. 1970. "Press Release from the Black and Puerto Rican Student Community." *CUNY Digital History Archive*. https://cdha.cuny.edu/items/show/6932. Accessed September 2, 2017.

Brodkey, Linda. 2012. "On the Subjects of Class and Gender in 'The Literacy Letters.'" *College English* 51 (2): 125–41.

Bruffee, Kenneth. 1986. "Social Construction, Language, and the Authority of Knowledge." *College English* 48 (8): 773–88.

Canagarajah, Suresh. 2013. *Translingual Practice: Global Englishes and Cosmopolitan Relations*. New York: Routledge.

Cooper, Marilyn M., and Cynthia L. Selfe. 1990. "Computer Conferences and Learning: Authority, Resistance, and Internally Persuasive Discourse." *College English* 52 (8): 847–69.

Fabricant, Michael, and Stephen Brier. 2016. *Austerity Blues: Fighting for the Soul of Public Higher Education*. Baltimore: Johns Hopkins University Press.

Flores, Nelson, and Jonathan Rosa. 2015. "Undoing Appropriateness: Raciolinguistic Ideologies and Language Diversity in Education." *Harvard Education Review* 85 (2): 149–71.

García, Ofelia, and Tatyana Kleyn. 2016. *Translanguaging with Multilingual Students: Learning from Classroom Moments*. New York: Routledge.

García, Ofelia, and Wei Li. 2013. *Translanguaging: Language, Bilingualism and Education.* Basingstoke: Palgrave Macmillan UK.

García, Ofelia, and Richard Otheguy, eds. 1989. *English across Cultures, Cultures across English: A Reader in Cross-Cultural Communication.* Berlin: Mouton de Gruyter.

Gilyard, Keith. 2016. "The Rhetoric of Translingualism." *College English* 78 (3): 284–89.

Gnevsheva, Ksenia. 2018. "The Expectation Mismatch Effect in Accentedness Perception of Asian and Caucasian Non-Native Speakers of English." *Linguistics* 56 (3): 581–98.

Guerra, Juan C. 2008. "Cultivating Transcultural Citizenship: A Writing across Communities Model." *Language Arts* 85 (4): 296–304.

Hancock, Lynnell, and Meredith Kolodner. 2015. "What It Takes to Get into New York City's Best Public Colleges." *The Atlantic*, January 13.

Hanson, Andrew, and Zackary Hawley. 2011. "Do Landlords Discriminate in the Rental Housing Market? Evidence from an Internet Field Experiment in US Cities." *Journal of Urban Economics* 70 (2–3): 99–114.

Horner, Bruce. 1996. "Discoursing Basic Writing." *College Composition and Communication* 47 (2): 199–222.

Horner, Bruce, Min-Zhan Lu, Jacqueline Jones Royster, and John Trimbur. 2011. "Language Difference in Writing: Toward a Translingual Approach." *College English* 73 (3): 303–21.

Inoue, Asao. 2015. *Antiracist Writing Assessment Ecologies: Teaching and Assessing Writing for a Socially Just Future.* Fort Collins, CO, and Anderson, SC: WAC Clearinghouse and Parlor Press.

Kells, Michelle Hall. 2007. "Writing across Communities: Deliberation and the Discursive Possibilities of WAC." *Reflections* 11 (1): 87–108.

King, Eden B., Saaid A. Mendoza, Juan M. Madera, Mikki R. Hebel, and Jennifer L. Knight. 2006. "What's in a Name? Multiracial Investigation of the Role of Occupational Stereotypes in Selection Decisions." *Journal of Applied Psychology* 36 (5): 1145–59.

Kirsch, Gesa. 1985. *Representing Writing Tasks/Gaining Authority: Development of a Writer.* San Diego: Third College Writing Program.

Kynard, Carmen. 2013. *Vernacular Insurrections: Race, Black Protest, and the New Century in Composition-Literacies Studies.* Stonybrook: State University of New York Press.

Lamos, Steve. 2000. "Basic Writing, CUNY, and 'Mainstreaming': (De)Racialization Reconsidered." *Journal of Basic Writing* 19 (2): 22–43.

Lee, Jerry Won, and Christopher Jenks. 2016. "Doing Translingual Dispositions." *College Composition and Communication* 68 (2): 317–44.

Lorimer Leonard, Rebecca. 2014. "Multilingual Writing as Rhetorical Attunement." *College English* 76 (3): 227–47.

Lu, Min-Zhan. 1991. "Redefining the Legacy of Mina Shaughnessy: A Critique of the Politics of Linguistic Innocence." *Journal of Basic Writing* 10 (1): 26–40.

Matsuda, Paul Kei. 2014. "The Lure of Translingual Writing." *PMLA* 129 (3): 478–83.

Medina, Douglas. 2014. "Oral History Interview with Khadija DeLoache," *CUNY Digital History Archive.* https://cdha.cuny.edu/items/show/6822. Accessed September 2, 2017.

Mills, Charles. 1997. *The Racial Contract.* Ithaca, NY: Cornell University Press.

"Newton Hall Statement." April 1970. *CUNY Digital History Archive.* https://cdha.cuny.edu/items/show/6942. Accessed September 2, 2017.

Ortmeier-Hooper, Christina. 2008. "English May Be My Second Language, But I'm Not 'ESL.'" *College Composition and Communication* 59 (3): 389–419.

Otte, George, and Rebecca Williams Mlynarczyk. 2010. *Basic Writing.* West Lafayette, IN: Parlor Press.

Rubin, Donald L. 1992. "Nonlanguage Factors Affecting Undergraduates' Judgments of Nonnative English-Speaking Teaching Assistants." *Research in Higher Education* 33 (4): 511–31.

Shor, Ira. 1996. *When Students Have Power: Negotiating Authority in a Critical Pedagogy.* Chicago: University of Chicago Press.
Trimbur, John. 2016. "Translingualism and Close Reading." *College English* 78 (3): 219–77.
Wright, William. 1991. "Students as Ethnographers: Encouraging Authority." *Teaching English in the Two-Year College* 18 (2): 103–8.
Yang, K. Wayne. 2017. *A Third University Is Possible.* Minneapolis: University of Minnesota Press.
You, Xiaoye. 2016. *Cosmopolitan English and Transliteracy.* Carbondale: Southern Illinois University Press.

7
TOWARD A DECOLONIAL TRANSLINGUAL PEDAGOGY FOR BLACK IMMIGRANT STUDENTS

Esther Milu

The 1884–85 Berlin Conference, organized by Otto von Bismarck, the first chancellor of Germany, brought together several European powers to deliberate how to conquer, occupy, and exploit Africa's human and economic resources. The conference marked the beginning of what has become known as the European Scramble for Africa. Once a single body of land occupied by a multiplicity of people with various ethnic and linguistic identities, Africa was subdivided into regions and countries. Since Europe's colonial agenda went hand in hand with its imperial racialization project (Omi and Winant 1994), Africans were racialized as uncivilized and barbaric—justifying their enslavement, colonization, and other forms of subjugation.

In Africa, racialization also involved ethnicization/tribalization practices aimed at classifying and controlling numerous ethnic and linguistic groups. These practices started to disrupt Africans' ethnic identification and multilingual practices, which were originally characterized by fluidity and overlapping complexities. Colonization also introduced raciolinguistic ideologies that framed European languages as culturally and intellectually superior to Indigenous languages. Such ideologies also introduced language homogenizing practices that "co-naturalized" the categories of language and race/ethnicity (Rosa and Flores 2017). African natives were forced to choose one language, one ethnicity, and one community. To stabilize the new ethnic and linguistic identities, African natives were forced to live in designated geographic areas called "African reserves" or "rural areas," similar to Indian reservations in the US. Each ethnic group was expected to live separately within clearly defined geographic boundaries, with its movement monitored by the colonial administrators. These racialization histories and raciolinguistic ideologies continue to shape continental and African immigrants' language identities, practices, theories, and ideologies. For example, although colonization ended, many African countries continue to define themselves based on the languages of Europe: for example, English-speaking, French-speaking, and Portuguese-speaking (wa Thiong'o 1986).

Given this context and considering the growing number of African immigrant students in American colleges (Anderson and Lopez 2018), it is becoming increasingly critical for US-based educators to ask: how might knowledge of Africa's colonial and racialized history inform the way we theorize and enact race-conscious translingual pedagogies that take into account raciolinguistic experiences of *all* Black students? What language pedagogies do writing and literacy instructors need to adopt to better address African and domestic Black immigrants' diverse language needs? Current research in the field of writing studies focuses on the racialization and raciolinguistic experiences of US-born Blacks—that is, descendants of enslaved Black people. This focus, while important and necessary, tends to homogenize not only Black students' raciolinguistic experiences but also Black students themselves.

James Kigamwa and Michael Ndemanu (2017) argue that the translingual approach to writing has the potential to address the language needs of African immigrant students because it (1) challenges monolingual and standard language ideologies, (2) recognizes language users as always borrowing semiotic resources from linguistic and non-linguistic systems to facilitate their everyday communication, and (3) calls for respect and tolerance of cultural and linguistic differences and the honoring of languages rights. This chapter builds on this work, arguing that while translingual approaches may have such potential, translingualism should also take into account the complex and diverse racialized histories and raciolinguistic experiences African immigrant students bring to American classrooms. Like other Black students, Black immigrants bring with them additional colonial baggage characterized by inferiority complexes (wa Thiong'o 1986), colonial mentalities (Fanon 1963), and double consciousness (Du Bois 1903). These factors can limit Black students' (immigrants and domestic) response to language-affirming and language-sustaining pedagogies. It is therefore important to ask: how can we teach translingualism in a way that helps Black students value and affirm their languages and also decolonize their minds?

This chapter proposes not only a race-conscious but also a decolonial translingual pedagogy. The pedagogy is not just for African immigrants but also for other Black immigrant students whose heritage languages are marginalized and disfranchised by European colonialism and imperialism. Enacting this pedagogy will require US writing instructors to teach about the implications of European linguistic imperialism in local and global contexts. Currently, US writing instruction focuses on English linguistic hegemony; yet other European languages—such as Spanish, Portuguese, Italian, German, and French—have historically marginalized heritage languages in various colonial contexts. Given the increasing numbers of immigrant, transnational, and international students in our classrooms, a decolonial translingual pedagogy should peel back the layers of European linguistic imperialism, considering its implications for students from former colonial contexts. It should also explore how the growing dominance of English globally continues to create hierarchies among European languages. Peeling back the layers is important, especially for minority students who navigate two and sometimes three colonial languages, as Aja Martinez shows in this collection (chapter 3). My chapter offers additional examples, using the experiences of two students from Angola who navigate two imperial languages, English and Portuguese, and one from Rwanda, who navigates French and English. These experiences illustrate that teaching translingual approaches in the context of historical and contemporary European colonization and imperialism can help heritage language speakers better understand how to resolve the language dilemmas, tensions, contradictions, shame, and guilt they experience as they navigate European and heritage languages, as also discussed by Tom Do (chapter 4), Aja Martinez (chapter 3), and Yasmine Romero (chapter 8) in this collection.

ADOPTION OF TRANSLINGUAL APPROACH IN COMPOSITION STUDIES

Ever since Bruce Horner and his colleagues (2011) called to adopt the translingual paradigm, scholars in rhetoric and composition have theorized and enacted translingual pedagogies that recognize, honor, and value linguistic diversity in American writing classrooms. The pedagogies show the limitations and injustices of monolingualism, recognizing all languages as equal and powerful. Outcomes of these pedagogies reveal students' agency in using their own languages to achieve various rhetorical goals (Lu and Horner 2013), show the potential to develop translingual dispositions or openness toward language differences (Lee and Jenks 2016), open opportunities for creativity in writing (Seloni 2014), allow students to practice specific textual negotiation strategies in their writing (Canagarajah 2013), and provide opportunities for writing instructors to teach genres as socially situated, fluid, negotiable, and performative (Gonzales 2015; Bawarshi 2016). Others have shown translingualism's many affordances when combined with multi/transmodality, since this approach allows students to move not only across languages but also various modalities in their compositions (Horner, Selfe, and Lockridge 2015; Shipka 2016).

Despite these developments, there are pushbacks against translingualism. Juan Guerra (2016) suggests that teachers should not to focus on teaching students to produce code-meshed writing. Instead, he proposes that they focus on raising students' critical awareness about language to help them reverse the internalized standard and monolingual beliefs they hold and to help them activate and practice the diverse "rhetorical sensibilities" about language they already possess. Similarly, Paul Kei Matsuda (2014, 483) has criticized translingual pedagogies, noting that teachers' approaches to addressing language difference focus on looking for "visible manifestations of translingual writing," what he calls "linguistic tourism." He also questions translingual theorizing, noting that it leaves no room to critically explore the complexities of how language works in people's everyday lives.

Keith Gilyard (2016, 286) has observed that translingualism's current theorization (1) flattens language differences by presenting the translingual subject as "as a sort of linguistic every person"; (2) fails to recognize that every person's or linguistic group's relationship to standard language norms is not the same; and (3) does not acknowledge that while all minority language users deal with language stigma, the experiences are not the same. Gilyard's critique draws attention to how the current theorization of translingualism takes a post-racial stance, ignoring students' racialization experiences; yet such experiences can reveal the "historical and unresolved struggles of groups that have been traditionally underrepresented in the academy and suffer disproportionately in relation to it" (286). Similarly, Lyons (2009) has critiqued hybrid pedagogies like code meshing and, by implication, translingualism, noting that they are not aligned with native communities' cultural goals of searching for sovereignty and decolonization. Like Gilyard, Lyons emphasizes the importance of examining race, ethnicity, and colonial histories when theorizing language pedagogies for native communities.

In this chapter, I echo Gilyard and Lyons to emphasize the need to center race, ethnicity, colonialism, and racialization practices when theorizing and enacting translingualism. Centering these issues can help writing instructors better understand how minoritized students continue to be impacted by historical and contemporary colonial and racialization histories and experiences. I ask writing scholars and teachers to consider the diverse raciolinguistic and colonial histories transnational and immigrant Black students bring to writing classrooms. Such knowledge can help writing instructors better understand how students can reap the full affordances of translingual pedagogies and also work toward helping them decolonize their minds. I do this by sharing my story and those of three African immigrant students. Our raciolinguistic experiences arise from British, French, and Portuguese colonization. Sharing my story, along with those of my students, aligns with Romero's argument in this collection (chapter 8) that co-storying students' and teacher-scholars' lived experiences with racialization can help *race* translingualism and also imagine race-conscious translingual pedagogies.

INSTITUTIONAL AND PEDAGOGICAL CONTEXT

The students whose voices are represented in this chapter participated in my spring 2016 first-year writing (FYW) class at a predominantly White institution in the Midwest.[1] Patrick and Jack were from Angola and identified Portuguese as their first language. They started learning English as their second language a year before joining the college in the US. They were among 500 young Angolans fully sponsored by their government to attend US universities. Both were majoring in mechanical engineering. John was from Rwanda and claimed literacy in three languages: French, English, and Kinyarwanda. He was attending a US college through a Mastercard Foundation scholarship, a program that supports talented African students from vulnerable backgrounds.

This FYW course was themed American Racial and Ethnic Experience. While many FYW courses at this institution were themed, instructors had the liberty to design the courses based on their own pedagogical and theoretical commitments, as long as they were aligned with the program's curriculum outcomes. The curriculum asked students to theorize, research, write, and reflect about literacy in all the core assignments: personal literacies, cultural literacies, disciplinary literacies, and multimodal literacies. In the first assignment of the curriculum, I saw an opportunity to work with students and help them debunk the myths of linguistic hegemony and monolingualism and instead develop translingual dispositions—that is, "a general openness to language plurality and difference" (Lee and Jenks 2016, 318). This assignment took the form of a literacy autobiography, which invited students to reflect on past and present events and practices associated with literacy and to consider their relationship to their lives now. I modified this assignment and made both language and literacy the subjects of inquiry. I asked my students to reflect on their language backgrounds, histories, and experiences and narrate how they have shaped their literacy development. Throughout the unit, students wrote critical reading responses to selected readings by Geneva Smitherman, Amy Tan, Gloria Anzaldúa, and Ofelia Zepeda. They also engaged in classroom and blog discussions of the same authors. I chose these readings because they have features of both a language and a literacy autobiography. Further, these authors discuss how their racialized histories and raciolinguistic experiences shaped their language journeys and literacy development. In addition to these readings, students also read selected critical pieces on literacy, including the introduction in *Elements of Literacy* by Julie Lindquist and David Seitz (2008). The excerpts analyzed in this chapter are from the students' literacy autobiographies, critical reading responses to the readings, and blog discussions.

RESEARCHER POSITIONALITY

As an African immigrant language scholar whose raciolinguistic history and experience is shaped by British colonization in Kenya, teaching students from various countries in Africa afforded me a specific connection and opportunity to interrogate the various histories of colonization in this continent and their repercussions for contemporary US writing classrooms. In reading about students' racialization and raciolinguistic experiences as represented in their literacy autobiographies and critical responses to the assigned readings, I realized that their experiences were very different from mine. For example, Patrick and Jack shared that they did not speak Angolan Indigenous languages because learning the languages was suppressed by Portuguese colonization. This was not my experience or John's, because we both speak African Indigenous languages. This led me to wonder how various forms of colonization in Africa contributed to our diverse language repertoires and experiences.

I decided to co-story my experience alongside that of my three students in this chapter because as an African immigrant language scholar, I noticed that transnational and immigrant African students' raciolinguistic experiences are not represented in language diversity scholarship. I began noticing this lack of representation as a graduate student—a general tendency to discuss Black language as monolithic and Black student as a homogeneous group. Yet I believe that for writing instructors to practice linguistically just pedagogies for all Black students, they must be aware of the diverse language differences and raciolinguistic experiences Black students bring to our classrooms. Writing instructors who lack awareness of African immigrants' language histories, for example, risk flattening, erasing, or subsuming their language repertoires and raciolinguistic experiences with those of other US and Afro-diasporic Blacks. While these groups share the same racial category—Black—each has experienced historically distinct racial and colonial projects (Omi and Winant 1994).

US-born Blacks, descendants of enslaved Black people, speak US Ebonics aka African American language, among other names. Their language repertoires are rooted in slavery history and US sociolinguistic order. In contrast, African immigrants' language repertoires are shaped by what Ali Mazrui (1986) calls Africa's triple linguistic heritage: African indigeneity, Arab-Islamic, and Europeanness. For example, my translingual identity is shaped by my mother tongue, Kikamba, an African Indigenous language; Kiswahili, a Creole-based language that arose through language contact among Bantu languages, Arabic, and Indo-Aryan languages such as Gujarati, Hindi, and Punjabi; and English, a European language. While this triple linguistic heritage represents the identity of many continental Africans, differences exist depending on where a country is located geographically in Africa, among other factors.

BRITISH RACIOLINGUISTIC EXPERIENCE

My aforementioned translingual identity does not mean that all the languages in my repertoire are equal. When I was growing up and attending school in Kenya, English occupied a higher status. In K–12 education, teachers enforced English hegemony and standard language ideologies through corporal punishment, public shaming, and humiliation. As students, we assumed this was normal. However, for students like me, who attended school in African reserves, mastering the English language was a challenge because our mother tongues and Swahili were always in the mix. I remember choosing to stay silent throughout the day for fear of slipping into the mother tongue and being punished. This was the case for many students, some of whom opted to drop out of school altogether.

It was not until I was exposed to decolonial language scholarship in graduate school, especially the work of Ngũgĩ wa Thiong'o, that I began to understand the history of standard language ideologies in Kenya. In *Decolonizing the Mind* (1986), wa Thiong'o, a product of colonial education, describes how colonial White teachers punished students for speaking Indigenous languages and rewarded those who spoke English. Colonial English pedagogy in Kenya introduced raciolinguistic ideologies by associating African Indigenous languages with a lack of intelligence and humanity, while English was associated with intelligence and prestige: "One of the most humiliating experiences was to be caught speaking Gikuyu in the vicinity of the school. The culprit was given corporal punishment—three to five strokes of the cane on bare buttocks—or was made to carry a metal plate around the neck with inscriptions such as I AM STUPID or I AM A DONKEY ... The attitude to English was the exact opposite: any achievement in spoken or written English was highly rewarded; prizes, prestige, applause; the ticket to higher realms" (11–12).

British colonization also introduced standard language ideologies for Swahili. Unlike other Indigenous languages, the British did not suppress Swahili because it was an important language for colonial administration across the eastern and central African regions. However, given the diverse Swahili dialects spoken in the region, British governors who ruled the East African region appointed the Inter-Territorial Language Committee to standardize it. At a 1928 conference held in Mombasa, Kenya, the Zanzibar dialect was adopted as the standard. These raciolinguistic and standard language ideologies introduced by British colonialists continue to be enforced and sustained through current formal education. Attending school in Kenya, I internalized these language ideologies, feelings of inferiority, colonial mentality (Fanon 1963), and double consciousness (Du Bois 1903)—additional language baggage I brought to my graduate classes in the US.

After moving to the US in 2008, I was confronted with another challenge. I was no longer African or Kenyan; I had to "become Black." Awad K. Ibrahim (2003, 170) explains how continental Africans undergo a new racialization experience of "becoming Black" when they immigrate to North America; in other words, they "enter a social imaginary—a discursive space in which they are already imagined, constructed, and ... treated as Blacks by hegemonic discourses and groups." These racialization practices force them to learn how to navigate new ethnic and racial identification practices, especially because dominant discourses expect them to act and speak Black. Some resist the racialization while others, as Ibrahim notes, embrace it and start using different varieties of Black English. Like other Blacks, I started experiencing racialization and discrimination based on my accented English. It was PTSD all over again; the language discrimination took me back to my K–12 experiences. I contemplated learning and speaking African American language (Black language) and acquiring what H. Samy Alim (2016) calls "normative Black identity," but

I knew it would be inauthentic, especially because I don't share its history and culture. As an emerging language scholar, I was also keen on affirming my African translingual heritage and using it to highlight the language diversity among Black students in US writing classrooms.

PORTUGUESE RACIOLINGUISTIC EXPERIENCE: PATRICK'S AND JACK'S STORY

Jack and Patrick are products of 500 years of Portugal's colonization of Angola. The country's racialization history and raciolinguistic experience began with the arrival of Portuguese traders in the West African coastal region in the 1480s. The Portuguese were initially interested in the transatlantic slave trade, which, according to W. G. Clarence-Smith (1979), saw the sale of between 5,000 and 10,000 Angolan slaves annually to various European nations and colonies. After the Berlin Conference and with the abolition of slavery, Portugal established aggressive settler colonial practices in Angola and six African states/territories. The Portuguese started homegrown enslavement practices that forced Angolan natives to provide free labor on sugar, coffee, maize, cotton, sisal, and palm oil plantations. The cash crops were then exported to Europe and their colonies in the Americas and elsewhere. Racialization practices were further consolidated through the passing of the 1926 Native Statute, legislation aimed at keeping European and African races separate. The categories of "citizen" and "Native" were established to facilitate the racialization process.

Like all European colonizing powers, Portugal engaged in a civilizing mission intended to make Angolans more like Europeans. The Portuguese introduced assimilation laws intended to help African natives achieve the legal status of a citizen, or *assimilado*. To qualify, one had to pass a special exam, demonstrate the ability to speak and write in Portuguese, show interest in Portugal, practice European mannerisms such as wearing European clothing and eating with a fork and knife, practice monogamy, and be a member of Roman Catholic Church (see Felipe 2013; Birmingham 2015). The assimilated parents were forbidden to teach their children African languages. In fact, the teaching of African languages in Angola was prohibited through the Decreto de Norton de Matos, or Decree Number 77 of 1927. Indigenous languages were taught only in catechism classes as a bridge to learning Portuguese (Manuel 2015).

This history is strongly present in Patrick's critical reading response to Geneva Smitherman's "From a Ghetto Lady to Critical Linguist" and Gloria Anzaldúa's "How to Tame a Wild Tongue." Patrick revealed how raciolinguistic practices in Angola shaped natives' attitude toward their Indigenous languages:

> After analyzing both texts, I realized something very similar that did happen . . . in my country, Angola . . . Portuguese government required Angolan people to forget their national language. There was a huge campaign of coercion for promoting Portuguese around the country as the most perfect language, and the national language as "inhuman" and "shameful." People who spoke Portuguese were seen as the "smartest" and "educated" while people who did speak Angolan languages [were] seen as "stupid" and "loser."

Like many independent countries in Africa, Angola sought to indigenize its education system by incorporating African languages in the curriculum. Of the forty-six Indigenous languages spoken in the country, six were designated as national languages (Kimbundu, Umbundu, Kikongo, Chokwe, Kwanyama, and Ngagela) and were standardized to be taught through transitional bilingual programs (Manuel 2015). However, as Patrick shared in one of his critical reading responses, the country's deeply entrenched Portuguese monolingual ideology discourages students and parents from learning the national languages:

> The ability of one to speak well [in] Portuguese was decisive to get a job or other social benefits . . . As one could expect, a great number of Angolan parents stopped teaching their children [a] national language. Nowadays, the generations who were born after independence of Angola, mainly the ones who live in urban areas . . . they just speak Portuguese (unfortunately, I am one of them). And even worst, they do not want to learn any national language, and they usually make fun of people who can speak one.

Luanda, the urban city Patrick alludes to, was the colonial and administrative capital of Angola, where wealth, power, and educational access were limited to Portuguese colonists and a few assimilated natives. Those living in rural areas were deliberately denied assimilado status. They were racialized as uncivilized to justify their forced labor, and they needed to carry a pass at all times and to pay poll (hut) taxes. While they retained their ethnic cultures and languages, they were denied formal education, which was only accessible through Portuguese. By the time Angola gained independence in 1975, it was estimated that between 85 and 90 percent of the population was illiterate (Warner 1989). After independence, rural populations that had been marginalized for years started immigrating to the city to look for economic and educational opportunities. Since independence, increased urbanization has seen many Angolans—particularly the younger generation—learn Portuguese, as Patrick confirms. According to "Ethnologue" (2010),

60 percent of Angolans speak Portuguese, with 40 percent as their L1. However, the social structures established during colonialism continue to exist, with those in urban cities gaining more access to Portuguese language and literacy compared to residents of rural communities—that is, African reserves. In a blog discussion, Patrick reminded Jack of how they made fun of their "Angolan brothers from rural areas who have difficulties speaking Portuguese."

Like many natives, Jack's family lived in rural areas during the colonial period and did not have access to formal education. He therefore located the history of his literacy journey beginning at end of the Angolan civil war, leading to the country's independence:

> Coming from a painful and dark time as civil war, all people wanted to think about was restarting, reconstructing, future, opportunities. My parents had to leave their loved homeland to immigrate to the capital city to look for a better life going through difficult times. However, looking all the way back to the elements that influenced my literacy in such a hard time, the word that sticks the most in my mind is surprisingly *privilege*. If I try to contextualize my literacy among the various definitions we read in the article "The Elements of Literacy," I would identify mine as what psychologist Sylvia Scribner defined as literacy as a state of grace.

Jack's contextualization of his literacy development as a "privilege," using the metaphor of literacy as a "state of grace," reveals a deeply embedded colonial mentality. In explaining this metaphor, Lindquist and Seitz (2008, 10) note that it implies that "if you're literate . . . you're smarter, more civilized, more ethical, more humane." European colonization and raciolinguistic ideologies in Angola associated these virtues with the privileged few, or those who could engage with the written word: Whites and assimilados. Jack continued to connect this metaphor to his literacy development journey, noting how learning to write in grammatically correct Portuguese forced him to develop virtues of "responsibility" and "accountability":

> In 2013 I remember working on my church's youth group. I was chosen to work with the person who had to write the report of all the activities done by the group and present it to the church leadership. The pastor was a very educated man who did his studies on Brazil and Russia, and I wanted to make sure that my writing wouldn't bother him. I started to learn the patterns of good writing on Portuguese, and work on my grammar and vocabulary, and it was very important for me because it helped me to account for responsibility and also the idea of growing over duties. That phase of working on my church's youth group was [a] very important time of my literacy because . . . it really encouraged me to take my writing more seriously since I had to write to an audience that was completely strange for me and I had to sound professional.

Jack's obsession with "good writing in Portuguese" that will not "bother" his immediate boss and "church leadership" reveals deeply embedded monolingual and standard language ideologies. These ideologies seemed hard to shake off, even after experiencing my translingual pedagogy. In a critical response to Anzaldúa's "How to Tame a Wild Tongue," he strongly believed it is the responsibility of the speaker of a non-dominant language to bear what Rosina Lippi-Green (1997) calls the "burden of communication." Jack therefore observed:

> It is important to realize that we have the burden of facilitating our communication within the society and principally to those that have a hard time understanding the language we speak . . . it is important to define the limits of our pride in order to not let it be an obstacle in our communication. I totally agree that we need to preserve our language because it is part of our identity, but in the same time we also need to realize that we are the ones responsible to make ourselves understood.

While Jack shows evidence of developing a translingual disposition or openness toward language diversity, his willingness to accept or put the burden of communication on the minority speaker reveals internalized racism and a colonial mentality. Jack's attitude calls for a decolonial translingual pedagogy that seeks to understand and help students like him reverse the deeply entrenched internalized racism, colonial mentality, and raciolinguistic ideologies. Patrick, on the other hand, showed the transformative potential of decolonial translingual pedagogy in one of his critical responses:

> This course really challenges me to think about how much I was disinterested about my culture . . . I am ashamed to admit that I cannot speak any Angolan language, or to identify myself with one Angolan ethnic group . . . My first language is a European one (Portuguese) I . . . talk much more as a European than Angolan . . . Now, I want[ed] to do the opposite . . . I want to appreciate my culture, exploring its beauty and singularity. I wanted to talk to my people using our own language.

FRENCH RACIOLINGUISTIC EXPERIENCE: JOHN'S STORY

In his literacy autobiography, John shared that his translingual repertoires draw resources from three language systems: Kinyarwanda, French, and English. Kinyarwanda is one of the national languages of and also the lingua franca in Rwanda. As such, it is the medium of instruction in grades 1–3. John remembered his "joyful" elementary years learning to read and write in Kinyarwanda. He also shared how English and French became part of his linguistic repertoire through formal schooling:

I got to learn how to write different words in my mother tongue, and more interestingly how to write my name. "Mom, look[,] that is the Kirehe district hospital, Kabare secondary school," I would tell my mom while reading posts through the bus window on our way traveling. I was so thrilled to understand the meaning of Kinyarwanda written posts . . . Meanwhile, in my early primary education, I got to experience learning both English and French as foreign languages. However, the official academic language for many schools including mine was French.

At the surface level, John's description of his translingual repertoires seems straightforward. However, those repertoires are rooted in a complex and traumatic racialization history and raciolinguistic experience. Rwanda was colonized by both Belgium and France, who introduced French to the country and made it the official language. Since Kinyarwanda was the country's lingua franca, the Belgians allowed it to be the language of instruction up to third grade and French the language of instruction from fourth grade through college. However, when Rwanda gained independence in 1962, the country sought to indigenize the curriculum, making Kinyarwanda the language of instruction for all eight years of elementary schooling. In 1991, the country reverted to the old system after students exhibited poor literacy performance levels in national exams.

After the 1994 Rwandan genocide, new language policies were proposed. President Paul Kagame's government, composed mostly of returning Tutsis refugees who had sought refuge in English-speaking countries, argued that French was not the ideal language for the country because it promoted a "genocide ideology" (Samuelson and Freedman 2010). By adopting English as the official language, Rwanda wanted to distance itself from Belgian/French colonial influence. With the introduction of the new language reforms, President Kagame also sought to unify the country by ending ethnicization and racialization practices introduced by Belgian colonists. Belgium's racialization practices, inspired by the Eugenics movement, had used practices like skull testing to advance the argument that the Tutsis had Caucasian ancestry and were morally, intellectually, and physically "superior" to the other two ethnic groups: Hutu and Twa. They also argued that because Tutsis were lighter skinned, had taller stature, and had Hamitic origins, they were closer to "Europeans." In 1931, these racialization practices were solidified with the introduction of identification cards that detailed each person's ethnicity. Throughout the colonial period, the colonists favored the Tutsis by giving them economic and political power and other privileges. Years of systematic exclusion and disenfranchisement led Hutu rebels to turn against the Tutsis, leading to the 1994 genocide.

Because of this racialization history, Kagame's government was keen on emphasizing the role language should play in unifying and bonding the three Rwandese ethnic groups. The Kagame government "asserted that all Rwandans are first and foremost citizens of Rwanda and that the sharp divisions over ethnicity are a legacy of colonization under the Belgians . . . since Rwandans share Kinyarwanda in common, they are therefore of the same ethnic group" (Samuelson and Freedman 2010, 196). Today, discussions of ethnicity are prohibited in Rwanda because they are seen as divisive or as seeking to promote a genocide ideology. The new leadership has also argued that because English is the language of the global economy, its use gives Rwanda a better chance of participating in the competitive global economy. In 2009, English was adopted as the official language of instruction in Rwanda. These language policy changes have not been easy for students like John, who are caught up in the transition. In his literacy autobiography, John shared the challenges he faced negotiating the use of French and English in his writing:

> As the system is in Rwanda, upon completion of three years of secondary school (9th grade in the US system), students have the opportunity to choose a combination of three classes for Advanced level secondary school. I chose Math, Chemistry and Biology; this might have been the easiest choice that I have ever made in my academic life, because I considered myself fitting exactly into that combination. However, I had to overcome a new language barrier. The education system was changed from French to English so I had to adjust to the new teaching medium. In the first assessment that I had, I was required to write names of certain chemical compounds, which I definitely knew in French. However it was a struggle to write them in English. For instance for NaCl (Sodium Chloride) I wrote Chlorure of Sodium, because in French it is Chlorure de Sodium and I knew that de literary [literally] meant of.

Rwanda's sociolinguistic landscape is as complex and diverse as that of any other African country. For example, returning Tutsi refugees brought with them Swahili from Tanzania, Lingala and Kikongo from Congo, and Kirundi from Burundi, among others. Given Swahili's prominence as the lingua franca in East Africa and the central African region, in Rwanda it is taught as an additional language and is considered the fourth national language. And while it may appear as if every Rwandese is onboard with Kagame's dominant English ideology and his detribalization efforts, this is not the case. Suffice is to say, Rwanda's racialization history and raciolinguistic experience is complex, and as one Rwandese elder recently told me, it needs to be told with care. As an outsider to the community, I am aware of my limitations in capturing the nuances. However, John's case is informative in helping us consider how we might theorize and enact race-conscious decolonial translingual pedagogy for students like him who bring traumatic racialization histories to the classroom. Such students may resist translingual pedagogies that invite them to discuss race and ethnicity in relation to language, particularly given the country's effort to detribalize. Further, students may also resist language pedagogies that ask them to reveal, affirm, or translanguage in their writing. For example, although French might be part of the students' language repertoire, they may associate it with the genocide, since that is the dominant ideology in their home country.

DISCUSSION, IMPLICATIONS, AND CONCLUSION

While our stories represent a small sample of sub-Saharan African immigrant experiences, they nevertheless reveal the diverse linguistic repertoires, racialized histories, and raciolinguistic experiences African immigrant students bring to American classrooms. Each country's colonial, racialized history and raciolinguistic experience discussed in this chapter suggest the need to rethink the translingual approach's sameness-of-difference tenet and develop bold approaches that seek to reverse the internalized racism and raciolinguistic ideologies immigrant Black students may harbor. Our stories therefore offer both theoretical and pedagogical implications.

Rethinking the Sameness-of-Difference Model

The four cases of racialization practices in Africa challenge translingualism's sameness-of-difference model. As evidenced in our stories, while my students and I may share the category "African" and have had experience with European colonization, we have very different language repertoires, various forms of linguistic marginalization, and diverse language ideologies. For example, Angola had very extreme raciolinguistic ideologies that enforced Portuguese monolingualism, as represented in Patrick's and Jack's experiences. Rwanda's and Kenya's colonial history produced different outcomes for John and me. Because I grew up in African reserves, or rural areas, I retained my mother tongue, and through formal education I acquired Swahili and English. Similarly, Jack developed a trilingual linguistic identity, since Kinyarwanda is the language of wider communication in his country and was the language of instruction up to third grade. Through formal education, John acquired French, the language of Belgian/

French colonialism in Rwanda. He also acquired English as a result of the language policy reforms introduced in the country after the 1994 genocide. These colonial histories and experiences not only reveal a diversity of language repertoires but also align with Gilyard's (2016) critique of translingual theory's sameness-of-difference tenet, since, as these experiences reveal, African immigrant students' histories and relationships with English are not the same. Patrick and Jack started learning English shortly before attending a US college, while John started learning English in high school. I started learning English in elementary school. As such, African immigrant students bring different English proficiency levels to American classrooms.

Our racialization histories and raciolinguistic experiences give rise to diverse language ideologies, which also challenge the sameness-of-difference model. Both Jack and Patrick believed in the superiority of Portuguese, since for many years in Angola it was racialized as the language of economic access, privilege, and Whiteness. Growing up in Angola, they had a very negative attitude toward Indigenous languages and their speakers. John had competing ideologies on the role of French as the language of genocide and English as the language of unity and decolonization for his country. Similarly, in Kenya, while standard language ideologies abound as I shared in my story, they are also being challenged by translingual practices, as I explain elsewhere in my research (see Milu 2018).

These complex and competing language ideologies give rise to contradictory theories and beliefs about monolingualism and multilingualism, a situation similar to what Nancy Bou Ayash (2016, 559) observed among her research participants in Lebanon, where their language theories revealed a "postmonolingual character in that established representations of language as a bounded, fixed entity preceding its use coexist side-by-side and compete with a translingual view of English as dynamic, mutable, and negotiated." These experiences in Africa and Lebanon challenge the largely celebratory tone in most translingual scholarship, which seems to suggest that language users no longer theorize and engage in language practices that follow the "traditional multilingual model" (Horner, NeCamp, and Donahue 2011)—a model that views languages as separate, discrete, and hierarchical. My experience and that of my three students suggests the need for more research in local and global contexts to better understand all factors that shape people's language theories, uses, and practices.

Teaching Language and/as Race and Ethnicity

Our experiences support recent research that suggests the need to teach language and race together. Drawing on Samy Alim's work on raciolinguistics, Geneva Smitherman (2017, 8) recently encouraged teachers to be bold in developing pedagogies that involve "conceptualizing, theorizing and analyzing race and language together." She argues that this will require teachers to draw knowledge from both language studies and race/ethnic studies to examine racialization experiences in local and global contexts. Our stories suggest the need for a race-conscious and decolonial translingual pedagogy that seeks to raise students' awareness of how European colonization and racialization practices contributed to shaping Africa's "linguistic cultures." Harold F. Schiffman (1996, 5) defines linguistic culture as the "set of behaviors, assumptions, cultural forms, prejudices, folk belief systems, attitudes, stereotypes, ways of thinking about language, and religio-historical circumstances associated with a particular language." Each African country has a particular belief system, attitude, and various ways of thinking about the role of European languages in that country. Consequently, each colonial history gives rise to specific raciolinguistic experiences and ideologies.

Writing teachers may ask: how can we learn the linguistic cultures of all the language systems students bring to the classroom and their respective raciolinguistic ideologies? As shown in my discussion, the literacy autobiography—a common assignment in first-year writing courses—can be redesigned to add a language component to it. Instructors can make both language and literacy the topics of inquiry and reflection by asking students to write about how their language histories and backgrounds shaped their literacy development. However, given the emphasis on centralizing race in the teaching of language and writing, such an assignment should also ask students to write about how their racialization experiences and colonial histories have shaped their literacy development. Instructors can also assign readings by authors whose language and literacy developments have been shaped by various racialization experiences and colonial histories. Such content can motivate students who have experienced colonial difference to share (through oral discussion and writing) how European colonization shaped the linguistic cultures of the language repertoires they bring to our classrooms.

Further, to understand and effectively respond to students' raciolinguistic experiences and ideologies, US-based educators need to combine their knowledge of translingual theory with what Kate Seltzer and Cati V. de los Ríos (2018) call "raciolinguistic literacies." This will require writing teachers to teach language, colonization, and racialization together. Seltzer and Ríos's proposal aligns with my vision of developing a race-conscious decolonial translingual pedagogy for Black immigrant students. This means that US-based educators must learn racialization and raciolinguistic experiences beyond the Americas, given calls in the field to research and teach composition as a transnational and global enterprise. For example, our stories demand that writing teachers develop raciolinguistic literacies that show awareness of how Africans have historically been racialized, tribalized, and ethnicized through European colonization and how European linguistic imperialism continues to shape African immigrant students' language identities and ideologies, as well as the colonial baggage they bring to US classrooms. Further, it is important for writing teachers to understand Black immigrants' racialization processes in Africa and the US, noting that Black students' linguistic practices are rooted in both individual and collective experiences that should be highlighted rather than erased.

NOTE

1. Portions of this chapter originally appeared as "Diversity of Raciolinguistic Experiences in the Writing Classroom: An Argument for a Transnational Black Language Pedagogy," *College English* 83 (6) (2021): 415–41. © 2021 by the National Council of Teachers of English. Used with permission.

REFERENCES

Alim, H. Samy. "Introducing Raciolinguistics: Racing Language and Languaging Race in Hyperracial Times." 2016. In *Raciolinguistics: How Language Shapes Our Ideas about Race*, ed. H. Samy Alim, John R. Rickford, and Arnetha F. Ball, 1–30. New York: Oxford University Press.

Anderson, Monica, and Gustavo Lopez. 2018. "Key Facts about Black Immigrants in the U.S." Pew Research Center. http://www.pewresearch.org/fact-tank/2018/01/24/key-facts-about-black-immigrants-in-the-u-s/. Accessed November 14, 2018.

Anzaldúa, Gloria. 1987. "How to Tame a Wild Tongue." In *Borderlands/La Frontera: The New Mestiza* by Anzaldúa, 53–64. San Francisco: Spinsters/Aunt Lute Press.

Augusto, António Filipe. 2012. *Assessing the Introduction of Angolan Indigenous Languages in the Educational System in Luanda: A Language Policy Perspective*. MA thesis, School of Literature and Language Studies, Department of Linguistics, University of the Witwatersrand, Johannesburg, South Africa. http://hdl.handle.net/10539/11378. Accessed July 15, 2018.

Ayash, Nancy Bou. 2016. "Conditions of (Im)Possibility: Postmonolingual Language Representations in Academic Literacies." *College English* 78 (6): 555–77.

Bawarshi, Anis. 2016. "Beyond the Genre Fixation: A Translingual Perspective on Genre." *College English* 78 (3): 243–49.

Birmingham, David A. 2015. *Short History of Modern Angola*. New York: Oxford University Press.
Canagarajah, Suresh. 2013. "Negotiating Translingual Literacy: An Enactment." *Research in the Teaching of English* 48 (1): 40–67.
Clarence-Smith, W. G. 1979. *Slaves, Peasants and Capitalists in Southern Angola 1840–1926*. Cambridge University Press.
Du Bois, W. E. B. 1903. *The Souls of Black Folk: Essays and Sketches*. Chicago: A. C. McClurg.
"Ethnologue: Languages of the World." 16th ed. 2010. Dallas: SIL International. http://www.ethnologue.com/region/Africa. Accessed March 12, 2018.
Fanon, Frantz. 1963. *The Wretched of the Earth*. New York: Grove.
Gilyard, Keith. 2016. "The Rhetoric of Translingualism." *College English* 78 (3): 284–89.
Gonzales, Laura. 2015. "Multimodality, Translingualism, and Rhetorical Genre Studies." *Composition Forum* 31. https://compositionforum.com/issue/31/multimodality.php. Accessed February 15, 2017.
Guerra, Juan. 2016. "Cultivating a Rhetorical Sensibility in the Translingual Writing Classroom." *College English* 78 (3): 228–33.
Horner, Bruce, Min-Zhan Lu, Jacqueline Jones Royster, and John Trimbur. 2011. "Language Difference in Writing: Toward a Translingual Approach." *College English* 73 (3): 303–21.
Horner, Bruce, Samantha NeCamp, and Christiane Donahue. 2011. "Toward a Multilingual Composition Scholarship: From English Only to a Translingual Norm." *College Composition and Communication* 63 (2): 269–300.
Horner, Bruce, Cynthia Selfe, and Tim Lockridge. 2015. *Translinguality, Transmodality, and Difference: Exploring Dispositions and Change in Language and Learning*. Intermezzo. http://intermezzo.enculturation.net/01/ttd-horner-selfe-lockridge/index.htm. Accessed July 15, 2018.
Ibrahim, Awad K. 2003. "Whassup, Homeboy? Joining the African Diaspora: Black English as a Symbolic Site of Identification and Language Learning." In *Black Linguistics: Language, Society, and Politics in Africa and the Americas*, ed. Sinfree Makoni, Geneva Smitherman, Arnetha Ball, and Arthur Spears, 169–85. New York: Routledge.
Kigamwa, James, and Michael Ndemanu. 2017. "Translingual Practice among African Immigrants in the US: Embracing the Mosaicness of the English Language." *Journal of Multilingual and Multicultural Development* 38 (5): 468–79.
Lee, Jerry Won, and Christopher J. Jenks. 2016. "Doing Translingual Dispositions." *College Composition and Communication* 68 (2): 317–44.
Lindquist, Julie, and David Seitz. 2008. *The Elements of Literacy*. New York: Longman.
Lippi-Green, Rosina. 1997. *English with an Accent: Language, Ideology, and Discrimination in*
Lu, Min-Zhan, and Bruce Horner. 2013. "Translingual Literacy and Matters of Agency." In *Literacy as a Translingual Practice: Between Communities and Classrooms*, ed. Suresh Canagarajah, 26–38. New York: Routledge.
Lyons, Scott. 2009. "The Fine Art of Fencing: Nationalism, Hybridity, and the Search for a Native American Writing Pedagogy." *Journal of Advanced Composition* 29: 77–106.
Manuel, Nicolau. 2015. "Language and Literacy Policies in Sub-Saharan Africa: Towards a Bilingual Education Policy in Angola." PhD diss., Washington State University, Pullman.
Matsuda, Paul Kei. 2014. "The Lure of Translingual Writing." *PMLA* 129 (3): 478–83.
Mazrui, Ali Al'Amin. 1986. *The Africans: A Triple Heritage*. Boston: Little, Brown.
Milu, Esther. 2018. "Translingualism, Kenyan Hip-Hop and Emergent Ethnicities: Implications for Language Theory and Pedagogy." *International Multilingual Research Journal* 12 (2): 96–108.
Omi, Michael, and Howard Winant. 1994. *Racial Formation in the United States: From the 1960s to 1990s*. 2nd ed. New York: Routledge.

Rosa, Jonathan, and Nelson Flores. 2017. "Unsettling Race and Language: Toward a Raciolinguistic Perspective." *Language in Society* 46 (5): 621–47.

Samuelson, Beth L., and Sarah W. Freedman. "Language Policy, Multilingual Education, and Power in Rwanda." *Language Policy* 9 (3): 191–215.

Schiffman, Harold. F. 1996. *Linguistic Culture and Language Policy*. New York: Routledge.

Seloni, Lisya. " 'I'm an Artist and a Scholar Who Is Trying to Find a Middle Point': A Textographic Analysis of a Colombian Art Historian's Thesis Writing." *Journal of Second Language Writing* 25: 79–99. https://doi.org/10.1016/j.jslw.2014.06.001. Accessed August 15, 2017.

Seltzer, Kate, and Cati V. de los Ríos. 2018. "Translating Theory to Practice: Exploring Teachers' Raciolinguistic Literacies in Secondary English Classrooms." *English Education* 51 (1): 49–79.

Shipka, Jody. 2016. "Transmodality in/and Processes of Making." *College English* 78 (3): 250–57.

Smitherman, Geneva. 2000. "From Ghetto Lady to Critical Linguist." In *Talkin That Talk: African American Language and Culture* by Smitherman, 1–12. New York: Routledge.

Smitherman, Geneva. 2017. "Raciolinguistics, 'Mis-Education,' and Language Arts Teaching in the 21st Century." *Language Arts Journal of Michigan* 32 (2): 4–14. https://doi.org/10.9707/2168-149X.2164. Accessed July 20, 2019.

Warner, Rachel. 1989. "The Society and Its Environment." In *A Country Study: Angola*, ed. Thomas Collelo, 53–110. Washington, DC: Library of Congress, Federal Research Division.

wa Thiong'o, Ngũgĩ 1986. *Decolonising the Mind: The Politics of Language in African Literature*. London: J. Currey.

8
MULTILINGUAL SPEAKER-WRITERS' CO-STORIES AS PART OF A RACE-CONSCIOUS TRANSLINGUAL PRACTICE

Yasmine Romero

Translingual and translanguaging orientations to language move away from monolingualist paradigms in language and writing studies, such as English-only (Auerbach 1993) or dualistic (Elbow 2002) approaches and policies that prioritize appropriateness (Flores and Rosa 2015), mastery (Fish 2009), erasure, and/or multiculturalist tokenism of minority students' linguistic and rhetorical practices (Kubota 2004; Lee 2016). This prioritization in language and writing studies has naturalized language ideologies of "ownership, purity, and even nativeness" (Canagarajah 2013, 43). Translingualism destabilizes these ideologies and their translations into language and writing classrooms; language becomes an emergent, collaborative practice in which language differences are the norm and "communicating across [these] differences" (Lorimer 2013, 163) involves interlocutors negotiating framings and footings in "situated interactions for new meaning construction" (Canagarajah 2013, 1). While translingual practices and literacy are not new, attention to and scholarship on performative competence, translocal spaces, translinguistic identities, and negotiation strategies in contact situations are currently the focus in translingual scholarship.

For instance, investigating what difference as norm means across contexts and identities is in current translingual work from Suhanthie Motha, Rashi Jain, and Tsegga Tecle's (2012) critically reflective narrative inquiry into translinguistic teacher identities to Nancy Bou Ayash's (2016) examination of monolingualist representations. However, with the catch-all use of difference in translingual scholarship, differences potentially become conflated. This conflation is problematic when it comes to race and racism in contact situations, as it re-inscribes the very notions that translingual scholarship works to transform: differences become sameness, a consequence for People of Color—many of whom are multilingual writers—then, is that the dialectic among language, race, and its inflections in a situated space is possibly forgotten or overlooked.

In this chapter I argue, like Keith Gilyard (2016), Tom Do (chapter 4, this volume), Steven Alvarez (chapter 11, this volume), and other contributors to this edited collection, for bringing students' lived experiences into translingual scholarship more thoughtfully so that nuanced and complex understandings can be gained about what "communicating across a lifetime of difference" (Lorimer 2013, 163) actually means in contact situations in which "race continues to covertly and overtly structure the lived experiences of millions of People of Color around the world" (Alim 2016a, 25). Further, by theorizing and incorporating lived experiences more explicitly, translingual scholars can *race* translingualism because White cis-male epistemological perspectives can no longer be centered and co-stories (narrations of their knowledges, repertoires, and backgrounds) of multilingual writers can be centered.

MAJOR CONCEPTS

Before showing more comprehensively how I engaged "co-stories" that emerged in interview data, I first discuss the major conceptualizations that shape the methodology, findings, and interpretations of the present study: lived experiences, race and racism, multilingual writer. I move on to the larger study from which this chapter draws and discuss my choice of focusing on one student's—Emma's—lived experiences bundled within dispositions, acts, and contexts.

Lived Experiences

In feminist theory, critical pedagogy, and critical race theory (CRT), lived experiences are day-to-day experiences of marginalized or non-privileged people (hooks 1994; Giroux 1996; Yosso 2006). By critically reflecting and imagining other possibilities based on these experiences, we can create theory or "mak[e] sense out of what is happening" (hooks 1994, 61) and ultimately *do* something about what is happening. For intersectional feminists, lived experiences allow us to "name [our] practice" in an effort to challenge systemic and everyday inequities facing marginalized groups and individuals (hooks 1994, 75; Mills and Mullany 2011). For critical pedagogues, teacher-scholars can foster classrooms in which student knowledges and experiences (*counter-narratives* from Giroux 1996) are central as opposed to marginal so as to transform their current social and political situations (Freire 2005; Kubota 2014). For critical race theorists, teacher-scholars can support counter-stories that work against majoritarian stories, which reproduce White privilege and interest through postracial and colorblind discourses (Solorzano and Yosso 2001; Yosso 2006).

Translingual scholarship has referenced lived experiences in a variety of ways as well. Suresh Canagarajah's (2013, 183–84) proposal to use performative competence over grammatical or communicative competence illustrates the ways our practices inform and are informed by our experiences with language, such as fostering "cooperative dispositions" and the many strategies of translingual learners such as "scaffolds." Arguably, these scaffolds and how these dispositions are fostered involve lived experiences because that is how they emerge—from past experiences into current interactions. Other references to lived experiences, explicitly or implicitly, include Paul Kei Matsuda's (2013, 136) call for teacher-scholars to be aware of the "multilingual reality"; Jerry Won Lee and Christopher Jenks's (2016, 320) description of the relationship between ideology and dispositions, that is, "bound to and shaped by discrete social conditions, *experiences* [emphasis added], and encounters"; Rebecca Lorimer's (2013, 163) exploration of rhetorical attunement for four participants "across a *lifetime* [emphasis added] of communicating across difference"; and Nancy Bou Ayash's (2016, 563) exploration of how dispositions are "influenced by" various (monolingual, translingual, multilingual) representations of English.

While all of the discussions above acknowledge that experience impacts writers' dispositions, rhetorical attunement, or performative competence, the only reference to racism or any form of discrimination is in the generalized reference to power relationships in language contact situations and the fact that these relationships are negotiable. None explicitly theorizes what lived experience is and how those lived experiences speak to race and racism specifically. As Gilyard (2016, 288) argues: "One of the strongest moves that translingualists can make is to document students' efforts. We need stories of struggle, as I have suggested, and those should include tales of triumph." In other words, translingual teacher-scholars need to more thoughtfully bring what students have *lived* into the classroom as pedagogical resources—lived experiences not only inform how we navigate our social worlds but also inform our very notions of identity, as feminists, critical race theorists, and critical pedagogues have discussed. As Eve Haque and Brian Morgan (2009, 282–83) assert, "The complex relation between the process of identification and the production and disruption of a stable ontological identity . . . must continually be at the forefront of our analysis and pedagogy if we are to move beyond the continual replay of essentialist explanations based on an ongoing project of delineating fixed identity categories."

Identity and identification processes are multifaceted and shaped by experiences. By making experience central to teaching and research, we can begin to reconceptualize our practices, our scholarship, and movements like translingualism. Similarly, teacher-scholars in language studies (Nelson 2011), critical race studies (Solorzano and Yosso 2001), and critical pedagogy (Giroux 1996) have made calls for (lived) experience to be brought into teaching and research more centrally. In her proposal for critical narrative studies, Nelson (2011) reimagines scholarship as a creative and critical practice by considering narrative as a learning tool. She writes, "[Narrative] can encourage learners to value their own experiential knowledge as important knowledge, which can be empowering" (467). Taking Nelson's (2011) assertion, experience allows us to reimagine knowledge and how it is disseminated and used. Furthermore, both learners and teacher-scholars can create meaning out of what Nelson terms classroom-life narratives or an arts-based form of analysis. Moreover, as Daniel Solorzano and Tara Yosso (2009) and Henry A. Giroux (1996) have shown, experience can then be a teaching and learning tool as well as a form of resistance. Lived experience, then, can be a way to critique our assumptions in the writing classroom; it can also bring the focus back to the intersections in students' social worlds, such as race and gender, that converge within and beyond our classrooms. This practice of using lived experiences as counter-stories or counter-narratives to the writing classroom has the potential to reimagine a translingualism that interrogates, critiques, and acts upon dimensions of difference—namely, race and its inflections for this present chapter. Alvarez (chapter 11, this volume) makes a similar argument: to "open students' lived experiences with racialized English-only ideologies."

Because lived experience is not fully theorized in translingual scholarship, I extend Nelson's (2011) call for storying in research on language learning to translingualism, which is similar to Canagarajah's (2012) call for story research or autoethnographies. Nelson's (2011) proposal incorporates important dimensions of CRT, critical pedagogy, and narrative studies. I build on work by Canagarajah (2012), Nelson (2011), and Matthew Prior (2016) to define narratives as collaborative and embedded. But in what context do these co-stories emerge, and how do we find or locate them as teacher-scholars? To begin to answer this question, it is important to address race and racism in language and writing studies.

Race in Writing Classrooms

Race has been discussed at length in language and writing studies. In language studies, Ryuko Kubota and Angel Lin (2009), Motha (2014), and H. Samy Alim and his coeditors (2016) have examined the relationship between language and race in classrooms, language policies, and speech styles. Victor Villanueva (1993), Vershawn Ashanti Young (2007), Morris Young (2015), and Mara Lee Grayson (2018) have examined how race and racism shape teaching and literacy practices in writing classrooms. In my writing classroom, students engaged conceptualizations of race throughout the term. One memorable example of that engagement happened at the end of the semester when students presented their projects to the class in group panels. These presentations involved firsthand research methods to gather narratives from their communities, family, and friends. At the end of each presentation, there was time for discussion. From that discussion, Long, a student who identifies as Vietnamese and as a heterosexual woman, vocally points to the differences between her interviewee and her peer's (Santiago) interviewee's perception and discussion of race: her interviewee says race exists, while Santiago's interviewee argues that race does not exist.

Long says, "Everyone has different opinions about [race] obviously, and it's—I mean, race is just a very abstract concept. It depends on how a person use [*sic*] it, you know . . . So, like, maybe for [Santiago's interviewee] race doesn't exist. For us, we feel, like, you know, it does. It does in the sense that—I mean, no one would be talking about it." Long acknowledges that race has multiple definitions at the beginning of her response, and while it may seem as though race does not exist for some like the White cis-male speaker interviewed by Santiago, for those in our class (whoever Long considers as "us"), race exists—that is, "no one would be talking about it" if race did not exist. My students spent most of the term discussing definitions of race: from race as biological or race based on a set of physical characteristics genetically linked (phenotypical; see the Human Genome Project 2018) to race as a social imaginary (Kubota and Lin 2009).

Students also discussed race using Kubota and Lin's (2009) concept of *racialization*. Racialization describes how people are categorized according to arbitrary features or values and how that categorization "carries a legacy of colonialism and often contains value judgments of the categories, although a scientific discourse masks such judgments with a neutral, objective, and even liberal humanistic tone" (5). Racialization, then, frames race "as a process of socialization in and through language, as a continuous project of becoming as opposed to being" (Alim 2016a, 2). Language as becoming is similar to Min-Zhan Lu and Bruce Horner's (2013, 27) discussion of how a translingual approach defines language: "not as something we have or have access to but as something we do. It centers attention on languaging: how we do language and why." However, their only explicit reference to race is in how it "emerge[s], inform[s], and [is] informed by individual acts of speaking-listening, reading-writing" (28). Lee (2016, 185) references "racial, ethnic, national, gender or sexual identification" when arguing for rethinking our assessment practices. Parallels exist in language and writing scholarship and translingual scholarship regarding race, but translingual scholarship needs to complicate its definition of difference and explicitly engage the ways identities, identification practices, and lived experiences—such as race, racism, and gender—texture contact situations.

In addition to race, the concepts of ethnicity and culture are difficult to separate (see Alim 2016a). Michael Omi and Howard Winant (1994) argue that race has been conflated with ethnicity, class, and nation. Kubota and Lin (2009, 4) offer a definition of ethnicity as a "relational concept" that separates groups. The criteria for maintaining this separation remain fuzzy and unclear. Similarly, culture overlaps with some conceptions of race, and even sometimes replacing "racial difference" with friendlier notions such as "cultural difference [is] a more benign and acceptable signifier than race" (Kubota and Lin 2009, 4). According to Jennifer Clary-Lemon's (2009) review of rhetoric and composition scholarship on race and racism, difference took the place of terms like *culture* and *diversity* when discussing race in the early 1990s. As a result, race in writing classrooms was either left unexamined or subsumed into difference. Therefore, using culture or even difference in place of the multiple dimensions and identities that are part of social interaction potentially elides what is unheard and unseen. Translingual scholarship also seemingly subsumes race and other dimensions under the catchall difference (Gilyard 2016).

Racism in Writing Classrooms

When discussing race in writing classrooms, we must engage the "serious and material consequences of race" (Motha 2014, 36); in other words, "the damage of racism" must be attended to in translingual scholarship beyond notions or constructions of race (Gilyard 2016, 287). Young's (2013, 140) response to Stanley Fish's (2009) argument against

Students' Right to Their Own Language captures the materiality or material impacts of race: teachers demand that students "speak black, when it's safe to do so, but not when your job, your grades, or your relationships with other non-black people (and sometimes other blacks who share the same prejudice) are on the line." To put Young's (2013, 145) statement in a different way, by only teaching what Fish and other educators like him refer to as the standard language, we reproduce a myth of a monolithic Standard English, a myth that everyone speaks and writes in the same way, and a myth that we and our students cannot work against "prevailing linguistic prejudice." Nelson Flores and Jonathan Rosa (2015, 250) engage this issue further in their critical examination of "additive approaches that promote the development of standardized language skills while encouraging students to maintain the minoritized linguistic practices they bring to the classroom." Students continue to be taught that their languages have no place in "academic settings" (150). These teaching moves and practices "conflate certain racialized bodies with linguistic deficiency unrelated to any objective linguistic practices;" that is, these practices are microaggressions or everyday forms of racism masked by discourses of appropriateness (150).

Many people may still see racism on the individual level, such as overtly discriminatory acts based on the person's racist beliefs, while others, like critical race theorists, see racism as systematic and fabricating our society (Delgado and Stefancic 2017). Kubota and Lin (2009, 6) suggest that seeing "racism [as] a discourse allows us to understand that most individuals are not racist; what is racist are the structured ideas that shape social reality." To put their suggestion another way, the individual and society are in a far more complex relationship to one another such that the ideas that shape our social worlds affect our interactions within those worlds. If we see racism as a discourse, then, according to Kubota and Lin (2009), we can engage with institutional or structural racism and epistemological racism. Institutional and structural racism refers to racist ideas that impact "every corner of society and shap[e] social relations, practices, and institutional structures" (6). This kind of racism is what CRT responded to as the grassroots movement argued against racist laws and legal practices that appear colorblind or post-racial. For translingual scholarship, discussing racism and its impacts on writing has been largely folded into language rights; while some scholars like Young (2013) have clearly identified that race matters, attending to race and racism explicitly remains unseen and in need of theorization and further research.

Another form of racism is epistemological racism that refers to how White cis-male perspectives are privileged in philosophical, educational, and scientific approaches, such as Pierre Bourdieu and Jean-Claude Passeron (1977) and Michel Foucault (1990). Throughout translingual scholarship, there has been reference to privileged perspectives, such as Canagarajah (2013), Lu and Horner (2013), and Asao Inoue (2015) who draw on Bourdieu's habitus or Anthony Giddens's (1984) theory of structuration. Even in my own classroom, I drew on Foucault's (1990) conceptualization of power—asking my multilingual students to navigate and challenge his perspective. Hunter reflected on his reading experience of Foucault: "When I was reading—is it heteronormativity? . . . because the first time I read [Foucault] I had no idea what he was talking about. And I think a few more times later it just felt like . . . this is different. This is something that . . . I could resonate with but the other part I just couldn't get."

Hunter was one of two students to actually engage with Foucault's work. This practice allowed him to consider parts of Foucault's theory but other parts not so much. This "other part" could have been the privileged way (and seemingly non-negotiable writing because you cannot speak with this author) Foucault writes or being unable to associate with Foucault's examples as a multilingual writer. Cloe, a Thai-identifying student, revised Foucault's concept of power to parallel her own understanding of peer pressure in a Thai community. Other students were more inclined to draw on the work of scholars of color such as Kubota and Lin (2009), including Sattar who presented on the history of racism in Kazakhstan between "Asians" and "Russians." He concluded: "Most of the world agreed that there is no place for racism and racist in the world, and I want to challenge that idea. Because even though most of the people agree that racism is bad and they don't think they are racists, I mostly agree with the idea of critical race theory." Sattar highlights the problem of what people desire (a world without racism and racists) and what in reality, according to his own experiences and CRT, actually happens (racist acts and everyday racism). Based on his findings for his final paper, he "mostly" sides with CRT: that is, racism is pervasive and systematic.

While translingual scholarship has built on privileged perspectives, Canagarajah (2013), Young (2013), and Vivette Milson-Whyte (2013) have brought in non-privileged perspectives as well, such as postcolonial theory, Lachman M. Khubchandani's (1997) linguistic work, and W. E. B. Du Bois's double consciousness. Lee and Jenks (2016) draw on Braj B. Kachru's (1997) World Englishes (WE) model to explore multilingual writers' translingual dispositions. Similar to Canagarajah (2013), Lee and Jenks (2016), and Ayash (2016), I bring lived experiences to the translingual conversation; however, I not only explicitly theorize lived experiences (see above) in translingual scholarship but also examine how co-storying students' lived experiences, as well as our (teacher-scholars in translingual scholarship) own, allows us to imagine a race-conscious translingualism. Before shifting to my study and methodology of co-storying, the emotionally charged label of "multilingual language learner" or "multilingual writer" needs to be defined for the purposes of building this chapter's framework.

Multilingual Language Learners or Multilingual Writers

Throughout this chapter, I make references to my students as multilingual language learners (MLL), or students whose home language(s) are non-English and who are learning English as a second, third, or other language (Matsuda and Jablonski 2000). I use MLL or multilingual writers to differentiate between the rhetorical situations, interpersonal relationships, and translingual practices my students experience and those situations, relationships, and practices that other, non-MLL students experience. This difference is important because "the claim that all students can develop translingual competence and do translingual dispositions should not . . . be taken to mean that monolingual students share, or can even fully understand, the sociolinguistic experiences of multilinguals" (Lee and Jenks 2016, 321–22). Lee's reference to "sociolinguistic experiences of multilinguals" echoes Matsuda's (2013, 136) use of *the multilingual reality* when describing his hope that "U.S. college composition scholars [will] try to develop advanced proficiency in multiple languages—both spoken and written—to understand firsthand what it is like to live the multilingual reality." MLL students, then, have specific realities and experiences that are inherently different than those of non-MLL learners: by theorizing lived experiences through multilingual writers' narrations of their realities and experiences, the ways race and racism texture contact situations can be more explicitly and clearly brought into translingual scholarship. In other words, I attempt to illustrate in this chapter:

1. Lived experiences *language* race and racism in contact situations: if the translingual orientation views "culture, ethnicity, nationality, race, geography and environments [as] seen as emerging in performance, informing and informed by individual acts of speaking—listening, reading-writing" (Lu and Horner 2013, 28), then we must open ourselves to lived experiences languaging how race, its intersections (culture, ethnicity, nationality, gender, sexuality, and other intersections), and racism texture contact situations in constrained (Milson-Whyte 2013) but not determined (Young 2007, 2013; Young 2015) ecologies.

2. Lived experiences *race* translingualism: our students' lived experiences, and our own as teacher-scholars, provide a way to speak *with* a translingual orientation founded on privileged White cis-male perspectives, such as Giddens's (1984) structuration theory (see Lu and Horner 2013) and Bourdieu's habitus (see Canagarajah 2013); in other words, we can create a conversation or dialectic between disciplinary and scholarly research and public, outside-the-classroom translingual practices that "provide checks and balances" (my extension of Matsuda 2013, 133) to foster a race-conscious translingualism.

OVERVIEW OF THE STUDY

This chapter shares a snapshot of what occurred throughout a ten-week term in an intermediate writing course for MLL. This course was the first of its kind, which resulted in numerous inquiries about whether it was for international students only, why a student learning Chinese as another language could not qualify, and how rigorous the course was because for most English monolingual speaker-writers who emailed me, MLL is collocated with remedial, deficient, and grammar. While the nuances and complexities of an MLL-only course were negotiated on a case-by-case basis, the actual classroom meetings and interactions were the focus of the larger study on intersectionality. Nineteen students enrolled who spoke and wrote in multiple language varieties across varying levels of proficiencies and competencies. According to a voluntary survey at the end of the term, these languages included Korean, Mandarin Chinese, Cantonese, Thai, Russian, Vietnamese, Spanish, and Kazakh. In the same survey, students disclosed their identities and/or identification practices. Eight students identified as women, eleven identified as men, and most identified as heterosexual, with one student choosing not to disclose. Some identified as international students with previous study abroad experiences in the United States (e.g., Eun and Rider), while others identified as American (e.g., Brody and Mateo). With the exception of Brody, eighteen students were of color. All students have been given pseudonyms to remain anonymous.

The course met twice per week, once in a seminar classroom and once in a computer lab. These modalities provided students with the means to interact across multiple platforms and genres—online, video, small group work, and group-authored documents. Further, their interactions in the traditional classroom and their conferences with me were recorded. Transcribing these recordings and then codifying them involved multiple steps: first, a big-picture memo-ing, with notes on times and the major topics and themes that emerged; second, line-by-line transcription and coding the transcriptions into the major topics and themes that emerged in my memos; and lastly, memo-ing once more to develop interview questions that attended to opening up the major topics and themes and how the students related to them through past and present experiences inside and outside the classroom. These questions led to six total interviews and one focus group.

How students related to major topics and themes is the focus of the present chapter, especially how this relationship is told through narrative or co-storying. I propose analyzing narratives as co-stories because the prefix *co-* before stories captures the collaborativeness of storying (Nair 2003; Prior 2016) and translingualism (Canagarajah 2013), as well as the negotiation involved in the storying process. I choose story over narrative to parallel critical race theory's use of counter-stories. While the original study innovated an intersectional framework for interrogating the relationships or inflections across multiple identities, identification practices, and more (Romero 2017), this chapter focuses specifically on the axis of race to see new, in-depth ways of reimagining translingual practice as anti-racist practice by "opening up" (Alvarez, chapter 11, this volume), upending, and re-seeing the ways my student and I co-story race and racism in the writing classroom and beyond.

METHODOLOGY: LOCATING CO-STORIES

To locate lived experiences or co-stories in classroom talk and text, focus groups, and interviews, teacher-scholars have to be able to recognize when co-stories begin. In narrative analysis, narratives begin with an abstract or preface as well as other signals (orientation narrative moves that contextualize where and when the experience took place) that cue that storying is about to start (Labov 1999). In Matthew Prior's (2016, 96) exploration of emotionality, interviewers may explicitly invite participants to story through questions of "strong, emotional, and memorable experiences." Therefore, co-stories, as narratives, sometimes begin with a preface to a narrative and/or questions (among other conversational moves) that invite storying. Co-stories can then take shape, as narrative analysis informs us, through different means. Means here means strategies such as orientation or those moves that give us time and place or evaluation, which are comments that can range from self-reflection to characterizing elements of the story.

Complicating action and resolution are moves that answer the questions "and then" and "final key event." The coda brings the speaker and listener back to the real world. These different moves vary, and while, at a minimum, a narrative must have two sequential clauses (Labov 1999), the kinds of stories speakers tell in interviews and how they tell them are of concern especially for translingual pedagogy centered around lived experiences: narratives not only *language* how race and racism can shape writing classrooms but also *race* pedagogical moves and strategies. These insights—as negotiated through co-stories or narratives from interviews, focus groups, and online and in-person classroom interaction—can help us, as teacher-scholars invested in translingual pedagogies and anti-racist praxis, center the lived experiences of our students within and across our praxis.

Co-stories emerged in our classroom conversations, follow-up interviews, journals, online discussion forums, and focus groups; each was categorized according to the kind of co-story narrated, as seen in table 8.1, in relation to topics and themes of race and racism specifically. Pedagogical co-stories are those in which students recall race and racism inside the classroom and how the teacher, student, and/or course content impacted their learning experiences. This definition is based on work on pedagogical memory; that is, how—emotionally, psychically, and physically—we remember our learning affects what we, in fact, learn (Jarratt et al. 2009). One common framing for these co-stories is the comparison of before and after: "*before [our course]* I really think that the race is biological . . . like, African people are good at sports [laughs], **but after taking this class** . . ." Sometimes the framing leads to a realization, while others find it leads to an awareness or added knowledge. Introspective co-stories, on the one hand, emerge in response to a raised topic or theme, such as race, and use self-reflexive critical reflection as a means for investigating the topic. This means is captured in evaluation narrative moves through the use of "**I feel**" or "I believe" to segue into reexamination of beliefs, values, and experiences. The self, as seen in table 8.1, is almost always defined for the listener to understand where the speaker is coming from so the reflective element is emphasized.

On the other hand, experiential co-stories recall moments in particular, which is most aligned with Labovian (1999) approaches to narrative (see Mosher, chapter 9, this volume). Experiential co-stories focus on developing a moment, scene, or event rather than a generalized experience; as such, the minimal narrative structure is necessary to locate this co-story—that is, two or more linear narrative moves, such as orientation and complicating action or complicating action and resolution. Emma, the focus of this chapter, shares an emotionally charged moment that is outside the pedagogical context—in the workplace—as seen in table 8.1.

Table 8.1. Co-stories coding scheme

Co-stories	Definitions	Example
Pedagogical	Students recall their experiences with race and racism inside the classroom and how the teacher and/or course content impacted their experience.	"Like, *before [our course]* I really think that the race is biological . . . like, African people are good at sports [laughs], **but after taking this class** I realize . . . how people categorize people, they just attach values to them." (Jack, Interview)
Introspective	Students recall their attitudes on race and racism, referencing experiences that are either their own or someone else's.	"I've always identified myself as Thai, as I've spent my childhood and most of my life in Thai communities. However, my face and complexion looks more Chinese than Thai (as my ancestors are part of Chinese), so much that I've always been mistaken as Chinese, especially when I'm overseas. However, **I don't feel** that it has a significant effect on both my private and public life though, which may be because I'm used to it by now." (Cloe, Journal Week 3)
Experiential	Students recall a specific episode, event, or happening involving race and/or racism.	"*There's one thing that really stood out.* Right now what the main job that I'm doing everyday is answering phone calls. So there was this guy who called in and they, well, I did my best explaining everything to him, and then he was, like, I can't understand you. Please put a native speaker on the phone." (Emma, Interview)

All three kinds of co-stories point to the relationship among language, race and racism, and education (and education here means broadly both academic and non-academic). This interrelation is the locus of the remainder of this chapter, and I have attempted to re-weave the co-stories I have gathered from one student's—Emma's—interview with me. Emma navigates multiple dispositions toward language and race across academic and non-academic contexts; further, she interrogates and negotiates the interrelation of these axes as they shape and are shaped by her identity as an MLL. Thus, a focus on her negotiations over those of other students allows us, my readers and me, to more carefully locate the ways co-stories not only inform one student's lived experiences but also provide an in-depth look at the possibilities of a co-storying framework for translingual scholars invested in anti-racist praxis.

In what follows, I co-story my experience interviewing Emma—that is, I locate her co-stories and retell our interview using narrative: I call this co-storying. I focus on major moments related to race and racism that emerged in our conversation. These moments illustrate how one multilingual writer negotiates dispositions, practices, and discourses through co-storying her lived experiences with me. I also critically reflect on my own moves and experiences "to explain how dispositions [and practices] develop in relation to social environment" textured by majoritarian discourses of race and racism (Canagarajah 2013, 180; Yosso 2016).

EMMA

Emma speaks, writes, and reads in five languages, with varying proficiencies. Her home languages are Cantonese, Mandarin Chinese, and Taiwanese Chinese. She evaluates her most proficient fourth language as English in our interview. This proficiency is followed by Korean, which she can "speak a little." Her least proficient language is French, which she studied for only a year. Emma preferred being called *multilingual language learner* as opposed to *English as a Second Language learner* or *English language learner*. She elaborated on this preference in our interview:

> EMMA: Among the three of them, I don't like English language learner?
> YAS: Uh huh. Why don't you like that one?
> EMMA: English . . .
> YAS: Just sounds weird to you or . . .
> EMMA: It feels like . . .'cause with the other two just the name of it. They put multilingual into it . . .
> YAS: Mmhmm.
> EMMA: So it . . . sort of in a sense it's recognizing you speak other language and then you're just learning another language.
> YAS: It's not like you're learning just English.
> EMMA: Yeah.

Emma describes her frustration with being known for her English proficiency and not her other language proficiencies. For Emma, MLL provides an opportunity to be identified as a speaker and writer who has multiple resources—linguistic, rhetorical, cultural, and experiential, to name a few—that are not "just English," as stated above. This label differs from translingual practices and orientations in that any speaker can practice translingualism; however, not all translingual practitioners share the same experiences and realities as multilingual writers. In this chapter, I focus on my interview with Emma and the co-stories that emerge from our conversation. By drawing on work in language and writing scholarship on race and racism, I narrate my experience navigating Emma's interview—especially moments in which she recalls lived experiences that impact her dispositions toward language. These experiences are inflected by race and racism.

CO-STORYING EMMA

October afternoon. I lean forward to start the audio recorder in front of me. It is an Olympus VN-702PC that fits easily in my hand. For now, it sits between my student, Emma, and me for our follow-up interview. I begin with the list of background questions that target students' home countries and residency, language histories and proficiencies, and educational and professional backgrounds:

> EMMA: When people ask me where I'm from, I would say I'm from Taiwan.
> YAS: Mmhmm.
> EMMA: But I would consider because I've lived in Shenzhen.
> YAS: Uh huh.
> EMMA: That's China. For like . . . four years?
> YAS: Uh huh.
> EMMA: So I consider that place as my second home.
> YAS: Ooh.
> EMMA: So when I meet people that [are] from Shenzhen, I can really easily connect to them.

Emma responds to my background questions with a "when . . . then" conditional clause. While Emma uses this clause to generalize her experiences when explaining where she is from, it also introduces particular geographic locations as part of her identity (or where she's from). This reference seems to connect race with place; that is, identity categories and languages "are almost always attached to locations" (Motha 2014, 41). These locations become more relevant throughout the conversation. Emma continues to add on to her explanation, while I give noncommittal responses like "mmhmm" and "uh huh" to indicate that I am listening. However, Emma's question with "four years" (along with her rising intonation) indicates that she may have wanted me to ask for more clarification. She responds more when I exclaim "ooh."

I ask for further clarification on her background as the interview continues, both constrained by the research interview genre and my formulaic questions. I do not know where Shenzhen is, and Emma explains that it is close to Hong Kong where "my mom's from." I say, "That's really cool, with the mixture of Chinese cultures." Emma confirms by saying, "So, I know a little bit of all of them. Like Hong Kong, China, and Taiwan." If we take what Emma said earlier, "when people ask me where I'm from," we see that she refers to co-stories of prior experiences (although she does not share these) in which she has had to explain and possibly point out *where* these locations are, such as Shenzhen (as she had to once again with me). Her openness to the various knowledges and experiences her interlocutors may bring, and negotiating that knowledge and experience to strengthen one's relationship with another, speaks to Canagarajah's (2013) disposition of openness to diversity.

In response to Emma's mixed cultures statement, I say "mmhmm." Emma then elaborates, "although they are maybe like the same country or not. I don't know." She laughs. "But we share all different, really different cultures." Again, her openness to diversity is seen here in "we all share different, really different cultures." Culture and place are also inextricably linked for Emma, suggesting that these different cultures and places shape her identities. Like place, culture has connections to race: it can be a nice way to say race (Clary-Lemon 2009); or, seemingly for Emma, culture implicates a racial identity that is made up of multiple Chinese locations, ideologies, and practices (Kubota and Lin 2009; Paris 2015; Alim 2016b).

For the next set of questions, I ask how Emma ended up in the United States and why she chose to study at this university. Emma says she moved to the US four years ago for her freshman year. She explains why:

> EMMA: Originally, 'cause this is the closest place to fly back to Asia. [Laughs]
> YAS: Ooh! [Laughs] So is your family still there?
> EMMA: Actually, my parents, they're in Michigan right now.
> YAS: Oh wow!
> EMMA: For his job, yeah.

Within two minutes, I learn more about Emma in our follow-up interview than I had ever learned in class. She was one of three students to participate in both the post-course focus group and the one-on-one interview for the study this chapter is based on. As I reflect on the moves I made during our interview, I see areas where I could have asked for more information. I needed to be more aware of her conversational cues. While these recognitions seem like minutiae, Emma's disclosures of her history, her racial, gendered, and sexual identities, her linguistic background, and her reactions to the course are part and parcel of this chapter's focus. After graduating with a degree in psychology, she was one of two students to find employment at a major corporation in the Pacific Northwest. Perhaps as a result of these conditions, she made clear connections between our course topics and her experiences post-university. Most especially, she interrogated the relationship between language and race in ways other students did not, as well as how certain spaces were impacted by social values that did not match her own. This disconnect impacted her positionality, dispositions, and racial identities according to two co-stories: "don't want to stand out" and "please put a native speaker on the phone." While these co-stories are by no means exhaustive, they are illustrative of the ways lived experiences reveal the relationships between language and race and how those relationships impact translingual dispositions and practices.

"Don't Want to Stand Out"

Emma and I are mid-interview. Like many other researchers, I invite co-stories related to our course topics through extreme case formulations (in bold for identification): "Have you, Emma, had **any significant or memorable** experiences that have helped you relate to our course topics?" Emma glances at the recorder and asks, "my personal experience?" I nod, waiting for her to share:

> EMMA: Now that I'm working and I think I have [laughs] I'm the only Asian in the building.
> YAS: Mmhm [laughs].
> EMMA: Sometimes I would try to avoid certain behavior that I think other people would categorize me as Asian. Not saying that Asian's not good. This is who I am but . . .
> YAS: Uh huh.
> EMMA: Sometimes I just don't want to stand out.
> YAS: You want to just kind of be like—
> EMMA: —Yeah, a low profile.

This preface to Emma's co-story is introspective. Emma examines her behavior and how that behavior is shaped by the racial category *Asian*. Because of my own background as half-White, half-Islander and being called oriental or Asian when growing up in Boise, Idaho, I laugh to communicate affiliation or a shared experience of avoiding certain behaviors. For me, I chose not to disclose that I ate rice and titiyas and had family from an island (Saipan) in the Pacific Ocean. I also identified exclusively as White until my post-baccalaureate studies. For Emma, she avoided eating rice when her coworkers were present (she co-storied this with her peers in a focus group before this interview; see Romero 2017 for more) and chose to keep conversation to non-Asian topics. For instance, Emma orients to language and rhetorical choices as constrained by racial identities, which include hers, her coworkers', and her friends': "I think a lot of people think that Asians are richer? . . . so just before I talk about things that are—share my life with my coworkers [who are White] I would be, like, extra careful with what I should say and shouldn't say . . . when I was in school, especially with the group of people that I hang out with, we come from similar backgrounds, so there would be less restriction on what you should say and shouldn't say" (Emma, Interview).

Emma presents her assumption that her White coworkers "think that Asians are richer." While she does not elaborate on this assumption (intersected by race and class), she does delve into her discomfort when speaking about her background. For instance, she has more freedom with friends "from similar backgrounds"; however, with people who are not part of that group, she must be "extra careful with what I should say and shouldn't say." For Emma, when interacting outside of her group that shares a racial identity, her linguistic and rhetorical choices may be constrained; she cannot be "Asian" or "who I am" in certain contact situations, as seen earlier. This introspective co-story speaks to the negotiation of language norms in contact situations. Language norms can also include what topics or themes are engaged in workplace conversations. Because Emma did not want her socioeconomic status to be assumed, she chose to take a more "careful" approach. What we see is that Emma has what Canagarajah (2013) calls a *cooperative disposition* toward language *and* conversation topics. She knows "what I should say and shouldn't say" in different situations and spaces. She is open to not choosing certain topics or themes. What becomes difficult to read is what Emma's cooperative disposition means in regard to her agency in these contact situations, that is, how her "sociolinguistic realities" (Ayash 2016, 557) shape her agency: is Emma adapting to situations "just so other people will feel comfortable" (Young 2013, 140), or is she adopting what Alim (2016b, 47) calls "strategic racialization" or "know[ing] when (and when not to) uphold, reject, and exploit racial categorization"? While I cannot answer these questions for Emma, I can draw on another important co-story in our interview that engages this problematic.

"Please Put a Native Speaker on the Phone"

After describing her "group of people" more fully, Emma recalls an experience that impacted her when she first started working at a multinational corporation in the Pacific Northwest. Emma begins the co-story with the preface, "there's one thing that really stood out." Before elaborating, she orients me, as her listener, to the context for the story: "right now what the main job that I'm doing everyday is answering phone calls." Emma then recalls her experience. "So, there was this guy who called in and they, well, I did my best explaining everything to him, and then he was, like, I can't understand you. Please put a native speaker on the phone." I respond with a disgusted "ugh."

Emma being asked to "put a native speaker on" is similar to Canagarajah's (2013, 164) informant who reflects on their interactions with Americans: "But I don't know, I feel like the Americans if you don't say exactly the way they say they can't hear. So it forces you to actually sound like them you know." This coercion to sound American or like a "native speaker" has been extensively investigated in language scholarship. Many teacher-scholars (Davies 2003; Shuck 2006; Romero 2010) have investigated the impacts of the native-non-native speaker dichotomy in contact situations and how the "existing racial hierarchy" textures these impacts for students and teachers (Liggett 2009, 31; Villanueva 1993; Curtis and Romney 2006; Kubota and Lin 2009). Emma's lived experience is initially similar to others who share her positionality and/or background, as seen in past scholarship, but her response diverges when she embeds another co-story and critical reflection:

> At the time, 'cause I think I just began work for—within a month of time so at that time I felt really bad. And then I talked to my coworker about it, and then he told me that, well, you don't have to care about that. Your English is native-like even though it's second language, but everyone comes from a different place . . . Everyone carries a different accent. So your English is your English that I can understand you. So don't worry about it.

Emma's evaluation can be interpreted in a variety of ways, such as her initial response of "I felt really bad." This response may be similar to Hoi-Yui in Lee and Jenks (2016, 334), who "consider[s] [her]self an inferior English speaker sometimes" because of her Hong Kong accent. Emma's response could also imply possible worry about her job security because she "just began work for—within a month of time." In addition to her initial reaction, Emma embeds a co-story of her conversation with a coworker. Emma's coworker appears to have a translingual disposition toward language, as they say "your English is native-like even though it's second language, but everyone comes from a different place. Everyone carries a different accent." This explicit reference to accent suggests that Emma felt bad because of her accent. Emma's coworker, however, "overlook[s] correctness and even unintelligible items in [a] spirit of collaboration"—that is, language norms are negotiable "as befits the interlocutors and their purposes" (Canagarajah 2013, 41). According to her coworker, when there is a failure to uptake, it was the customer's fault, *not* Emma's, because the customer did not attempt to negotiate.

Instead, the customer foreclosed that possibility, so Emma shouldn't "worry about it."

Their conversation is similar to Canagarajah's (2013) conversations with African migrants in the US, Australia, UK, and South Africa. Their comments suggest that translocal spaces entail translingual orientations to language, or "interlocutors are expected to collaborate and, presumably, adopt the 'let it pass' principle to accommodate non-intelligibility" (162). For example, one informant says: "I don't feel any tension about my ability to communicate in English and I think that it is sloppy when people say that they do not understand a person due to accent etcetera" (161). Similar to Emma's coworker, this informant takes a cooperative disposition toward language, emphasizing negotiation over so-called native correctness.

To the co-story and the embedded co-story, I respond to Emma's emotions and agree with her claims. I also respond to the way accent determines positive and negative perceptions in emotional ways—"ugh" and "that's so true!" While this relationship stands out in Emma's co-story, the ways race and racism texture the moment emerge in her subsequent discussion of after-school English courses and tutoring in Taiwan. Emma shares:

> Especially in Taiwan, we put a lot of effort on trying to sound American. Like all those English courses that we teach after school and stuff like tutoring . . . the main goal is to sound, to speak English with American accent or without an accent. I feel like that's wrong . . . makes it sound like speaking an American it's so much superior and it's just how, yeah, you. It's like you won't ask a foreigner to speak Chinese as good as you are because it's not their first language.

Her experiences are generalized in this description of learning English in Taiwan. She points to the importance of speaking "English with American accent or without an accent." As Rosina Lippi-Green's (1993) work demonstrates, accents are arbitrarily tied to social and cultural values (similar to the scales model Canagarajah 2013 problematizes). Attitudes toward these accents reproduce unequal power relationships, that is, systematic racism. When these particular ideologies translate into interlocutors' dispositions, racism effectively works against translingual dispositions and students may or may not resist these monolingualist dispositions being mapped onto them. Emma's evaluative comment toward the end indicates her resistance: "I feel like that's wrong . . . makes it sound like speaking an American it's so much superior." Her concluding statement marks a point in which she takes a translingual disposition—"it's just how, yeah, you" as a result of her lived experiences. In addition, she describes her expectations in a contact situation in China that parallel Canagarajah's (2013) definition of the "let it pass" principle or the listener does not "disrupt" moments of unintelligibility in the conversation. Instead, the listener lets the conversation progress and makes meaning of the unintelligible moment or item using conversational cues or other translingual strategies.

This superiority of accentless-ness that Emma engages was seen in other interactions throughout our course. Most memorable for me was Jack's discussion of his inspiration for studying Chinese American and Chinese student communities. Hunter, a peer of Jack's, was his inspiration. Jack said, "[Hunter] speaks perfect English, [and] I didn't know whether he was Chinese or Chinese American or his ethnicity when I first [*sic*] until I could get to know him better." Eun also questioned Hunter's identity as a Mainland Chinese student because of his seemingly "accentless" English during a focus group interview (see Romero and Shivers-McNair 2018). These conversations reflect the relationship Emma constructs between language and race as sounding American and accentless as positive while sounding less American is negative and is foreigner talk. Therefore, someone's accent should not determine a person's abilities and respect for that person, yet accent seemingly influences the relationship between language and race in the form of "native and non-native speaker" discrimination for Emma and other MLL (Motha 2014; Shuck 2006). This discrimination is racial, cultural, and social. However, Emma's evaluation of this relationship as negative suggests that she remains resistant to such notions. She also emphasized that she only felt bad "at the time," so the temporality of a colonial mentality was critically engaged and then effectively forgotten because Emma, as has been shown in her conversation with me, is incredibly proud of her mixed cultures. She seems to view, like Ayash's (2016, 570) informants, "English as a resource closely connected to different parts of their lifeworlds and treating translingual practice as necessary for their personal and intellectual development in language contact situations." The problem lies in accent discrimination and topic choice; for Emma, as seen in her co-stories, that links culture, race and ethnicity to language (Lippi-Green 1993; Shuck 2006; Kubota and Lin 2009).

"YOUR ENGLISH IS YOUR ENGLISH"

I have attempted to co-story my interview with Emma in a semi-linear fashion by narrating my reactions and incorporating her peers' overlapping co-stories—pedagogical, introspective, and experiential—as well as scholarship in translingualism and language and writing studies that attends to lived experiences. From her strategic avoidance to bring up topics and themes that would make her White coworkers uncomfortable to her emotionally charged experiences with accent discrimination, Emma reveals the "lived" aspects of negotiating with monolingual, White speaker-writers in the workplace. These lived aspects remind us that language and literacy are always intersected by multiple dimensions. What has remained with me throughout this process is the comment from her coworker: "your English is your English." This comment has both intrigued and bothered me. While it reaffirms that Emma, at least to her coworker, is equal, the comment also carries implications of race and racism: it is easy for a coworker who is White and most likely cis and whose home language is English to make this kind of statement. It is just as easy for translingual scholars to say that multilingual students' linguistic repertoires, their ability to adapt to English contact situations through syntax, pronunciation, and their diversity of experiences, are meaningful; however, it is just as misleading if racism and other forms of discrimination are not considered to be part and parcel of each contact situation. It is also misleading to assume that translingual scholarship, as it is practiced now, is, in fact, anti-racist.

Translingualism is a "rejection of the monolingual paradigm" (Gilyard 2016, 289). And while all speakers and writers are translingual, speaker-writers whose home language is not English experience this paradigm differently (Matsuda 2013; Lee 2016). As seen across Emma's co-stories, she experiences this paradigm differently because of her racial and cultural identities. Therefore, translingual teacher-scholars can no longer, as this collection argues, ignore the relationships between language and race that our students orient to in contact situations, such as the workplace or the writing classroom; my interview with Emma and the conversations from my students have illustrated that if teacher-scholars continue to do so, then we participate in the ideology of colorblindness or "Your English Is Your English" (see Rowan, chapter 1, this volume). This collection has pointed to strategies, theories, and dispositions that can reimagine a race-conscious translingualism. This chapter adds to this conversation by capturing the concept of co-stories as a living, collaborative process, composed of many different experiences, perspectives, and notions of race and racism. Race and other dimensions (gender and sexuality) and injustices (heterosexism) inflect the lived experiences of myself and my multilingual students who are of color. However, the scope of this chapter (race and racism) limits my engagement with these inflections (see Crenshaw 1993 for more on intersectionality; see Romero 2017 for more on intersectional approaches in language studies).

If translingual teacher-scholars co-story (write with the co-stories they learn) multilingual writers' lived experiences, then teacher-scholars may potentially see the gaps, dissonances, and misunderstandings that take place across *multilingual realities* (Matsuda 2013) or the *sociolinguistic experience* or *realities* of multilinguals (Lee 2016; Ayash 2016). If they interrogate co-stories about race and racism in particular, teacher-scholars invested may better understand how multilingual students' dispositions, competencies, and practices toward language develop in situ systemic and everyday racism. In other words, dimensions of language, racialization, culture, geography, nationalism, sexuality, gender, and more shape and are shaped by multilingual speaker-writers' translingual practices and competencies. If we wish to understand the complexity of their lived experiences and what those experiences mean in relation to translingual orientations to language, then translingual teacher-scholars should actively listen to how multilingual speaker-writers theorize race and racism to make sense of language dispositions and competencies—both their own and others. In this way, we can begin to build a race-conscious translingualism that is founded on students' co-stories that speak *with* dominant perspectives in translingual scholarship and that comprehensively explore how and why "we don't all differ from said standard in the same way" (Gilyard 2016, 286).

REFERENCES

Alim, H. Samy. 2016a. "Introducing Raciolinguistics: Racing Language and Languaging Race in Hyperracial Times." In *Raciolinguistics: How Language Shapes Our Ideas about Race*, ed. H. Samy Alim, John R. Rickford, and Arnetha F. Ball, 1–30. New York: Oxford University Press.

Alim, H. Samy. 2016b. "Who's Afraid of the Transracial Subject? Raciolinguistics and the Political Project of Transracialization." In *Raciolinguistics: How Language Shapes Our Ideas about Race*, ed. H. Samy Alim, John R. Rickford, and Arnetha F. Ball, 33–50. New York: Oxford University Press.

Alim, H. Samy, John R. Rickford, and Arnetha F. Ball, eds. 2016. *Raciolinguistics: How Language Shapes Our Ideas about Race*. New York: Oxford University Press.

Auerbach, Elsa. 1993. "Reexamining English Only in the ESL Classroom." *TESOL Quarterly* 27 (1): 9–32.

Ayash, Nancy Bou. 2016. "Conditions of (Im)Possibility: Postmonolingual Language Representations in Academic Literacies." *College English* 78 (6): 555–77.

Bourdieu, Pierre, and Jean-Claude Passeron. 1977. *Reproduction in Education, Society, and Culture*. London: Sage.

Canagarajah, Suresh. 2012. "Autoethnography in the Study of Multilingual Writers." In *Writing Studies Research in Practice: Methods and Methodologies*, ed. Lee Nickoson and Mary P. Sheridan, 113–24. Carbondale: Southern Illinois University Press.

Canagarajah, Suresh. 2013. *Translingual Practice: Global Englishes and Cosmopolitan Relations*. New York: Routledge.

Clary-Lemon, Jennifer. 2009. "The Racialization of Composition Studies: Scholarly Rhetoric of Race since 1990." *College Composition and Communication* 61 (2): W1–W17.

Crenshaw, Kimberlè W. 1993. "Beyond Racism and Misogyny: Black Feminism and 2 Live Crew." In *Words That Wound: Critical Race Theory, Assaultive Speech, and the First Amendment*, ed. Mari J. Matsuda, Charles R. Lawrence III, Richard Delgado, and Kimberlè W. Crenshaw, 111–32. Boulder: Westview.

Curtis, Andy, and Mary Romney. 2006. *Color, Race, and English Language Teaching: Shades of Meaning*. New York: Routledge.

Davies, Alan. 2003. *The Native Speaker: Myth and Reality*. Tonawanda, NY: Multilingual Matters.

Delgado, Richard, and Jean Stefancic. 2017. *Critical Race Theory: An Introduction*. New York: New York University Press.

Elbow, Peter. 2002. "Vernacular Literacies in the Writing Classroom? Probing the Culture of Literacy." In *ALT/DIS: Alternative Discourses and the Academy*, ed. Christopher Schroeder, Helen Fox, and Patricia Bizzell, 126–38. Portsmouth, NH: Boynton/Cook.

Fish, Stanley. 2009. "What Should Colleges Teach? Part 3." *New York Times*, September 7. https://opinionator.blogs.nytimes.com/2009/09/07/what-should-colleges-teach-part-3/. Accessed April 4, 2019.

Flores, Nelson, and Jonathan Rosa. 2015. "Undoing Appropriateness: Raciolinguistic Ideologies and Language Diversity in Education." *Harvard Education Review* 85 (2): 149–71.

Foucault, Michel. 1990. *History of Sexuality*. New York: Vintage.

Freire, Paulo. 2005. *Pedagogy of the Oppressed*. New York: Continuum.

Giddens, Anthony. 1984. *The Constitution of Society: Outline of the Theory of Structuration*. Berkeley: University of California Press.

Gilyard, Keith. 2016. "The Rhetoric of Translingualism." *College English* 78 (3): 284–89.

Giroux, Henry A. 1996. *Counternarratives: Cultural Studies and Critical Pedagogies in Postmodern Spaces*. New York: Routledge.

Grayson, Mara Lee. 2018. *Teaching Racial Literacy: Reflective Practices for Critical Writing*. New York: Rowman and Littlefield.

Haque, Eve, and Brian Morgan. 2009. "Un/Marked Pedagogies: A Dialogue on Race in EFL and ESL Settings." In *Race, Culture, and Identities in Second Language Education: Exploring Critically Engaged Practice*, ed. Ryuko Kubota and Angel Lin, 271–85. New York: Routledge.

hooks, bell. 1994. *Teaching to Transgress: Education as the Practice of Freedom*. New York: Routledge.

Human Genome Project. 2018. "What Is the Human Genome Project?" Last modified October 28, 2018. https://www.genome.gov/12011238/an-overview-of-the-human-genome-project/. Accessed April 4, 2019.

Inoue, Asao. 2015. *Antiracist Writing Assessment Ecologies: Teaching and Assessing Writing for a Socially Just Future*. Fort Collins, CO, and Anderson, SC: WAC Clearinghouse and Parlor Press.

Jarratt, Susan C., Katherine Mack, Alexandra Sartor, and Shevaun E. Watson. 2009. "Pedagogical Memory: Writing, Mapping, Translating." *WPA: Writing Program Administration* 33 (1–2): 46–73.

Kachru, Braj B. 1997. "World Englishes and English-Using Communities." *Annual Review of Applied Linguistics* 17: 66–87.

Khubchandani, Lachman M. 1997. *Revisualizing Boundaries: A Plurilingual Ethos*. New Delhi: Sage.

Kubota, Ryuko. 2004. "Critical Multiculturalism and Second Language Education." In *Critical Pedagogies and Language Learning*, ed. Bonny Norton and Kelleen Toohey, 30–52. New York: Cambridge University Press.

Kubota, Ryuko. 2014. " 'We Must Look at Both Sides'—But a Denial of Genocide Too? Difficult Moments on Controversial Issues in the Classroom." *Critical Inquiry in Language Studies* 11 (4): 225–51.
Kubota, Ryuko, and Angel Lin. 2009. "Introduction to Research and Practice." In *Race, Culture, and Identities in Second Language Education: Exploring Critically Engaged Practice*, ed. Ryuko Kubota and Angel Lin, 1–24. New York: Routledge.
Labov, William. 1999. "The Transformation of Experience in Narrative." In *The Discourse Reader*, ed. Adam Jaworski and Nikolas Coupland, 221–35. New York: Routledge.
Lee, Jerry Won. 2016. "Beyond Translingual Writing." *College English* 79 (2): 174–95.
Lee, Jerry Won, and Christopher Jenks. 2016. "Doing Translingual Dispositions." *College Composition and Communication* 68 (2): 317–44.
Liggett, Tonda. 2009. "Unpacking White Racial Identity in English Language Teacher Education." In *Race, Culture, and Identities in Second Language Education: Exploring Critically Engaged Practice*, ed. Ryuko Kubota and Angel Lin, 27–43. New York: Routledge.
Lippi-Green, Rosina. 1993. *English with an Accent: Language, Ideology, and Discrimination in the United States*. New York: Routledge.
Lorimer, Rebecca. 2013. "Writing across Languages: Developing Rhetorical Attunement." In *Literacy as Translingual Practice: Between Communities and Classrooms*, ed. A. Suresh Canagarajah, 162–69. New York: Routledge.
Lu, Min-Zhan, and Bruce Horner. 2013. "Translingual Literacy and Matters of Agency." In *Literacy as Translingual Practice: Between Communities and Classrooms*, ed. A. Suresh Canagarajah, 26–38. New York: Routledge.
Matsuda, Paul Kei. 2013. "It's the Wild West Out There: A New Linguistic Frontier in U.S. College Composition." In *Literacy as Translingual Practice: Between Communities and Classrooms*, ed. A. Suresh Canagarajah, 128–38. New York: Routledge.
Matsuda, Paul Kei, and Jeffrey Jablonski. 2000. "Beyond the L2 Metaphor: Towards a Mutually Transformative Model of ESL/WAC Collaboration." *Academic.Writing*. https://wac.colostate.edu/aw/articles/matsuda_jablonski2000.htm. Accessed April 4, 2019.
Mills, Sara, and Louise Mullany. 2011. *Language, Gender, and Feminism: Theory, Methodology, and Practice*. New York: Routledge.
Milson-Whyte, Vivette. 2013. "Pedagogical and Socio-Political Implications of Code-Meshing in Classrooms: Some Considerations for a Translingual Orientation to Writing." In *Literacy as Translingual Practice: Between Communities and Classrooms*, ed. A. Suresh Canagarajah, 115–27. New York: Routledge.
Motha, Suhanthie. 2014. *Race, Empire, and English Language Teaching: Creating Responsible and Ethical Anti-Racist Practice*. New York: Teachers College Press.
Motha, Suhanthie, Rashi Jain, and Tsegga Tecle. 2012. "Translinguistic Identity-as-Pedagogy: Implications for Language Teacher Education." *International Journal of Innovation in English Language Teaching and Research* 1 (1): 13–28.
Nair, Rukmini Bhaya. 2003. *Narrative Gravity: Conversation, Cognition, Culture*. 2nd ed. London: Routledge.
Nelson, Cynthia D. 2011. "Narratives of Classroom Life: Changing Conceptions of Knowledge." *TESOL Quarterly* 45 (3): 463–85.
Omi, Michael, and Howard Winant. 1994. *Racial Formation in the United States: From the 1960s to the 1990s*. 2nd ed. New York: Routledge.
Paris, Django. 2015. " 'They're in My Culture, They Speak the Same Way': African American Language in Multiethnic High Schools." In *Students' Right to Their Own Language: A Critical Sourcebook*, ed. Staci Perryman-Clark, David E. Kirkland, and Austin Jackson, 305–23. Boston: Bedford/St. Martin's.
Prior, Matthew. 2016. *Emotion and Discourse in L2 Narrative Research*. Bristol, UK: Multilingual Matters.
Romero, Yasmine. 2010. "The Native Speaker Re-Examined: The Ideal ELT in Japan." *Educational Studies* 52: 217–25.

Romero, Yasmine. 2017. "Developing an Intersectional Framework: Engaging the Decenter in Language Studies." *Critical Inquiry in Language Studies* 14 (4): 320–46.

Romero, Yasmine, and Ann Shivers-McNair. 2018. "Encountering Internationalization in the Writing Classroom: Resistant Teaching and Learning Strategies." *Across the Disciplines: A Journal of Language, Learning, and Academic Writing* 15 (2): 47–60.

Shuck, Gail. 2006. "Racializing the Nonnative English Speaker." *Journal of Language, Identity, and Education* 5 (4): 259–76.

Solorzano, Daniel, and Tara Yosso. 2001. "Critical Race and LatCrit Theory and Method: Counter-Storytelling." *International Journal of Qualitative Studies in Education* 14 (4): 471–95.

Villanueva, Victor. 1993. *Bootstraps: From an American Academic of Color.* Urbana, IL: NCTE.

Yosso, Tara J. 2006. *Critical Race Counterstories along the Chicana/Chicano Educational Pipeline.* Hoboken, NJ: Taylor and Francis.

Young, Morris. 2015. *Minor Re/Visions: Asian American Literacy as a Rhetoric of Citizenship.* Carbondale: Southern Illinois University Press.

Young, Vershawn Ashanti. 2007. *Your Average Nigga: Performing Race, Literacy, and Masculinity.* Detroit: Wayne State University Press.

Young, Vershawn Ashanti. 2013. "Keep Code-Meshing." In *Literacy as Translingual Practice: Between Communities and Classrooms*, ed. A. Suresh Canagarajah, 139–46. New York: Routledge.

9
"THE ALTERNATIVE IS SORT OF AN ENDLESS MULTIPLICITY"
Narrative and Negotiating the Translingual

Stephanie Mosher

The stories we tell—about ourselves, to ourselves, about and to others—are inextricable from our identities, beliefs, and actions. These stories are based not only in our individual experiences but also on other people's stories, which we have heard and chosen to believe, not believe, or modify to suit our purposes. Moreover, the master narratives and sometimes counter-narratives of our cultures and communities have powerful influence. Storytelling is a uniquely human endeavor, and the tales someone tells, the narratives they spin, help paint a small picture of their humanity. Yet while the positions we build through narrative *guide* our interactions with the world, these positions are *fluid*, not *fixed* (Davies and Harré 1990, 46). When introduced to challenging new narratives, we have options: engage with and attempt to learn from the new stories, pretend not to hear, lose our sense of self, or become defensive (Condon 2011, 1–2; Corder 1985, 16–19). As Jim W. Corder (1985) argues, narrative is inextricably linked with identity, guiding our responses to new information. In this chapter, I explore how five college writing instructors use storytelling with conversation to position themselves, process new ideas, and demonstrate their understanding of the intersection of race and language difference.

Translingualism provides a new narrative to compositionists. It challenges many of the stories we have assembled about what it means to be a successful writer. For too long, our default setting as a profession has been to teach and assess based on a White norm, including the expectation for students to master the White, middle-class–based Standard English (SE). Some of the ideologies that contribute to the prominence of this default Whiteness in composition include "Appropriacy Reasoning" and the "white listening subject" (Flores and Rosa 2015),

https://doi.org/10.7330/9781646422104.c009

the "white habitus," and "color-blind racism" (Bonilla-Silva 2014). Full treatment of these ideologies is beyond the scope of this project, but each contributes to a worldview in which, in the US, conventions based on White communicative practices are generally perceived as correct, appropriate, and desired—not only by mainstream society but also by college writing instructors, between 84 percent and 88 percent of whom are European American (National Center for Education Statistics 2008).

I see translingualism as more a way of thinking about language and language diversity that has material consequences for how we teach and write than as a particular set of practices. However, our perceptions of language influence our teaching decisions, including the paradigms of correctness and appropriateness we convey in course materials, formative assessment, and summative assessment. In debates about what *translingualism* means, we have seen calls to resist associating the paradigm only with linguistically minoritized writers (Lu and Horner 2013). However, I am more interested in Keith Gilyard's (2016, 284) call to avoid the "flattening of language differences" by falsely equating, say, the muddy linguistic waters an African American English (AAE) user must navigate and the discrimination they often face with the no-less-intellectually stimulating, typically less hazardous challenges and opportunities the linguistically privileged—among them, White native SE users—face. I agree that we should resist focusing solely on racially, ethnically, or language-minoritized writers and am aware that it is important to challenge the conflation of SE and/or monolingualism only with White writers. Keeping that in mind, we simply cannot neglect the prominence of Whiteness in standardization ideology and monolingual ideology in the US—a prominence well established by research (Bonilla-Silva 2014; Flores and Rosa 2015; Ball and Lardner 1997) and which survives in much training of writing teachers.

In K–12 and higher education, training in the understanding of linguistic diversity does exist, but it is far from widespread. Kim Brian Lovejoy and his colleagues (2015, 382) find that composition programs usually ignore language diversity, and Arnetha F. Ball and Rashida Jaami' Muhammad (2003, 79–81) found few opportunities for pre-service teachers to study variety. When new educators do study language variety, results are usually mixed. Some research reports the effectiveness of courses and training in promoting positive attitudes about language difference (Canagarajah 2016; Okawa 2015; Richardson 2003), but other research—even at times the *same* research—notes teachers' resistance to incorporating variation (Ball and Lardner 1997; Canagarajah 2016).

In contrast to the work available on pre-service K–12 educators, veteran K–12 educators, and novice composition teachers, little professionalization research focuses on experienced composition instructors. But the latter constitute an important group: they are a large part of the composition teaching population; they are often overworked, multiple-institution contingent faculty with little time and few resources for professional development; and the longer they've taught, the longer they've had time to independently ask questions about language variety and/or solidify existing beliefs. Learning more about these group members' dispositions toward language variety can better prepare us to create meaningful, sustainable translingual professionalization opportunities in higher education.

STUDY DESIGN AND METHODOLOGY

In fall 2015, I recruited[1] PhD students in American literature from a mid-sized, research-focused, flagship university in the American South; each was then working, or had worked, as instructor-of-record in the school's composition program. Six volunteered, and five were selected for narrative analysis.[2] All were White (non-Hispanic), middle class,[3] in their mid-twenties to mid-thirties, with between two and eight years' experience as instructor-of-record in college writing, and native speakers of American English. They met with me individually throughout the semester to discuss linguistic experiences and beliefs, responses to scholarly texts on linguistic variety and translingualism, and three student texts by non-mainstream writers: two African American English (AAE)–strong writers[4] and an English language learner (L2 writer). I chose these texts because each deals with translingual ideas and/or serves as an artifact prompting discussion about translingual concerns, such as writing across difference and the communicative burden. For my purposes in this chapter, the most relevant aspects of translingualism are, first, the interrogation of preexisting beliefs about language (Trimbur 2016, 226) and, second, the incorporation of race consciousness into considerations of language difference, including examples of how Whiteness shapes dominant language ideologies.

I conducted five interviews with each participant. In the first, I asked about demographic information and previous experiences of and beliefs about language variety. The second centered on Chris M. Anson's (1999) "Reflective Reading," including an essay by an L2 writer, along with an excerpt from Bruce Horner and colleagues' (2011) "Language Difference."[5] For Interview Three, we discussed a section of Arnetha Ball and Ted Lardner's (2005) *African American Literacies Unleashed* that features an AAE-strong student essay and the book authors' commentary on it; for the fourth, we talked about Vershawn Ashanti Young's (2009) "Nah, We Straight" paired with an AAE-strong student text written at the university where my research was conducted. The fifth interview provided an opportunity to discuss initial impressions of participation in the project.

My interview methodology was influenced by Participatory Design (Spinuzzi 2005), while data analysis was shaped by principles of Grounded Theory (Maxwell 2008). I made participants aware of my research questions and drew from qualitative human-participants research methods and theories that emphasize both rapport (Williams quoted in Webb-Sunderhaus 2016, 14) and non-threatening environments (Okawa 2015, 335; Corder 1985, 20). I used active listening strategies such as backchanneling,[6] and interviews took the form more of conversations between colleagues than traditional data collection.

NARRATIVE STUDY AS ANALYTICAL FRAMEWORK

I employ narrative analysis to examine how instructors respond to translingualism. We use narrative to shape a coherent identity, an understanding of the self with which we can live happily (Corder 1985). But then, "What happens if a narrative not our own reveals to us that our own narrative was wanting all along, though it is the only evidence of our identity" (19)? When beliefs have long been part of our practice and validate our sense of professional efficacy, they become part of our identities. If a person senses a threat to their very *self*, it isn't easy to get that person to consider change. No matter how logical an argument, it "may be totally ineffectual when employed in a rhetorical situation where the audience feels its beliefs or values are being threatened" (Bator quoted in Corder 1985, 23–24). No wonder experienced instructors confident in their educational personae, including reliance on default Whiteness, hesitate to reconsider beliefs about language difference.

We think we know how something works until we are confronted with a contrary storyline, a new and contradictory set of rules. Though we may not be obligated to abandon former ways of being, the rhetorically responsible action is to learn, let the new narrative broaden our worldviews and, if necessary, change our minds and influence our behaviors. "Sometimes we turn away from other narratives," Corder (1985) writes. "Sometimes we teach ourselves *not to know that there are other narratives*" (19, my emphasis). Or, we can engage: "Sometimes—probably all too seldom—we encounter another narrative and learn to change our own" (19). Engagement is difficult, and willful ignorance tempts us. Faced with new narratives:

> Sometimes we lose our plot, and our convictions as well; since our convictions belong to our narratives . . . Sometimes we go to war . . . [or] sink into madness, totally unable to manage what our wit or judgment has shown us—a contending narrative that has force to it and charm and appeal and perhaps justice and beauty as well . . . a contending narrative that shakes and cracks all foundations and promises to alter our identity, a *narrative that would educate us to be wholly other than what we are*. (19, emphasis added)

On one hand, we have options of willful ignorance, confusion, anger, or existential crisis; on the other, we have the options of learning and perhaps appropriating.[7] The different reactions are interconnected and complementary. To borrow from popular psychology, they recall the commonly cited five stages of grief: denial, bargaining, anger, depression, and acceptance. Psychologists argue that this streamlined model of the grieving process helps us understand how people cope with trauma. People don't necessarily cycle through each stage in the order listed, but they do experience most or all of those stages. Based on my participants' stories, I suggest that something similar happens when we encounter new narratives: we may for a time willfully ignore them or aggressively defend our previous positions, but upon further introspection, we may find value in an idea that initially offended us.

I also used William Labov's (1973) narrative paradigm to select and analyze data. Though a full treatment is beyond the scope of this chapter, three aspects of Labov's paradigm are key to understanding the work these instructors did. They are the *complicating action*, the conflict or unexpected event in a story; the *evaluation*, indicating why the story is worth telling, the "so-what" factor—which sometimes means evaluating characters or ideas in the narratives; and the *result* or *resolution*, telling how the complicating action is resolved (363).

FINDINGS

Each instructor showed some degree of willingness to "lean in and learn" (Condon 2011, 2), though at first, each resisted the new concepts. A negative reaction does not necessarily indicate someone's final position on a matter but is part of the construction of discursive self. After a brief overview of general trends, I share a sample of narratives demonstrating anger, confusion, and/or willful ignorance or rejection of new information. These narratives often utilized what Eduardo Bonilla-Silva

(2014) calls the frames of "color-blind racism." I then share narratives indicating the speaker's commitment to learning from the new discourses, including by problem solving. The selected narratives are meant to represent the types of responses that occurred, not individual instructors' final positions.

"Lean[ing] in" (Condon 2011, 2) includes openly embracing translingual ideas, grappling with them through confusion, uncertainty, and anger, or all three. The instructors generally let translingualism *trouble* them, and "to be troubled is a necessary condition for learning and for change" (7). Ultimately, composition instructors may be willing and able to incorporate translingualism into their professional thinking, given the time, space, and opportunity to do so in a dialogic environment that values their professional knowledge and experiences. Such an approach is supported by Suresh Canagarajah's (2016, 268) argument that in the college writing practicum, acknowledging the resources new instructors bring to the classroom is essential: "If the pedagogical content and professional knowledge" (266) introduced in the graduate classroom "are not negotiated in relation to instructors' current beliefs and past experiences or appropriated in relation to the professional identities they are developing, their professionalization won't be effective" (266). That is, ignoring or dismissing instructors' prior knowledge and beliefs, even if they are based on inaccurate myths about language, is counterproductive.

Such an environment invites instructors to answer John Trimbur's (2016, 226) call for "readers—teachers and students alike—to come to terms with their responses to language differences." Vital to utilizing translingualism is confronting how we read quality into varieties of linguistic expression. Dialogic components may help instructors engage responsively with translingualism, make room for this new paradigm in their professional understanding, and even incorporate translingual concepts into pedagogy.

Barry, Martin, Oliver, Thea, and Wally were my five principal participants. All four men initially indicated ambivalence about SE's prominence, but Thea firmly espoused a belief in SE's primacy and even associated correctness with cognitive ability. My participants' narratives indicate that they were influenced by one or more ideologies that contribute to default Whiteness. By project's end, all five indicated *some* way their perception of language variety had been influenced and/or increased awareness of inequities resulting from language's intersections with power.

Wally saw a change in his response practices, rethinking why he might be confused by a student text. Instead of presuming the student made errors because of sloppy thinking, he raised the possibility that the student had a deliberate meaning that he, Wally, misunderstood. He said he was attempting more face-to-face conversation, rather than direct corrective written feedback, to help clear up communicative confusion: "Maybe a phrase that I think that they used that was inappropriate was used for a completely different goal and they had a real motive behind it and I missed it."[8] Martin said, "I think I would just maybe be more open to the students who (were) {long pause} sincerely trying to be productive and different with their language." Oliver, who already had a few translingual instincts at the start of the project, said he was more prepared to adopt those instincts in practice: "It's just giving me like one more sort of dimension on how to talk about how to negotiate these kinds of things, or how writing is connected to our identity." Barry noted, "I would probably say that my conception [of SE] is a little more capacious maybe now" and referred to "widening the confines of standardized English." Thea, who firmly reasserted her commitment to teaching and assessing for SE at the end of the final interview, did acknowledge increased awareness of power imbalances: "I guess in the way that it might influence me might be . . . just more awareness, like of language and what kind of {short pause} what kind of power I guess, kind of goes along with that or can be exercised by not recognizing differences."

Each participant expressed concerns about the practicalities of translingual pedagogy. They include fairness in assessment, institutional expectations, a White SE-using instructor's ability to effectively and ethically teach and assess works incorporating AAE, and training. Wally said, "I'm still just sort of bothered by how to strike a balance . . . obviously you do wanna be inclusive, but . . . it seems like you've got to set some sort of objective bar." He also pointed out that the departmental-required textbook instructed students to use SE: "I kind of accept a lot of the key tenets of [the translingual approach], but at the same time, my textbook is telling me that I have to encourage my students to white-wash their prose."

Martin and Oliver said that their Whiteness made them unsure about their ability to teach translingually. Martin asked, "Do I, as a middle-class white male, get to say what is or what is not African American English? And how do I assess whether or not this is a successful employment of that vernacular . . . in an academic paper?" Oliver expressed similar concerns. Barry explained that he hadn't been trained to teach translingually. Each of these is a valid concern that needs to be addressed in professionalization. While translingual approaches are certainly not impossible for White instructors to adopt, perhaps awareness of our linguistic privilege makes this group hesitant to address language difference; ironically, increased awareness of Whiteness as linguistic power may make White instructors feel alienated from and insecure about translingual practice. Further articulating translingualism's relevance to monolinguals and Whites could help address these concerns.

A note here on my participants' association of translingualism and race: the reader will likely notice that speakers often connected translingual ideas with the teaching of African American college writers. This could be seen as a predisposition for White instructors to associate translingualism with the intersection of race and language difference, but such a hypothesis would need to be tested in a different study design. I suggest it is more likely that they made these connections because of this project's study design. I had explicitly asked them to consider translingual approaches as a method of reevaluating assumptions about AAE writing.

USING NARRATIVE TO FIT A NEW STORY INTO PRIOR UNDERSTANDING

The first type of narratives I discuss are those in which instructors either ignored translingual and race-conscious concepts or struggled to reconcile them with existing beliefs. The most prominent example of outright rejection came from the following discussion with Thea. When we came to the excerpt from *African American Literacies Unleashed*, I asked if Thea had ever heard of AAE before reading the text; instead of commenting on the text or providing a simple "yes" or "no" answer, she told a story about discussing the Oakland Ebonics controversy several years previously in an undergraduate introductory linguistics class:[9]

In narrative terms, Thea performs *evaluation* of the story and the people and ideas involved; the tale is worth telling because it is "funny" (line 2) and because Thea had encountered "a really racist" idea (line 7), which she counters with a "really good zinger" (line 25), which earns outside approval in the moment (line 30). The *complicating action* is the racist comment by Thea's classmate; the *resolution* is that Thea shut the classmate down with a zinger that references and rejects negative stereotypes about the intelligence and language variety of American southerners, including Whites like Thea.

The narratives of resistance or rejection frequently feature what Bonilla-Silva (2014) identifies as one or more of "four central frames" of "color-blind racism" (74); *frames* in this context are "*set paths for interpreting information*" (75, original italics), that is, ways of thinking about

Line	Speaker	Utterance
1	Thea	Well,
2		sort of a funny story about this debate that I got into with this girl,
3		who was white....
4		We [the class] were talking about Ebonics,
5		and about how teachers should talk in Ebonics...
6		And I don't know I found that silly and said I thought that was actually,
7		a really racist,
8		that's how I felt about some things in here{indicates *African American Literacies Unleashed*},
9		and that it's saying that if you are a Black student,
10		let's say,
11		that you are incapable of learning Standard English...
12	Stephanie	mmhmm
13	Thea	So this girl, [from lines 2–3]
14		(I think) she was from like [elite northeastern city]...
15		and she goes well–
16		'cause I was sitting in the back,
17		and actually the Black kids were sitting with me,
18		(because we were all friends),
19		and she goes well they just can't help it,
20		they can't learn it,
21		it's not their fault...
22		And [she and I] start yelling and getting (mad)
23	Stephanie	yeah
24	Thea	and then she's talking about special standards, [negative connotation of "special," as synonym for "deficient," is clear from full context of conversation]
25		and then for once in my life I actually thought up a good zinger...
26	Stephanie	{laughter}
27	Thea	... I just looked at her and I said,
28		well I guess I need to go to a special [same negative connotation of "special"]... school [for students from the American South]

continued on next page

continued from previous page

Line	Speaker	Utterance
29		because I could never understand such a smart person from [elite northeastern city].
30		And an African American student next to me started laughing so hard he cried.
31		So I won,
32		I'd say!

phenomena we counter. Two of these frames include "cultural racism," which relies on "culturally based arguments," usually stereotypes, "to explain the standing of minorities in society" (76); and "abstract liberalism," which is more complex but often involves relying on the notion that everyone *should* have equality and generating a kind of wishful thinking that such equality exists in reality, allowing for the willful ignorance of, for instance, "savage inequalities between whites and blacks" (79).

Tellingly, Thea's instinct was to repeat popular misinformation about AAE (in contrast to the scholarship she had just read) while presenting herself in as positive and non-racist a light as possible. In detailing her opposition to a classmate who said something that was overtly racist and telling us she sat with African American students she considered friends and who endorsed her takedown of the northeastern interloper, she gives us Thea the non-racist White ally.[10] Yet Thea ignores Ball and Lardner's scholarship on AAE; she "turn[s] away from other narratives" (Corder 1985, 19), returning to a common but incorrect story about the aims of the Oakland School Board resolution.

Several of Bonilla-Silva's (2014) "frames" can also be found in this stretch of discourse. The student from the Northeast demonstrates the "cultural racism" frame (76–77) by arguing that African Americans are *unable* to learn SE because of an inherent and unchangeable quality. Thea takes the opposite position; by reading into the Oakland School Board's resolution and Ball and Lardner's (2005) book—arguments based in cultural racism—she challenges them by using the "abstract liberalism" frame, which relies on colorblind notions of equal opportunity (Bonilla-Silva 2014, 76). In this frame, individual choice is separated from social context (76). Most likely unconsciously and in an attempt to fit the Ball and Lardner piece into her existing understanding of language difference, she misreads their work as claiming that "if you are a black student . . . you are incapable of learning Standard English" (lines 9–11). She also zeroes in on the common misconception that the Oakland School Board resolution *required teachers to use AAE* as problematic; another tenet of "abstract liberalism" is "the idea that force should not be used to achieve social policy" (Bonilla-Silva 2014, 76).

Although this analysis of Thea's engagement with Ball and Lardner is based in part in her experience as an undergraduate student, not an instructor, it is worth drawing attention to for several reasons. First, when asked during the study, in her capacity as an instructor engaging with new pedagogical scholarship, to discuss that scholarship, she changes course and volunteers the undergraduate story. Based on other interview data, the undergraduate experience aligns with and perhaps influenced her language ideology and approach to processing new information. In professional development and in academia in general, we are expected to question common knowledge and engage with new developments in our field. Yet Thea clearly rejects this opportunity to learn from Ball and Lardner's (2005) esteemed *African American Literacies Unleashed*. Other comments she made support my analysis that a colorblind mentality has shaped her teaching. For example, she cites a former student as a model of an African American student who wrote in SE: "I've had varying writing abilities and writing styles from African American students . . . And I was actually thinking about one kid I taught. . . . he was African American. He wrote beautifully. He was a music major, and I kept telling him dude you gotta do something with English. You write too well."

In another case, instructor Barry struggled to make his reading about translingualism fit into his existing pedagogical worldview. While he also frequently utilized a "colorblind" frame, "naturalization," he did not ignore the reading from Horner and his colleagues' (2011) "Language Difference." He initially responded with anger; like Thea, he "go[es] to war" (Corder 1985, 19). But he also lets Horner and colleagues' (2011) work *trouble* him, even though it challenges his privileging of SE *and* his identity as an informed teacher. "Naturalization" is primarily used to describe how Whites justify a preference for socializing with other Whites (Bonilla Silva 2014, 84–85). However, naturalization can also be used as justification for deferring to a racist status quo: "The word 'natural' or the phrase 'that's the way it is' is often interjected to normalize events or actions that could otherwise be interpreted as racially motivated . . . or racist" (85). The full exchange shows Barry's use of a narrative constructed within a conversation to ruminate on new ideas using narrative strategies and colorblind frames:

Line	Speaker	Utterance
1	Barry	But you know I found this one to be {long pause}
2		{sigh},
3		I found it to be sort of offensive {laughs}
4	Stephanie	Okay.
5		Why did you find it offensive?
6	Barry	Maybe I'm just taking it too personally.
7		But,
8		I mean obviously I don't subscribe to the translingual
9	Stephanie	mmhmm
10	Barry	Approach um,
11		you know we talked about this last time,
12		about how I do sort of push for these ideas of correctness and polish you know in my class so obviously I felt like they were kind of attacking me.
13		A little bit. {laughter}
14	Stephanie	{laughter}
15	Barry	Or people like me.
16		Um,
17		but what I,
18		okay,
19		so you know I understood you know their basic points,
20		that um,
21	Barry	you know,
22		there is no one version of English,
23		and if we try to teach it that way we're really teaching a fiction.
24	Stephanie	mmhmm
25	Barry	Uh,
26		there's no uniform standard.
27		But,
28		you know,

continued on next page

continued from previous page

Line	Speaker	Utterance
29		I mean I'll kind of agree with those ideas in the abstract,
30	Stephanie	mmhmm.
31	Barry	but then over like on page three oh four, {sound of turning pages}
32		when,
33		again this is just probably my own ignorance of,
34		of trends in composition,
35		because when they talk about the "Students' Right to Their Own Language,"
36	Stephanie	mmhmm
37	Barry	this big sort of landmark {laughter} declaration in 1974,
38		um,
39		I've never heard of it.
40	Stephanie	Yeah
41	Barry	You know until,
42		until today I'd never heard of that,
43	Stephanie	yeah
44	Barry	never been told about that.
45		Never read about that.
46		Um,
47		so they,
48		they treat it as if,
49		um,
50		Standard English is gone.
51		We've done away with it.
52		We've all come together,
53		we've all decided that teaching Standard English is just,
54		it doesn't work,
55	Stephanie	mmhmm

continued on next page

continued from previous page

Line	Speaker	Utterance
56	Barry	and it's a fiction and it's counterproductive.
57		So now we're gonna accept all different kinds of English,
58		all different kinds of languages,
59		And that's just not true . . .
60		And again I'm not sure what year this was written,
61		Um
62	Stephanie	I think it was two thousand eleven,
62		Yeah two thousand eleven.
63	Barry	Yeah
64		I mean I know it varies widely from institution to institution
65	Stephanie	mmhmm
66	Barry	but
67		at all the institutions I've ever {pause}
68		been at,
69		not once have I ever heard this idea circulated or advocated for.
70	Stephanie	mmhmm
71	Barry	You know I've never heard–
72	Barry	it's never been pushed on me,
73		or even,
74		I've never even been uh,
75		exposed to it.
76		You know I've never even had anybody hand me an article and say "you should really check this out"
77		And again maybe that's my own failing for not,
78		for not you know reading more in the field,
79		but,
80		the way they characterize it,
81		to me it's just,
82		I even (wrote) to say "I think you failed" {laughter}
83	Stephanie	{laughter}
84	Barry	I mean if your goal was to make this sort of a universal,
85		universally accepted new paradigm
86	Stephanie	mmhmm

continued on next page

continued from previous page

Line	Speaker	Utterance
87	Barry	it's not.
88		I mean it hasn't worked.
89		I mean I'm sure composition people are aware of it,
90		I'm sure it's talked about at–
91		at composition conferences
92	Stephanie	mmhmm
93	Barry	And um,
94		and that's great,
95		and I'm sure it has value.
96		But to treat it as if it's,
97		it's this–
98		it's the new paradigm that we've all accepted,
99		that struck me as inaccurate,
100	Stephanie	mmhmm
101	Barry	and that struck me as idealistic,
102		and it struck me as just as monolithic and um {long pause}
103		sorta totalitarian as
104	Stephanie	mmhmm
105	Barry	what they were actually fighting against.

Based on the definition of naturalization presented above, we can find several examples here: "So now we're gonna accept all different kinds of English, all different kinds of languages, and that's just not true" (lines 57–59); "not once have I ever heard this idea circulated or advocated for" (line 69); "but to treat it as if it's this– it's the new paradigm that we've all accepted, that struck me as inaccurate" (lines 96–99). To Barry, Horner and colleagues' (2011) claims are inaccurate because they have not been widely circulated and because the majority of institutions agree that SE is "the way it is" (Bonilla-Silva 2014, 85).

However, Barry struggles to reach a single resolution; he combines resolution with evaluation, arguing that translingual advocacy has failed (lines 80–88, 96–99) but—by suggesting that his having not studied translingualism before is his own shortcoming (77–78)—also recognizing his responsibility to consider such viewpoints. The primary resolution he settles on is that scholars have tried and failed to advance translingualism; but Barry's frustration at never having been exposed to a concept important to his profession indicates another resolution: if teachers like him are expected to incorporate translingualism into their pedagogy, it should be explicitly introduced during professionalization and training.

Barry demonstrates how we can use narrative to process the unfamiliar. Unlike Thea's reaction to Ball and Lardner, Barry has no prepared stance because he is still building this story. His positioning is ambivalent; at times he evaluates *himself*, first as an experienced educator, referencing his work at multiple institutions (line 67), then as a novice with insufficient knowledge of language movements in composition (lines 77–78). Through such moves, he expressed confusion, uncertainty, and willingness to learn. But "naturalization" is also part of the existing narrative that Barry is allowing himself to trouble, and it is particularly hard to let go of.

In another stretch of discourse, Barry's discussion of Ball and Lardner shows how the introduction of "a contending narrative that shakes and cracks all foundations" (Corder 1985, 19) can lead to confusion, indecision:

Line	Speaker	Utterance
1	Barry	I feel like the assumption was,
2		you the instructor who don't know much about African American vernacular,
3		so far you have been holding everybody to (this) same Standard English standard
4	Stephanie	yeah,
5		I get what you're saying
6	Barry	and,
7		and what we want you to adjust . . .
8		is this mind-set that everything that fails to conform to certain Standard English conventions is automatically and necessarily wrong.

Barry said, "I accept all that as probably being, you know, as valid. But I just think that opens up a whole lot of other questions." He raised the issue of other non-mainstream varieties, saying: "So you want me to be familiar with African American vernacular, okay fair enough, I can probably do that" but asked, "How many other vernaculars do we need to be familiar with?" He explained: "I'm not necessarily opposed to it, I'm just a little bit unsure of how to proceed." His questions recall Elinor Ochs and

Lisa Capps's (1996) distinction between *relativistic* and *fundamentalistic* responses to new narratives. The relativistic may open infinite possibilities, while the fundamentalistic limits us to one story (32); thus, "the relativistic tendency" may "lead to a paralyzing sense of indeterminacy" (32). Barry doesn't know what to do—how many dialects must he learn to be a good teacher? Presumably attracted by the possibility of "lay[ing] down one coherent, correct solution to the problem" (32), Barry defers to SE:

Line	Speaker	Utterance
38[11]	Barry	I do think there's some merit even though it kinda squashes individuality to some extent,
39		I think there is some merit to having a standard,
40	Stephanie	mmhmm
41	Barry	right?
42		You have a standard that applies to everybody,
43		and yeah I get that the standard's a white man's standard.
44		We're obviously,
45		are asking them to conform to
46	Stephanie	and somewhat class-based
47	Barry	sure,
48		sure.
49		And uh,
50		yeah that is troubling {laughter}.
51		I guess.
52		I guess I just don't see any easy way around it,
53		because,
54		uh,
55		the alternative is sort of an endless multiplicity,
56		it seems
57	Stephanie	{laughter} that's like my dream
58	Barry	{laughter} and that seems great,
59		but it seems hard to evaluate.

In this dialogue, Barry takes up the more familiar solution of following the status quo. Yes, students are all expected to follow "a white man's standard" (line 43) because such is the current expectation, the way things are. But he is not entirely comfortable with this solution, and in calling SE "a white man's standard," he acknowledges the inherent racism at hand.

USING NARRATIVES TO LEARN ABOUT AND EXPLORE TRANSLINGUALISM

Colorblind racist frames were less present, if at all, in the narratives instructors used to focus more on incorporating translingual ideas into their thinking or teaching instead of resisting them. For example, here is Martin's description of being convinced by Young's (2009) argument:

Line	Speaker	Utterance
1	Martin	The purpose of the piece is to make a very sort of stark well-reasoned even legalistically based and ideologically based argument against code switching.[12]
2		And,
3		I find it more persuasive than I was expecting.
4	Stephanie	why,
5		um,
6		can you point to any parts
7	Martin	yeah
8	Stephanie	that you may have just found particularly persuasive?
9	Martin	I thought the comparison to integration and segregation was really helpful.
10		Um,
11		more so than I expected.
12		Um I'm not entirely certain that I'm sold or persuaded or fully understand what code *meshing* is
13	Stephanie	Mmhmm.
14	Martin	but that's,
15		again I'm not,
16		I don't wanna split hairs about that.
17		The,
18		just like really,

continued on next page

Line	Speaker	Utterance
		continued from previous page
19		just in some senses it was very repetitive,
20		but again he was trying to produce a lot of evidence to prove that look this is a racist logic
21	Stephanie	yeah
22	Martin	and by the end of it,
23		by the end of part one I was like yup,
24		it is a racist logic.
25		He is correct. {laughter}
26	Stephanie	{laughter}
27	Martin	I am one hundred percent persuaded by this.

Martin "encounter[s] narrative and learns to change [his] own" (Corder 1985, 19)—to incorporate the narrative that the expectation of code switching stems from "a racist logic." While it would be easy for Martin to take up the naturalization frame, he indicates rejection of "the way things are" after recognizing that they are racist. Based at least in part on Young's (2009) comparison of the separate-but-equal mentality of segregation—commonly acknowledged today as "a racist logic"—to the separate-but-equal demand for AAE users to adopt SE, Martin openly acknowledged that racism plays a role in dominant writing norms. Martin is unclear on how code meshing is practically applied, but that is not the point—he is engaging with race in language difference, a first step to learning more about how to incorporate race consciousness and translingualism into pedagogy.

Instructors also talked about times when they'd allowed a new Whiteness- or monolingual-challenging discourse to influence them, positioning themselves as reflective teachers open to change or empathetic to linguistically diverse students facing discrimination. In our first interview, Martin recalled tutoring a native English speaker from the Caribbean whose instructors frequently belittled her English. "I worked with a student . . . she was uh, Caribbean. I can't remember if it was Jamaica or it was one of the other islands . . . but she was an Anglophone," Martin said. He further explained, "She thought of herself as a native English speaker, and she was being told by all her professors that she didn't understand English. And it devastated her. . . . she was being told that she didn't speak English, when every day of her life she spoke English. And she would cry. While we were working on her writing." As Martin recalls her being possibly Jamaican-born, it is likely that she was Black, and race may well have played a role in professors' reactions to her variety of English. Though Martin made several arguments in favor of adherence to SE in academic writing early in our interview sessions, he did not conceive of varieties of English as deviant. "It's a really difficult thing," he said. "I would never tell a student that he or she (did) not actually speak a language. . . . certainly not English. I might say to a student 'you're having trouble writing in the way I need you to write to do well in this class,' and explain to that student why, but I would never tell a student he or she couldn't speak English."

In another example of an instructor being influenced by interactions with students, Barry described adapting his teaching in response to a challenge in the classroom. His first teaching experience was as an adjunct at a technical college with a large population of African American adult learners whose writing was Gullah-based and who resisted his attempts to teach or assess based on SE grammar. For several reasons, primarily that as a twenty-something he wasn't comfortable challenging strong-willed, linguistically self-confident, middle-aged people on their ability to use their native language, he deferred to their authority and abandoned SE teaching. Instead, he focused on critical thinking and discussing literary texts, which the students *were* eager to do:

Line	Speaker	Utterance
1	Barry	They were super engaged.
2		They all did the reading . . .
3		And I was really surprised,
4		and it was my own probably,
5		my own prejudice. . . .
6		at first I was like,
7		these people aren't gonna read,
8		man.
9		They're not gonna want to read and they're not gonna want to talk about it,
10		but I was wrong.
11		On both points. . . .
12		So I just kinda changed my expectations . . .
13		you know they are critically thinking . . .

continued on next page

Line	Speaker	Utterance
14		and if that's our goal is to increase their critical thinking ability and to make them formulate arguments,
15		they're doing it.

Barry acknowledged a bias he held and told of how he quickly recognized that he was wrong. This experience, which came up often during our conversations, appears to have been formative, inspiring an interest in linguistic diversity that lay relatively dormant until he had the chance to participate in my study—he explicitly said that his interest in learning more about how compositionists view language difference was his primary motivation for volunteering.

Finally, instructors used hypothetical future narratives to problem-solve. In the following narrative, Wally's growing appreciation for language variation clashes with a desire to avoid conflict related to race:

Line	Speaker	Utterance
1	Wally	I kinda do like the idea here,
2		it just seems like it'd be extremely hard to justify,
3		you know if two students are peer reviewing each other's essays,
4		and you had one student who had just reviewed somebody's paper written in,
5		I don't know like a code-switched dialect,
6		and that got turned in,
7		and that grade got potentially higher than somebody who wrote in standard written English . . .
8		it would be very hard to defend that point,
9		I think,
10		if (they) came to me like I peer-reviewed so-and-so's paper . . .
11		and he got so-and-so grade,
12		and I got so-and-so grade,
13		how did that happen?
14		There were these misspellings,
15		there were these sort of strange idiomatic phrases in there.

continued from previous page

Line	Speaker	Utterance
16	Stephanie	yeah
17	Wally	How do you justify that?
18		Like,
19		I'd feel really uncomfortable looking that student in the eye and being like,
20		well,
21		it's a dialect.
22		And just expecting that student to understand it.
23		Which I guess is why it needs to be discussed in class . . .
24	Stephanie	mmhmm.
25		Well so in this hypothetical scenario,
26		'cause I can see that being a problem. . . .
27		would it have been a matter of,
28		the,
29		let's say if there's an African American student AAE speaker who gets a higher grade,
30		is the reason they got the higher grade because their ideas were better,
31		or–
32	Wally	yeah it's likely gonna be content,
33		it's gonna be argument.
34		Um whereas the other student might have a lesser argument,
35		but they just convey the conventions more properly.
36	Stephanie	Then couldn't you just say that?
37		Like you know–
38	Wally	You could,
39		but I'd still feel pretty uncomfortable . . .
40	Stephanie	mmhmm.
41	Wally	I'd feel okay giving that grade . . .
42		but it would still be very uncomfortable to tell that student,
43		to try to confront (him) one-on-one and just be like no no no,

continued on next page

continued from previous page

Line	Speaker	Utterance
44		this is acceptable,
45		this is okay.
46		Your ideas just need to improve.
47		Um.
48		I don't know if that's properly justifiable on my part,
49		but at least that's my own apprehension towards it.

Factoring linguistic diversity into assessment doesn't bother Wally; he worries about awkwardness as a White teacher explaining to a White SE user why they received a lower grade than an AAE user. Such discomfort is common (Kim and Olson 2013, 12), yet Wally knows it is not a sound reason to avoid race consciousness. He problem-solves by positing that discussing linguistic diversity in class could help prevent or mitigate such encounters.

Another future narrative comes from Oliver. We had discussed the teaching of code meshing as something any writer can do, but Oliver indicated his discomfort with the "flattening of language differences" (Gilyard 2016, 284) and conveyed a perception of code meshing as more familiar for language-minoritized students than for White, SE-using instructors. He said, "I don't even know if I'd be comfortable saying, like, 'I code mesh, too,' 'cause it sort of implies that I have this double consciousness or whatever." He sees his straight-White-maleness as an obstacle:

Line	Speaker	Utterance
1	Oliver	Demographically I'm like the world's worst thing,
2		white heterosexual male. . . .
3		so I mean that's always a strange kind of situation,
4		where it's like,
5		I know about code meshing,
6		and I'm introducing you to code meshing,
7		even though you're the one who's doing it,
8		and I really don't know how to practice it. . . .
9		but I mean that's my problem as a teacher to figure out.

Oliver's awareness of his Whiteness as a complicating variable and his willingness to be troubled indicate race-conscious thinking using the translingual paradigm.

The logic of narrative structure may help Wally and Oliver reach these resolutions; the instinct to include some kind of resolution in narratives, to solve the complicating actions we've introduced, is ingrained. Sometimes, as in Thea's story about the argument with her classmate or Martin's stories of being persuaded by an academic essay and sympathizing with a non-SE English user, we have a resolution ready when we start talking. Other times, especially with conflicts we're still processing, we get to the part of the story where we intuitively sense we need to provide a resolution and struggle to find one—so we reach back to what is comfortable, as Barry did in concluding that an unfair but easy-to-grade standard is better than the chaos of "endless multiplicity." Or like Oliver and Wally, we use the resolution to challenge ourselves to solve or acknowledge the need to continue interrogating a problem. Understanding the power of narrative in shaping how one uses translingualism as a mode of thinking (or not) helps us see the positive potential of dialogic professional methods.

CONCLUSION

During final interviews, I asked participants why they'd volunteered. Most cited the desire to help a colleague; Barry and Wally also cited subject-matter interest. Regardless of motivation, each participant was intrigued by the readings and engaged fully in the project. I initially allotted fifteen to thirty minutes for each interview, but we rarely finished within this time frame; whenever I offered to stop at the thirty-minute mark, even if we still had a few questions to cover, participants tended to decline—they wanted more time to share their perspective on a reading, ask questions, or tell another story.

My stance is that promoting translingualism as a possible way of thinking for college faculty is a worthy goal. And perhaps the prospect of translingual professionalization in composition studies is not so bleak as previously believed. The problem may not be that English teachers are particularly stubborn in their views about language; instead, those seeking to incorporate translingualism and race consciousness more fully into composition practice, or at least provide them as available ways of approaching language difference, must do more than simply present facts and expect anything to change. Using narrative techniques drawn from work of scholars such as Corder (1985), we should provide skeptical colleagues with the time and space to grapple with discourses new to them. As Corder points out, some of this grappling might involve a bit of anger, hesitation, or rejection. But as suggested by my participants' comments and narratives, those initially unfamiliar with principles of diversity in language can find value in translingual study—an expanded definition of "correctness," increased awareness of power and language difference, a new appreciation for marginalized discourses, and even the adoption of translingualism into their pedagogical thinking. In our conversations, I found that these instructors generally like and respect their students, are conscientious about their work, and want to learn more ways to be effective teachers. Professionalization that keeps these factors in mind and invites instructors to work through new information using their own stories will be one step closer to sustainably promoting appreciation for linguistic diversity.

NOTES

1. I sent a formal invitation over the graduate English listserv, outlining the study protocol and noting the fifty-dollar incentive.
2. After initial data analysis, I focused on instructors engaging with translingualism for the first time; as "Josephine" (all names are pseudonyms) had studied translingualism at a prior institution, her data were not used for this analysis.
3. I didn't limit by race or class background, but only White middle-class instructors volunteered (likely due to institutional demographics). Participants *were* limited to students of American literature: studying participants from the same discipline reduces confounding variables, American literature is a popular area of inquiry, and many Americanists teach composition after graduation.
4. "AAE-strong" is inspired by Coleman's (1997) "Ebonics-strong" as a label for writing with AAE characteristics.
5. Conscious of time commitment, I asked them to read only the first three pages, which provide a basic introduction to translingualism.
6. "Backchanneling involves interjecting small utterances like *Mmmhmm, Uh-huh, Yeah,* and *Right*—or even just nodding the head—into conversation in order to let the current speaker know that he or she may continue" (Wolfram and Schilling-Estes 2006, 99, original italics). Though I attempted to backchannel neutrally, it's possible that I sometimes conveyed agreement or disagreement and/or that participants interpreted utterances as such.
7. Assuming it is not a morally reprehensible narrative, such as one promoting racism, xenophobia, or sexism.
8. My transcription style is modified from that favored by sociolinguists such as Bucholtz (2011) but incorporates aspects of MLA citation conventions. Shorter transcripts are presented within the regular text. Longer transcriptions are set apart with lines numbered by utterance. Text in parentheses ( ) indicates uncertain transcription; a comma (,): speaker paused briefly; a period (.): speaker paused after falling intonation, and for slightly longer than after a comma, suggesting the end of an utterance. Question marks (?): same as periods (.), except that speaker voices or cites a question. Information in {braces} indicates nonverbal action, including {laughter}; a single dash (-) indicates self-interruption by the speaker.

    Ellipses (. . .): the removal of part of a single utterance or with (. . . .) of removal of text that includes part(s) of more than one utterance. Brackets [ ]: substitution of synonymous wording needed to clarify meaning, for example, if the speaker uses a pronoun but reader understanding requires a noun; brackets [ ] are also used to obscure information that might compromise confidentiality, for example, Chicago would be replaced with [major American city]. All transcripts include "filler" words such as "um" and "like." Participants often used their turns-at-talk to work through an idea and expressed varying degrees of certainty. The inclusion of these "filler words" helps demonstrate that process.
9. Longer transcripts appear in chart format, broken up by pause, self-interruption, or end of turn-at-talk by interviewee; *or* interruption, cross-talk, or turn-at-talk by interviewer.
10. Bonilla-Silva (2014, 156) describes Whites' claims of friendship with Blacks as a way of enacting colorblindness, pointing out Whites' tendency to "promote" Black acquaintances to friends for non-racist credibility; note that Thea's friend is not identified by name but as "an African American student next to me" (line 30).
11. I start this line with 38 because it is the 38th line of the narrative that began in the previous transcript excerpt.
12. An assimilationist practice of expecting language-minoritized students to "switch" to SE and White-based discourses at school and in other "formal" situations (Young 2009).

REFERENCES

Anson, Chris M. 1999. "Reflective Reading: Developing Thoughtful Ways to Respond to Students' Writing." In *Evaluating Writing: The Role of Teachers' Knowledge about Text, Learning, and Culture*, ed. Charles R. Cooper and Lee Odell, 302–24. Urbana, IL: NCTE.

Ball, Arnetha F., and Ted Lardner. 1997. "Dispositions toward Language: Teacher Constructs of Knowledge and the Ann Arbor Black English Case." *College Composition and Communication* 48 (4): 469–85.

Ball, Arnetha F., and Ted Lardner. 2005. *African American Literacies Unleashed: Vernacular English and the Composition Classroom*. Carbondale: Southern Illinois University Press.

Ball, Arnetha F., and Rashida Jaami' Muhammad. 2003. "Language Diversity in Teacher Education and the Classroom." In *Language Diversity in the Classroom: From Intention to Practice*, ed. Geneva Smitherman and Victor Villanueva, 76–88. Carbondale: Southern Illinois University Press.

Bonilla-Silva, Eduardo. 2014. *Racism without Racists: Color-Blind Racism and the Persistence of Racial Inequality in America*. 4th ed. Lanham, MD: Rowman and Littlefield.

Bucholtz, Mary. 2011. *White Kids: Language, Race, and Styles of Youth Identity*. New York: Cambridge University Press.

Canagarajah, Suresh. 2016. "Translingual Writing and Teacher Development." *College English* 78 (3): 265–73.

Coleman, Charles F. 1997. "Our Students Write with Accents: Oral Paradigms for ESD Students." *College Composition and Communication* 48 (4): 486–500.

Condon, Frankie. 2011. "A Place Where There Isn't Any Trouble." In *Code-Meshing as World English: Pedagogy, Policy, Performance*, ed. Vershawn Ashanti Young and Aja Y. Martinez, 1–8. Urbana, IL: NCTE.

Corder, Jim W. 1985. "Argument as Emergence, Rhetoric as Love." *Rhetoric Review* 4 (1): 16–32.

Davies, Bronwyn, and Rom Harré. 1990. "Positioning: The Discursive Production of Selves." *Journal for the Theory of Social Behavior* 20 (1): 43–63.

Flores, Nelson, and Jonathan Rosa. 2015. "Undoing Appropriateness: Raciolinguistic Ideologies and Language Diversity in Education." *Harvard Education Review* 85 (2): 149–71.

Gilyard, Keith. 2016. "The Rhetoric of Translingualism." *College English* 78 (3): 284–89.

Horner, Bruce, Min-Zhan Lu, Jacqueline Jones Royster, and John Trimbur. 2011. "Language Difference in Writing: Toward a Translingual Approach." *College English* 73 (3): 303–21.

Kim, Dae-Joong, and Bobbi Olson. 2013. "Deconstructing Whiteliness in the Globalized Classroom." *Across the Disciplines* 10 (3). http://wac.colostate.edu/atd/race/kim_olson.cfm. Accessed March 15, 2017.

Labov, William. 1973. *Language in the Inner City: Studies in the Black English Vernacular*. Philadelphia: University of Pennsylvania Press.

Lovejoy, Kim Brian, Steve Fox, and Katherine V. Wills. 2015. "From Language Experience to Classroom Practice: Affirming Linguistic Diversity in Writing Pedagogy." In *Students' Right to Their Own Language: A Critical Sourcebook*, ed. Staci Perryman-Clark, David E. Kirkland, and Austin Jackson, 381–403. Boston: Bedford/St. Martin's.

Lu, Min-Zhan, and Bruce Horner. 2013. "Translingual Literacy, Language Difference, and Matters of Agency." *College English* 75 (6): 582–607.

Maxwell, Joseph A. 2008. "Designing a Qualitative Study." In *The SAGE Handbook of Applied Social Research Methods*. 2nd ed., ed. Leonard Bickman and Debra J. Rog, 214–53. Thousand Oaks, CA: Sage.

National Center for Education Statistics. 2008. "Table 315.80: Full-Time and Part-Time Faculty and Instructional Staff in Degree-Granting Postsecondary Institutions, by Race/Ethnicity, Sex, and Program Area: Fall 1998 and Fall 2003." https://nces.ed.gov/programs/digest/d15/tables/dt15_315.80.asp. Accessed April 1, 2017.

Ochs, Elinor, and Lisa Capps. 1996. "Narrating the Self." *Annual Review of Anthropology* 25: 19–43.

Okawa, Gail Y. 2015. "From 'Bad Attitudes' to(ward) Linguistic Pluralism: Developing Reflective Language Policy among Preservice Teachers." In *Students' Right to Their Own Language: A Critical Sourcebook*, ed. Staci Perryman-Clark, David E. Kirkland, and Austin Jackson, 324–37. Boston: Bedford/St. Martin's.

Richardson, Elaine. 2003. "Race, Class(es), Gender, and Age: The Making of Knowledge about Language Diversity." In *Language Diversity in the Classroom: From Intention to Practice*, ed. Geneva Smitherman and Victor Villanueva, 40–66. Carbondale: Southern Illinois University Press.

Spinuzzi, Clay. 2005. "The Methodology of Participatory Design." *Technical Communication* 52 (2): 163–74.

Trimbur, John. 2016. "Translingualism and Close Reading." *College English* 78 (3): 219–27.

Webb-Sunderhaus, Sara. 2016. "'Keep the Appalachian, Drop the Redneck': Tellable Student Narratives of Appalachian Identity." *College English* 79 (1): 11–33.

Wolfram, Walt, and Natalie Schilling-Estes. 2006. *American English: Dialects and Variation*. 2nd ed. Malden, MA: Blackwell.

Young, Vershawn Ashanti. 2009. "'Nah, We Straight': An Argument against Code-Switching." *JAC* 29 (1–2): 49–76.

10
SEGREGATED SPACE AND TRANSLINGUAL PEDAGOGY

Jaclyn Hilberg

The scholarly lineage of translingualism as a new linguistic paradigm for US college composition is typically traced through two abiding concerns in the field: the implications for social justice that emerge when language difference comes into contact with monolingual ideology and the regularity of that contact in the context of globalization. Put another way, contact—among languages, cultures, economies, identities—creates the conditions under which translingualism has emerged as an orientation toward language difference that promotes inclusion. The central tenet of a translingual approach to linguistic and literate practice—that difference is, in fact, the norm of language use—seems particularly well-suited to twenty-first-century writing instruction. Given that constantly evolving communication technologies and the permeability of traditional barriers between nation-states have become commonplaces of literate life, translingualism can help teacher-scholars to ethically approach the attendant contact between languages and cultures that can no longer be considered discrete.

The notion of writing classrooms as spaces of linguistic contact, often theorized as (loosely) analogous to Mary Louise Pratt's (1991) contact zones, has become a mainstay in composition scholarship, with translingualism now standing as perhaps the most prominent and promising manifestation of what a contact-oriented approach to classroom space has to offer. This dominant imagining of classrooms as spaces of linguistic contact, however, risks obscuring the significant extent to which literacy education in the United States occurs under conditions of racial and socioeconomic segregation. Indeed, much recent data indicates that US schools are becoming increasingly segregated, a trend deeply interconnected with the ongoing residential segregation that, while no longer legally condoned, has yet to be meaningfully redressed. While segregated schools and communities certainly do not exist outside the contact zones of globalization—not least because affluent, White suburbs and their neighborhood schools are, after all, segregated—the language and literacy learning that occurs in segregated spaces may be characterized more by a *lack* of contact than a translingual approach to such learning might suggest.

In this chapter, I argue that translingual writing scholarship might benefit from (re)considering composition classrooms as complex spaces of both linguistic contact *and* segregation. Accordingly, I consider what a translingual pedagogy might look like when approached against the reality of racially and socioeconomically segregated spaces as a prevalent context for literacy learning in the United States. To be clear, my aim is not to reject the insights afforded through contact-centered conceptions of literacy education but rather to point out that any single spatial rendering of writing classrooms foregrounds certain contexts and concerns while eliding others. Compositionists have already thoughtfully undertaken the work of extending and refining the conception of writing classrooms as contact zones; it may now be productive, I suggest here, to give similar consideration to our classrooms as segregated spaces. Indeed, the work of complicating our notions of classroom spaces to account for which languages and language users are permitted to come into contact and which are excluded entirely may be central to the project of "racing" translingualism.

To make this argument, I begin by locating translingualism within a disciplinary tradition of contact-oriented approaches to writing pedagogy. While such approaches have certainly helped writing instructors ethically address linguistic difference in their classrooms, I argue that a fuller consideration of the ways classrooms function as segregated spaces can complement contact-oriented notions of classroom space, sketching out a brief history of educational segregation and analyzing the case of the University of Louisville to complicate the contact zone metaphor. A consideration of multiple framings of classroom space, I hope to show, invites us to adopt translingual pedagogies that more explicitly account for linguistic *exclusion* alongside the typical focus on inclusion. My intervention, then, is ultimately pedagogical: I conclude by proposing a series of moves composition instructors can make to foster a race-conscious translingual pedagogy for the segregated classroom.

LOCATING TRANSLINGUALISM IN THE CONTACT ZONES OF COMPOSITION

In their manifesto introducing translingualism as a new approach to "language difference in writing," Bruce Horner, Min-Zhan Lu, Jacqueline Jones Royster, and John Trimbur (2011) trace the scholarly lineage of this approach through the 1974 "Students' Right to Their Own Language" resolution released by the Conference on College Composition and Communication (CCCC). Summarizing the work performed by "Students' Right," they describe the resolution's defense of "the right of students (and all other writers) to use different varieties of English"; its opposition to "the common, though inaccurate, view that varieties of English other than those recognized as 'standard' are defective," along with the users of those languages; and its recognition of "the logicality of all varieties of English, the meanings to be gained by speakers and writers in using particular varieties of English, and the right of speakers and writers to produce such meanings" (304). They also note a number of prominent efforts by CCCC and the National Council of Teachers of English to expand on the initial "Students' Right" resolution (304). Horner and his colleagues locate their articulation of a translingual approach to writing alongside these sustained efforts to foster linguistic inclusivity in writing classrooms. As they explain it, "The translingual approach we call for extends the CCCC resolution to differences within and across all languages . . . Further, this approach insists on viewing language differences and fluidities as resources to be preserved, developed, and utilized" (304).

This view of language difference and flexibility as not only the norms of language use but also as resources for the user echoes the scholarship on global Englishes that also significantly informs the translingual approach. As Horner and colleagues (2011, 303) note, despite the monolingual ideology that inaccurately posits the existence and desirability of a uniform Standard English, the actual use of language "in our classrooms, our communities, the nation, and the world has always been multilingual," especially given that the boundaries between languages have always been fluid. While this porousness of linguistic boundaries is nothing new, as Horner and colleagues make clear, globalization has made the reality of linguistic heterogeneity undeniable and simultaneously intensified the breakdown of perceived linguistic barriers. Whether through the greater access to higher education that prompted "Students' Right" or through the information flows of globalization, then, increased linguistic contact and its attendant implications for linguistic justice serve as the primary exigencies for a translingual approach to language difference in writing.

Although a translingual approach to these issues is relatively new to composition theory, the exigencies themselves are not. Compositionists have been parsing the ethics of linguistic contact and linguistic difference since at least the 1970s, as the foundational "Students' Right to Their Own Language" resolution makes clear. Indeed, while the resolution now represents a broad statement of disciplinary values, it was initially crafted in response to a specific institutional problem concerning language difference. "Students' Right," as Keith Gilyard (2016, 285) reminds us in "The Rhetoric of Translingualism," responded to a "particular political problem, the harsh penalizing of students who were firmly tethered linguistically to an institutionally discredited heritage." This political problem is most often associated in disciplinary lore with the open admissions policy of the City University of New York (CUNY) in the 1970s and the rise of basic writing as an institutional requirement for certain language users.

We might see in the CUNY example an early instance of the institutional power dynamics that would later lead composition scholars, in the 1990s and early 2000s, to theorize writing classrooms as akin to Pratt's (1991) contact zones. Pratt's initial articulation of the concept as "social spaces where cultures meet, clash, and grapple with each other, often in contexts of highly asymmetrical relations of power, such as colonialism, slavery, or their aftermaths" (34), and her reflections on the function of language(s) in such spaces resonate with descriptions of CUNY classrooms during the era of open admissions. Historical context, as Gilyard (2016) reminds us, is important here; when we situate open admissions and the "Students' Right to Their Own Language" resolution as specific responses to institutionalized racial segregation—and, thus, the legacy of slavery—Pratt's spatial metaphor seems particularly apt. But compositionists have also refined and extended the term to better fit the broader situation of literacy education and writing classrooms across institutions of higher education. Notably, Patricia Bizzell (1994, 164), in " 'Contact Zones' and English Studies," calls for the reorganization of English studies "in terms of historically defined contact zones, moments when different groups within the society contend for the power to interpret what is going on," reworking Pratt's term as a heuristic for investigating the social struggle surrounding the act of interpretation. Composition scholarship has also utilized the concept of the contact zone to productively examine how language difference clashes with monolingual ideology in institutional spaces. Min-Zhan Lu's (1994) oft-cited "Professing

Multiculturalism: The Politics of Style in the Contact Zone" perhaps best exemplifies the theoretical and pedagogical fruits born of such an approach; her critical examination, in her essay and with her students, of one student's "can able to" structure elucidates the invention of new meaning that can arise for both writers and readers when language difference is regarded as a resource instead of a limitation (and foreshadows her later work on translingualism). These notable reworkings of Pratt's (1991) contact zone led Joseph Harris to charge his colleagues with "proclaim[ing] Pratt the 1990s 'patron theorist of composition'" (quoted in Hall and Rosner 2004, 103).

Significantly, while composition scholars may have largely moved past explicitly refining Pratt's (1991) concept, the contact zone remains a prominent and productive metaphor for spaces of literacy learning and literate negotiation in the context of globalization. Suresh Canagarajah (2013) perhaps most explicitly articulates the connection among contact zones, globalization, and translingualism—taking the cultural contact zones produced by globalization to be a central impetus for a translingual approach to all literate practice. Much of his work examines the ways "people are developing relevant strategies and dispositions for translingual literacies" in spaces he characterizes as "global contact zones" (8, 6). Canagarajah and Yumi Matsumoto (2017, 1) also call for a Pratt-inspired pedagogy that enables translingual literate interaction by providing "ecological affordances for the negotiation of competing norms and the emergence of new genres." Indeed, given the undeniable global proliferation of linguistic contact zones, especially with increased access to the internet, the moment might seem particularly ripe for such a pedagogy.

At the same time, I worry that envisioning educational spaces primarily in terms of contact zones—even though the metaphor is often apt—can obscure the ways such spaces have been designed to exclude and thus to *preclude* contact. The contact zone as a spatial metaphor, in other words, risks becoming a terministic screen that reflects particular features of our classrooms—such as linguistic difference and cultural mediation—while deflecting others. More troubling, the features *reflected* by this metaphor, like broader cultural inclusion and even conflict, tend to be those most literacy educators prize in educational spaces. But the metaphor's *deflections*, as I demonstrate below, may inhibit us from recognizing the significant extent to which our writing classrooms, particularly those at traditional four-year institutions, function as racially and socioeconomically segregated spaces.

THE SEGREGATED SPACES OF LITERACY EDUCATION IN THE UNITED STATES

To complement the affordances of contact-oriented approaches to literacy pedagogy, I contend that we need to more thoroughly examine the conditions of racial and socioeconomic segregation that characterize many spaces of literacy learning in the United States. If CUNY's open admissions experiment, the CCCC's "Students' Right to Their Own Language" resolution, globalization, and now the move toward translingualism have, in combination, tended to support one prominent narrative about composition as a discipline, then an investigation of segregation as a spatial practice structuring many writing classrooms can add important nuance to that narrative. This section, accordingly, considers the broad context of racial and socioeconomic segregation in the US in which institutions of higher education—and thus composition classrooms—unavoidably find themselves. I draw upon legal decisions and educational data to make the case that we cannot separate the politics of our classroom spaces from the politics of the broader institutions—institutions extending beyond and encapsulating the university—that profoundly structure them.[1]

Mainstream cultural narratives concerning school segregation in the United States typically situate the phenomenon in the Jim Crow South and celebrate its demise with the 1954 US Supreme Court decision in *Brown v. Board of Education*, oversimplifying the more insidious and ongoing reality of school segregation in the US. The unanimous *Brown* decision overturned the "separate but equal" precedent established by the Court in the infamous *Plessy v. Ferguson* (1896) decision by declaring "separate educational facilities" to be "inherently unequal" (*Brown*). Implementation of the desegregation mandated by *Brown*, ordered to proceed with "all deliberate speed" in a 1955 follow-up case known as *Brown II*, infamously met with "massive resistance" from governors, legislatures, school boards, and White citizens in the South. This "massive resistance" amounted to massive—and largely effective—foot-dragging on the part of state and local governments to forestall desegregation. An extensive compilation of data published by the Harvard Civil Rights Project assessing the legacy of the *Brown* decision on its fiftieth anniversary indicates that in 1954, when the Supreme Court handed down the *Brown* verdict, 0 percent of Black students in the South attended majority White schools; ten years later, by 1964, that figure had risen to a paltry 2.3 percent (Orfield and Lee 2004, 19). However, with the passage of the 1964 Civil Rights Act and subsequent Supreme Court decisions in

Green v. New Kent County (1968), *Alexander v. Holmes* (1969), *and Swann v. Charlotte-Mecklenburg* (1971), the political and legal challenge to segregated schools mounted. Supreme Court rulings were especially effective in obligating southern school districts to enact desegregation in a manner that was "thorough, comprehensive, [and] immediate" (Orfield and Lee 2004, 18), such that by 1970, nearly one-third of Black students in the South attended majority White schools (19). That number continued to rise until 1988, at which point 43.5 percent of southern Black students attended majority White schools (19).

Yet even amid the fiftieth anniversary celebrations lauding the *Brown* decision, southern public schools were quietly continuing a decade-long trend toward re-segregation. As the Harvard Civil Rights Project report, titled "*Brown* at 50: King's Dream or *Plessy*'s Nightmare," notes, this trend can be "linked to the impact of three Supreme Court decisions between 1991 and 1995 limiting school desegregation and authorizing a return to segregated neighborhood schools, decisions which were interpreted by a number of Southern courts as prohibiting even voluntary race-conscious plans to maintain desegregated schools where local authorities believed integration to be a crucial local goal" (Orfield and Lee 2004, 18). The most notorious among these Supreme Court cases was *Dowell v. Oklahoma City* (1991), which ended the earlier desegregation orders put in place for many districts under the premise that their integration obligations had been met. Many districts quickly moved to return to segregated neighborhood schools, such that the percentage of Black students in majority White southern schools had fallen from 43.5 percent in 1988 to 30.2 percent in 2001 (19). While the phenomenon of re-segregation has been most pointed in the South, other regions of the country are far from exonerated by the available data. A decade after the *Dowell* decision, re-segregation was occurring in every region of the United States except for the Northeast. Significantly, the Northeast currently houses the most racially and socioeconomically segregated schools in the nation, and re-segregation is not a prominent trend in the region largely because a legally mandated *desegregation* of intensely segregated neighborhood schools never took place.

Neighborhood schools are not inherently problematic, but the intense residential segregation across the United States—much of it initially promoted and subsidized by federal, state, and local governments[2]—very often ensures that such schools are racially and socioeconomically segregated. The precise nature of this segregation, moreover, reveals a disturbing, though unsurprising, correlation between race and poverty. Explicating this link, the Harvard Civil Rights Project report states:

In the 2001–2002 school year, 43 percent of all U.S. schools were intensely segregated white schools or schools with less than a tenth black and Latino students. Only 15 percent of these intensely segregated white schools were schools of concentrated poverty, or schools with more than half of the students on free or reduced priced lunch. In contrast, 88 percent of intensely segregated minority schools (or schools with less than ten percent white [students]) had concentrated poverty, with more than half of all students getting free lunches. That means that students in highly segregated [minority] neighborhood schools are many times more likely to be in schools of concentrated poverty. (Orfield and Lee 2004, 21)

According to data compiled by UCLA's Civil Rights Project / Proyecto Derechos Civiles,[3] as of 2013, 18.6 percent of all public schools were classified, following these criteria, as intensely segregated White schools; 18.4 percent of all public schools were classified as intensely segregated minority schools (Orfield et al. 2016, 3). Thus, in 2013, a full 37 percent of American public schools were considered to be intensely segregated, with intensely segregated minority schools reporting substantially higher rates of student poverty than intensely segregated White schools.

Although I have thus far focused primarily on the segregation of K–12 schools, the link among race, poverty, and educational attainment bears directly on higher education. For example, if high-poverty, intensely segregated schools do not offer college preparatory courses, as the Harvard Civil Rights Project report suggests is often the case (Orfield and Lee 2004, 22), then students receive a powerful institutional message about societal expectations for their futures. Students from so-called apartheid schools who do go on to attend college will not have nearly the same degree of preparation to enter into the White middle-class discourse(s) of higher education as their more affluent peers—many of whom, as the data offered above indicate, will have attended low-poverty, segregated White schools. Students from high-poverty schools where college attendance is not the expectation face disadvantages at multiple stages of the college application and admissions process; for example, they are less likely to receive guidance about the college application process and less likely to be informed about the range of options available to them. Not to be overlooked, they are also likely to have lower standardized test scores than their more affluent peers, and while such tests are far from racially or socioeconomically neutral, they nonetheless serve a gate-keeping function at many institutions of higher education (23–24).

Colleges have attempted to mitigate against these disadvantages through affirmative action policies. But such policies, which allow institutions to consider race as a factor in determining which similarly qualified applicants should be granted admission as a means of countering the effects of systemic racism, have been subject to legal challenge and may face a precarious future under a conservative US Supreme Court. While the Supreme Court upheld affirmative action policies in the 2003 *Grutter v. Bollinger* decision, citing the well-established benefits of racially integrated educational spaces for *all* students, recent decisions have been more ambivalent. For example, in the 2016 *Fisher v. Texas* opinion, the justices upheld affirmative action generally but declared that "strict scrutiny" should apply to individual institutions' affirmative action policies—hardly the full-throated endorsement of integrated educational spaces the Court offered in 2003. With the future of affirmative action far from certain and the effectiveness of such policies far from adequate to the task of redressing educational discrimination, institutions of higher education—especially traditional four-year schools that charge tuition—may need to reckon more fully with the extent to which they operate as racially and socioeconomically segregated spaces.

CASE STUDY: RACIAL (RE-)SEGREGATION AT THE UNIVERSITY OF LOUISVILLE

Thus far, I have relied extensively on legal precedent and educational data to make the case that a large number of K–12 public schools in the contemporary United States serve as racially and socioeconomically segregated spaces—and often intensely so. I have also shown that such segregation necessarily impacts who makes it through the admissions gate at higher education institutions, especially at traditional four-year colleges that charge tuition. In addition to being situated within a broad culture of racially and socioeconomically segregated educational spaces and thus inheriting the consequences of a fundamentally racist K–12 educational system, college classrooms may further exacerbate racial segregation, as a case study of my current institution, the University of Louisville, demonstrates.

The University of Louisville (U of L) is located in Jefferson County, Kentucky, the largest and most densely populated county in the state, with a population that is 72.3 percent White and 22.0 percent African American (with the remaining population identifying with other race[s] or ethnicities) based on July 1, 2017, estimates ("Quick Facts" 2017). In a discussion of racial segregation, Jefferson County is notable in two ways: it boasts some of the most racially integrated public schools in the US while its major city, Louisville, contains some of the most deeply segregated neighborhoods in the nation. The coexistence of school integration with profound residential segregation is made possible through a district-wide bussing policy that Jefferson County Public Schools (JCPS) has fought to maintain despite its constant targeting by conservative state lawmakers. Thus, Jefferson County provides an interesting case study for this analysis given the high degree of racial integration in the public school system, enabling us to glean particular insight into the segregationist practices that structure higher education in the county. In other words, because JCPS provides well-integrated public schools, we cannot simply assume that any racial segregation occurring through admissions processes at U of L results "naturally" from the segregated K–12 public education system.

U of L enrolled 13,764 in-state undergraduate students in fall 2017, with 9,455 of those students hailing from Jefferson County ("Profile" 2018). While U of L does not provide demographic data for this specific subset of students, the university's website does indicate that of a total student population of 22,459, 10.4 percent identified as African American, 71.1 percent identified as White, and the remaining 18.5 percent were grouped together under the category "all other minority." Thus, at a public university that draws well over half of its undergraduate population from the county in which it is located, there is a major discrepancy between the proportion of African American residents in the county (22.0%) and African American students at the university (10.4%). Out-of-state students and students residing outside of Jefferson County certainly have some role in this discrepancy, but it remains important to question why U of L's African American student population is so out of sync with Jefferson County demographics, especially given the high proportion of Jefferson County students at the university.

Data from the local community college system, Jefferson Community and Technical College (JCC), further complicate the picture. JCC reports that of its total student population of 12,259, 19.1 percent identify as African American and 61.8 percent identify as White, with the remaining student population identifying with other race(s) or ethnicities ("Fast Facts" 2018). JCC's student population, then, more closely matches broader Jefferson County demographics concerning African Americans (19.1% vs. 22.0%) but includes a lower proportion of Whites than the county at large (61.8% vs. 72.3%). Whatever else we take away from these data, it's clear that JCC has a much more significant minority population than U of L, which has a significantly lower Black student population than we might expect of a largely regional public university located in a county known for its well-integrated public schools.

Why do Black students seem to be underrepresented at U of L when we situate the university in its local context? While a full exploration of the sociological and educational literature examining the connections among race, socioeconomic status, and educational attainment is outside the scope of this chapter, it's worth considering how Louisville's intense residential segregation might contribute to racial disparities in higher education. Louisville's affluent East End (population 71,291) has a median household income of $59,360, a median home value of $228,500, an unemployment rate of 3.1 percent, and a population that is 4 percent African American and 91 percent White. By contrast, the West End (population 64,735) has a median household income of $22,471, a median home value of $58,150, an unemployment rate of 11.7 percent, and a population that is 77 percent African American and 19 percent White ("East vs. West" 2017). This stark divide earned Louisville eighth place on *Time* magazine's 2017 list of most economically segregated cities in the United States, and clearly, segregation in Louisville is not merely economic.

U of L is more racially diverse than East Louisville, although its African American population looks much more like East Louisville's than West Louisville's. Given the dramatically lower socioeconomic status of West Louisville residents than East Louisville residents and the strong correlation between race and socioeconomic status, it is not surprising that has a much higher proportion of Black students than U of L; in 2018, JCC charged $169 per credit hour for in-state students, while U of L charged $478 per credit hour ("Tuition and Fees" 2018a, 2018b). The ever-dwindling state support for higher education in Kentucky has led to tuition increases and financial aid reductions at U of L over the past several years, a trend unlikely to be reversed in the foreseeable future. Cost, then, likely serves as a significant barrier to racial integration at U of L, an institution that is much less racially integrated than the public school district in which it is located.

As this case study has demonstrated, college classrooms—at least at the University of Louisville—are not necessarily the contact zones that some approaches to translingual pedagogy invite us to celebrate. This is not a problem for translingual theory; as Lu and Horner (2013) have demonstrated, translingual approaches account even for writing that seems to (re)produce the norms posited by monolingual ideology. However, in practice, translingual pedagogies risk relying too heavily on the contact zone metaphor for classroom space without critically examining the extent to which our classrooms both inherit and perpetuate broader social processes of racial segregation. The project of "racing" translingual pedagogies, then, pushes us to look beyond the contact zone as a metaphor for classroom space—even as we recognize the pedagogical benefits of such an approach—to ask uncomfortable questions about the spatial organization of our institutions, both in the narrow sense of our universities and in the broader sense of our public school systems, legal systems, and government at all levels. To be clear, accounting for segregation in our composition pedagogies in no way requires us to throw out contact-oriented approaches to literacy education but rather to complement and complicate those approaches with a more complex rendering of classroom space that accounts for the pervasiveness of de facto segregation across higher education institutions. Race-conscious translingual pedagogies, as I demonstrate below, may offer a way of addressing the complex interplay between contact and segregation that structures many college composition classrooms.

TOWARD A TRANSLINGUAL PEDAGOGY FOR SEGREGATED SPACES

As translingual writing programs and pedagogies become more common (e.g., Horner and Tetrault 2017), composition instructors and writing program administrators may be increasingly called upon to justify the apparent mismatch between the traditional institutional impetus for the first-year writing requirement—usually bound up in monolingual ideology—and the decision to pursue a translingual pedagogy. While the increasing linguistic contact characterizing workspaces and digital arenas due to globalization and the impressive body of scholarship on global Englishes, English as a lingua franca, and now translingualism provide a compelling economic justification for a translingual approach to writing, I have argued that the racial and socioeconomic realities *within* the United States also lead us to an additional set of pedagogical and administrative concerns. Put simply, the institutionalized segregation governing American society—which universities and thus composition classrooms cannot escape—creates particular imperatives for literacy educators concerned with linguistic justice. The CCCC "Students' Right to Their Own Language" resolution took up these imperatives in the 1970s, and its revisions and reiterations have performed that work in the intervening decades, with translingualism as the most prominent and perhaps most important such revision. Yet translingual pedagogies could respond even more effectively to the specific forms of racism structuring US society by more thoroughly considering segregation and its impact on composition classrooms.

The project of racing translingualism to account for segregated spaces of literacy education, as I see it, requires three pedagogical moves: (1) explicitly (re)framing our classrooms as complex spaces of contact and de facto segregation, (2) intentionally bringing into the classroom voices and language practices that systemic racial segregation excludes, and (3) consciously adopting strategies that minimize the instructor's role in perpetuating the violence of segregation. I want to emphasize that none of these moves requires making an interrogation of monolingual ideology—or even of structural racism—the central focus of the composition class (although I certainly believe these are important and productive foci). Rather, these are moves *all* instructors can make to foster a race-conscious translingual pedagogy regardless of specific course content.

The first move, explicitly (re)framing the composition classroom as a complex space of both linguistic contact and segregation, entails getting to know who our students are *and aren't*. That is, in addition to taking the usual measures to get to know our students at the beginning of a new semester, we need to be conscious of the students who will never set foot in our classrooms because they are systematically excluded. Instructors might investigate some of the following questions: From where does my present institution draw its student population? How well does the demographic composition of recent entering classes reflect the broader demographic makeup of the community, state, or country? How might the particular admissions and financial requirements at this institution contribute to this (mis)match? Is an implied linguistic norm evident in the admissions requirements? What additional burdens does the university place on students who diverge from that norm? How does the university support (or fail to support) such students? What is the role of first-year writing in any of this? Of course, we must also attend to the particular backgrounds of the students in our classrooms, some of whom will represent racial and/or linguistic identities US society is structured to largely exclude from higher education. Heightening our awareness of these structures of exclusion and their relationship(s) to our particular institutions—to the extent that our classrooms operate as segregated spaces—will better attune us to the specific challenges these students face.

The process of (re)framing the classroom as a segregated space need not include explicit class discussions with students—again, my goal is to outline pedagogical moves that do not presume particular course content—but instructors who do want to raise issues of race and language ideology in the classroom can involve students in the (re)framing process. For instance, instructors could provide readings and data that invite students to investigate the ways American universities, as institutions situated within a broadly segregated society, are designed to *exclude* linguistic and racial difference even while typically upholding a vague notion of "diversity" as an institutional value. Students' investigations of linguistic and racial exclusion could then set up the exigence for pursuing a pedagogy that maximizes *inclusion* within the complex space of the composition classroom—paving the way for composition instructors to introduce a translingual pedagogy geared toward such aims. For example, composition instructors might ask students to examine both the financial costs and admissions requirements at their university. Comparing these data with the demographic composition of recent entering classes would enable students to make inferences about the connections among language, race, and access to higher education—especially if coupled with a broader investigation of the correlation between race and poverty in the United States. By asking students to consider how race and language are related and how these relationships impact who can access and afford to pursue higher education, composition instructors can help shed light on the workings of monolingual ideology in higher education institutions and US society more broadly.

For instructors interested in using the classroom to explore the relationship(s) between segregated spaces and higher education in more depth, the common assignment of the literacy narrative—often the culminating project of the first unit in first-year composition classes—could provide one fitting opportunity to do so. This assignment could ask students to consider the degree of racial and socioeconomic segregation or integration that structured their own schooling experiences and to further reflect on how such segregation or integration contributed to their literacy development. What educational opportunities were provided to or withheld from them? How has this personal history led them to their particular university and program of study? And how might race—and, more specifically, racial segregation—have played a role?

Regardless of whether instructors choose to discuss racial segregation in their classes, (re)framing the classroom as a segregated space leads to the second pedagogical move outlined above: intentionally bringing into the classroom voices and language practices that segregation excludes. This move, of course, would need to be adapted to fit the particular aims and content of the course. For example, I taught a first-year writing course at U of L in which we investigated the rhetorical construction of "West Louisville" in local public discourse from a variety of different angles. The class, which included two African American students, two Asian American students, and seventeen White students—reasonably representative, in terms of racial demographics, of U of L's broader student population—consisted overwhelmingly of Jefferson County residents; sixteen of the twenty-one students were from Jefferson County, and three more were from neighboring Kentucky counties. Yet none of these students were from West Louisville, and only a handful had even *been* to West Louisville. To bring West Louisville voices into the classroom, we read selections from a collection of narratives written by West End high school students and published by a local nonprofit organization. Obviously, including such texts in a composition course does not nearly remedy the exclusion of West Louisville residents from the classroom through various processes of de facto segregation; however, I argue that it's better than leaving these voices unacknowledged entirely. Community-engaged pedagogies, if thoughtfully implemented, could perhaps better accomplish the goal of bringing those voices and language practices into the classroom that segregation systematically excludes (e.g., Grobman 2017).

Finally and perhaps most important, a translingual pedagogy for segregated spaces requires that instructors consciously adopt strategies that minimize their role in perpetuating the violence of segregation. Assessment plays a key role here. As Asao Inoue (2017, 120–21) has argued, "A classroom cannot view language difference (from a hegemonic norm) as a resource for learning while at the same time penalizing students for practicing that difference. Thus, the ecologies created by our writing assessments are the conditions in which translingual pedagogies will succeed or fail." An anti-racist, translingual assessment ecology for the segregated classroom avoids imposing monolingual ideological standards on student writing, such as through labor-based grading contracts (Inoue 2017), with the goal of minimizing the linguistic violence perpetrated against those students whose language practices are most likely to have been historically—and, in many cases, contemporarily—shut out from higher education.

The pedagogical moves I have explored here will not, of course, redress the structural racism and monolingual ideology that figure many college composition classrooms as segregated spaces. Nor will these moves necessarily produce students who are prepared to critique the fundamentally racist nature of American institutions writ large. Rather, it is my hope that these moves can help promote translingual pedagogies that take racial difference seriously while still acknowledging linguistic difference as the norm of language use. By situating composition classrooms within the broader structures of racially and socioeconomically segregated literacy education in the US, composition instructors can teach with greater awareness of the connections among language, race, class, and access to opportunities that remain central to the project of promoting linguistic and social justice in the United States.

NOTES

1. One logical extension of this argument is that distinctions between de jure and de facto segregation in higher education may miss the point. That is, while the overt, de jure racial segregation of educational institutions is no longer legal, the de facto segregation that persists cannot be separated from the history and legacy of de jure segregation.
2. For a full account of governments' implication in residential segregation, see Rothstein (2017).
3. Gary Orfield moved from Harvard University to UCLA in 2007 and took the Civil Rights Project with him.

REFERENCES

Bizzell, Patricia. 1994. "'Contact Zones' and English Studies." *College English* 56 (2): 163–69.
Canagarajah, A. Suresh, ed. 2013. *Literacy as Translingual Practice: Between Communities and Classrooms.* New York: Routledge.
Canagarajah, A. Suresh, and Yumi Matsumoto. 2017. "Negotiating Voice in Translingual Literacies: From Literacy Regimes to Contact Zones." *Journal of Multilingual and Multicultural Development* 38 (5): 390–406.
"East vs. West." 2017. *Louisville Magazine*, 54–55.
"Fast Facts." 2018. *About: Jefferson Community and Technical College*, Jefferson Community and Technical College. https://jefferson.kctcs.edu/about/college-at-a-glance/index.aspx. Accessed March 25, 2018.
Gilyard, Keith. 2016. "The Rhetoric of Translingualism." *College English* 78 (3): 284–89.
Grobman, Laurie. 2017. "'Engaging Race': Teaching Critical Race Inquiry and Community-Engaged Projects." *College English* 80 (2): 105–32.
Hall, R. Mark, and Mary Rosner. 2004. "Pratt and Pratfalls: Revisioning Contact Zones." In *Crossing Borderlands: Composition and Postcolonial Studies*, ed. Andrea A. Lunsford and Lahoucine Ouzgane, 95–109. Pittsburgh: University of Pittsburgh Press.
Horner, Bruce, Min-Zhan Lu, Jacqueline Jones Royster, and John Trimbur. 2011. "Language Difference in Writing: Toward a Translingual Approach." *College English* 73 (3): 303–21.
Horner, Bruce, and Laura Tetrault, eds. 2017. *Crossing Divides: Exploring Translingual Writing Pedagogies and Programs.* Logan: Utah State University Press.
Inoue, Asao. 2017. "Writing Assessment as the Conditions for Translingual Approaches." In *Crossing Divides: Exploring Translingual Writing Pedagogies and Programs*, ed. Bruce Horner and Laura Tetrault, 119–34. Logan: Utah State University Press.
Lu, Min-Zhan. 1994. "Professing Multiculturalism: The Politics of Style in the Contact Zone." *College Composition and Communication* 45 (4): 442–58.
Lu, Min-Zhan, and Bruce Horner. 2013. "Translingual Literacy, Language Difference, and Matters of Agency." *College English* 75 (6): 582–607.
Orfield, Gary, Jongyeon Ee, Erica Frankenberg, and Genevieve Siegel-Hawley. 2016. "*Brown* at 62: School Segregation by Race, Poverty, and State." *Civil Rights Project / Proyecto Derechos Civiles*, UCLA, May 16.

Orfield, Gary, and Chungmei Lee. 2004. "*Brown* at 50: King's Dream or *Plessy*'s Nightmare?" *The Civil Rights Project*, Harvard University, January 18. https://www.gse.harvard.edu/news/04/01/brown-50-kings-dream-or-plessys-nightmare. Accessed April 1, 2018.

Pratt, Mary Louise. 1991. "Arts of the Contact Zone." *Profession*: 33–40.

"Profile." 2018. *About UofL*, University of Louisville. http://louisville.edu/about/profile. Accessed March 23, 2018.

"Quick Facts: Jefferson County, Kentucky." 2017. *United States Census Bureau*. Washington, DC: United States Census Bureau. https://www.census.gov/quickfacts/fact/table/jeffersoncountykentucky/PST045217. Accessed March 17, 2018.

Rothstein, Richard. 2017. *The Color of Law: A Forgotten History of How Our Government Segregated America*. New York: Liveright.

"Tuition and Fees." 2018a. *Affording College*, Jefferson Community and Technical College. https://jefferson.kctcs.edu/affording-college/tuition-costs/index.aspx. Accessed March 15, 2018.

"Tuition and Fees." 2018b. *Office of Admissions*, University of Louisville. https://louisville.edu/admissions/cost-aid/tuition. Accessed March 12, 2018.

11
THE RACIOLINGUISTICS OF TRANSLINGUAL LITERACIES

Steven Alvarez

The liberatory potential of translingual literacies—literacy practices that move beyond and between standardized language systems—is the power to demystify monolingualist ideologies that dominate the lived, meaning-making experiences of communities. Translingualism presents an alternative paradigm to monoglossic language ideologies that understand language as a standardizable entity. Translingualism instead understands the fluidity of languages and literacies as social practices, interactions, and negotiations, all embedded in dynamic relations of power. Too often overlooked, I believe, are the dynamics of race in these power dynamics when we use a translingual lens. That is, even with the liberatory potential to embrace students' sophisticated translingual repertoires, for certain people this movement poses different rewards, different risks, different levels of policing—even when certain bodies perform the dominant, standardized English. Further, for language minoritized students of color, their language and literacy practices are constantly pathologized, even when they perform standardized English on assessment measures. As Nelson Flores and Jonathan Rosa (2015) argue, this discourse of semilingualism—a type of bilingual extraction—or of subtracting students' home languages particularly affects communities of color whereas White students are celebrated for their additive multilingualism, which becomes cause for multicultural celebration. In this way, language policing happens in unequal ways, thus reinforcing and reproducing social inequalities. The "natural" policing of translingual movement across borders is a tactic that reifies borders, the militarization and policing of borders specifically, as well as the reality that this policing is not only linguistic but also racialized. Despite the liberatory potential for translingual literacies to challenge monolingualist ideologies, we must always remember that language, race, and identity are intertwined and that liberation is inextricable for all experiences of oppression. For this reason, each of the chapters in this collection has spoken to approaches for realizing a race-conscious translingualism, what I identify as a raciolinguistic framework for translingual literacies.

A raciolinguistic perspective opens critiques of how translingual policing across contexts becomes inscribed as practice and how standardization as practice becomes a tool to mask systemic inequalities as individualized deficiencies, especially those that sustain "English-only" ideologies. To this end, I propose a raciolinguistics frame that examines when racially minoritized language practices are policed publicly for racialized people. This element of public policing of race and language starts critical dialogues that challenge relations in the ideologies of race and language "to the ways that race is socially constructed through language but also to the ways that language is socially constructed through race" (Rosa 2019, 7). Critical challenges to misguided, racialized notions of linguistic "deficiency" offer analytical tools for examining the ways "English-only" beliefs further modes of racialized domination. The creativity and criticality of translingual literacies offer some tools in this anti-racist work of imagining a transformed world, a critical translingual approach with a raciolinguistics orientation of naming for social justice. In the case I present, I demonstrate how multilingual individuals of color are targeted for speaking Spanish in public but also how they use their cell phones to document the incident. The all too common videos of such encounters are teachable texts for students to critically study how race and multilingualism are experienced by People of Color.

This sense of criticality layered on top of a translingual orientation builds off the work theorized further by Kate Seltzer's (2017) and Seltzer and Cati de los Ríos's (2018) notion of a "critical translingual approach." A critical translingual approach challenges monolingualist norms that name languages, directly problematizing language ideologies as learned by lived experiences or bordered by ways of thinking about so-called correctness regarding language and the performances of power. These performances call into question the instructor's racialized positionality in productive ways, as well as the demographics of classrooms and, even more broadly, of institutions. The questions expand as the contexts expand, and following students in their research into the social circumstances at their university positions instructors differently. This type of orientation speaks to teachers and researchers to position themselves in a Freirean approach to teaching that de-centers classrooms into student-centered spaces—problematizing dialogues about languages, literacies, and race. Students' voices begin with problematizing experiences in dialogue and by listening and learning—learning from the teaching students shape for themselves. The work of Seltzer and de los Ríos (2018) is important to examine, specifically from the side of English educators doing important literacy research, who should ask how they can transform these structural inequalities in their pedagogies. A critical translingual approach "calls for teachers to shift their stances and resulting instructional designs to make space for students' diverse language practices, voices, and experiences as racialized speakers" (72). This transformative potential begins by recognizing how the dominant forms of racialized standardizing happen in classrooms, across schools, in communities, and in larger policies—becoming a critical perspective that asks more questions, with extended analysis and dialogue.

The theorization of critical translingual literacies builds off this attention to problematizing local historical moments while also turning to the liberatory potential of critical literacy to challenge dominant ideologies about race and language in the lived experiences of people in dialogue. The element of transforming problematized local conditions learned alongside students has been geared toward social justice and using literacy to transform social conditions. Raciolinguistics is grounded in social justice, with a focus of embracing critical literacy research in the practices, performances, and activities of communities that honor the languages of all students—which impacts literacies in classrooms, challenging the sanctioned ordering of socially structured inequalities. I argue for critical translingual pedagogies that demystify raciolinguistic structures, opening students' lived experiences with racialized English-only ideologies (Alim, Rickford, and Ball 2016; Baker-Bell 2017; Flores and Rosa 2015; Seltzer and de los Ríos 2018; Smitherman 2017). This raciolinguistic turn in translingual literacy pedagogy is attuned to the ways dominant narratives about race in the United States frame, conceptualize, police, and silence the plurality of histories and social struggles.

A raciolinguistics positionality layered with a critical translingual orientation has the potential to intersect race, language, power, and local issues of social justice, seeking to look deeper at how race and language cooperate to reproduce hegemonic ideologies and material inequalities—how Whiteness becomes complicit in English-only ideologies specifically. This approach also means learning about historical movements toward bilingual education in the United States led by People of Color and challenging the racialized assumptions of English-only teaching and learning in schools that reproduced social inequalities.

The tradition of critical pedagogy as a means of reading the word to reread the world and the opportunity to rewrite it is where rhetoric and composition offer the liberating potential to envision social justice across languages with attention to racialized identities. I nod to a translingual orientation toward translanguaging practices of students, extending the asset-based K–12 bilingual educational research that honors, explores, and builds on the strengths of communities (García et al. 2013; García and Kleyn 2016; Rosa 2019). I offer a theoretical reconsideration of critical translingual literacies that attends to a raciolinguistics framework. A raciolinguistics frame, however, grounds the work of translingualism in the systemic racial inequalities structured in institutions, in language ideologies that become the smokescreens for racialized injustices (Flores and Rosa 2015). This framework, analyzing English-only ideologies, for example, demystifies ideological promises of upward mobility, assimilation, and diversity with the lived realities of the languages and bodies of People of Color—bodies and languages that are profiled, criminalized, and policed. Where language, race, and power find expression across and between systems, there we can begin to think about border where we challenge colorblind, meritocratic playing fields while also potentially moving to alternative models to understand how "standards" are used as a form of discrimination, both ideologically and in practice. Critical translingual literacy research into the language practices of communities offers methods for de-linking from standardizing notions of English-only ideologies to challenge the reproduction of racialized inequalities inherent in those types of policies as policing. I advocate for literacy researchers to join in dialogue with scholars whose works lead rhetoric and composition and literacy studies further in a "trans" (-lingual, -languaging, -national, -literacies, -generational, -cultural) analytic framework across disciplines and speak to research about race, especially literacy and race research in education and the social sciences.

RACIALIZED TRANSLINGUAL LITERACIES

Rather than ignore multilingualism or perceive it as a problem, translingual literacy begins with an understanding that communication is always negotiated, mobile, and diverse (Canagarajah, 2013b; Lu and Horner 2013; Horner et al. 2011). As semiotic practice, Suresh Canagarajah (2013a, 41) defines translingual literacy as "an understanding of the production, circulation, and reception of texts that are always mobile; that draw from diverse languages, symbol systems, and modalities of communication; and that involve inter-community negotiations." In practice, individuals extend their literacy repertoires as they develop stocks of practical, translingual experiences from which to strategically perform daily activities, forming different power relations in highly mobile contexts.

Emi Otsuji and Alastair Pennycook (2018) further conceptualize translingualism as distributed linguistic and learning practices, which are advantageous under certain circumstances. Pennycook (2019, 170) further elaborates that a translingual advantage "may occur when a student is able to use a variety of linguistic and other resources in their learning but will not do so when these resources are denied or denigrated." This sense of exclusion or self-censorship of a multilingual student's full translingual repertoire has been a key focus for translingual researchers and educators who turn to approaches that instead honor students' language diversity, even if this has meant debunking long-held purist assumptions about standardized English and forms of "proper" writing.

The translingual view may remain contrary to that of language purists, but the translingual orientation also acknowledges the hybridity of the everyday practices plurilingual communities develop in their situated contexts. Translingual literacies acknowledge ethical values associated with pluralism and power and the suitability of negotiating differences and navigating strategies for reception and interpretation. This dimension of translingual literacies enables a consideration of communicative competence as not restricted to predefined meanings of individual languages but instead as practices that shuttle across languages in situated interactions. Communicative shuttling, however, does not account for the ways race affects and impacts translingual literacy practices.

Canagarajah (2013a) contends that translingual literacies are always negotiated and exploratory in social contexts. He further theorizes these translocal practices "as routinized sets of activities relating to specific forms of literacies in specific bounded communities. These data suggest that the practices involved in negotiated literacy are of a different order. Rather than being routinized, they are more exploratory. Rather than being sedimented by the history and culture of local literacies, they are more heuristic in negotiating difference in the contact zone" (61). The structuring of routines to practice is body-specific but also cultural in its communication-generating possibilities for knowing and for making. Further, because these literacies that are critical and creative are not bound to history, they have the potential for hybridity. For Canagarajah, this aspect of negotiating the personal and communal as a translingual practice becomes a tool for remixing and disrupting language ideologies.

While we can appreciate Canagarajah's (2013a) argument for mixing languages, we also have to account for the notions of "native" and what mixing means historically in the Americas and whether his idea of "being sedimented by the history and culture of local literacies" can truly be a possibility. That is, historically, European forms of literacy have been used as tools for warfare and the policing of "native" peoples for over 500 years, including those forms of literacy used to classify racial mixture in the Americas. Indeed, a critical translingual orientation is important to consider so we treat "languages as always in contact and mutually influencing each other, with emergent meanings and grammars" (41), but while being attentive to power dynamics in contexts and to history. We should also use these critical translingual literacies to challenge ideologies that encourage standardizing forms of language practices that sustain racialized inequalities and that have been used to police peoples and their languages throughout history and in the present. For this, understanding how White supremacy has been associated with European languages across the hemisphere can extend the historical project into larger questions regarding colonial rule in the Americas, including the United States.

Canagarajah and Xuesong Gao (2019) make a point about future translingual scholarship turning to diverse language histories beyond English or moving away from an "English+" in this type of research. No doubt, understanding racial dynamics in those contexts will also be important to contextualize globally, as will the ways languages and contact have historically been sites of contention in struggles for dominance—that is, standardization. Canagarajah and Gao also point to a common misunderstanding about translingualism "disregarding established norms of communication" (2). This critique reinforces notions about doing a "disservice" to students who come to writing courses with hopes of improving their standardized language performance for educational mobility. These critiques, however, completely miss the mark regarding translingual orientations to teaching and regarding students' language practices. In fact, translingualism conceptualizes the ways language norms are always both present and implied, articulated and not, but always engaged in power dynamics with different language systems. Further, translingualism looks to the real ways multilingual people "creatively and strategically renegotiate the norms for voice" (2), locating this negotiation as the site of struggles that happen on micro- and macro-scales.

Translingual literacy studies has contributed to a necessary shift in literacy studies by discussing ways such an orientation treats heterogeneity in contact zones as the norm rather than the exception. From the historical legacies of race in the United States, however, translingualism has much to address with regard to racialized ideologies masked by language, ideologies that are masked both intentionally and not. April Baker-Bell (2017, 101) describes this as linguistic racism, a racialized policing of language and literacy practices that reproduces inequalities "normalized in classrooms every day through disciplinary discourses, curricular choices, and pedagogical practices." On this point, Keith Gilyard (2016, 285) critiques translingual scholarship for eliding issues of race and racism in its construction of the "linguistic everyperson," a construct that flattens linguistic difference, overlooks the material and political consequences of linguistic differences, and ignores the struggles of racialized minorities for linguistic legitimacy. No doubt, the "linguistic everyperson" is a theoretical construct imagined as having the privileges of Whiteness.

Critical translingual literacies from a raciolinguistics turn position the discourses of race as front and center and as symptomatic of larger systems of racialized inequalities that permeate the social order. The linguistic inequalities a translingual orientation takes as a given, raciolinguistics notes, also further racialize inequalities mapped onto the social structure. A raciolinguistic approach that is critical challenges the ways language and race further dehumanize projects that reproduce domination. According to Rosa (2019, 6), "A raciolinguistic perspective must be informed by a theory of change that is focused on reconstituting or eradicating systems of domination, such as racial capitalism, white supremacy, and the normative modes of colonial subject formation that organize these systems rather than modifying the embodied communicative behaviors of racially minoritized individuals." Raciolinguistic ideologies "produce racialized speaking subjects who are constructed as linguistically deviant even when engaging in linguistic practices positioned as normative or innovative when produced by privileged white subjects" (Flores and Rosa 2015, 150). That is, the privileged position of Whiteness always has additive elements for translingual learning while dismissing and/or "subtracting" the translingual practices of communities of color. People of Color, even if practicing standardized language and literacy forms, are socially marked as "deviant" because of their bodies by a normative White gaze. Flores and Rosa describe the normative gaze as one that idealizes the linguistic practices of Whiteness and forms categories of deviance for minoritized communities.

Flores and Rosa's (2015) theory of raciolinguistics de-focalizes racialized ideologies masked by language. Indeed, for decades, sociolinguists have warned that political struggles between and across languages serve as smokescreens for other inequalities (Zentella 1997). For Flores and Rosa (2015), the ideological position and mode of perception that shape a racialized society constitute the "white gaze." A core tenet of raciolinguistics is to demystify this White gaze. They write: "A raciolinguistic perspective seeks to understand how the white gaze is attached both to a speaking subject who engages in the idealized linguistic practices of whiteness and to a listening subject who hears and interprets the linguistic practices of language-minoritized populations as deviant based on their racial positioning in society as opposed to any objective characteristics of their language use" (151). Probing these "deviant" practices as ideological constructions, linked to the system of racialized oppression; policing; languaging; and demystifying the White gaze are at the heart of a raciolinguistics pedagogy. Critical translingual literacies offer a useful theoretical orientation that can assist in challenging the White gaze as it permeates monolingualized assumptions for language education policies. From a raciolinguistics perspective, the contact zones of translingual literacies have the potential to dismantle minoritizing orientations that arbitrarily assume the existence of linguistic borders and structured inequalities linked to race. But a translingual orientation that does not give critical attention to the dynamics of race overlooks the ways social practices by different groups are socially structured to reproduce and police inequalities.

I propose that raciolinguistics represents another avenue by which rhetoric and composition can further add to conversations that examine how critical translingual literacy practices and cultural rhetorics can potentially offer open spaces for intersectional theorizing and pedagogies. Raciolinguistics and critical translingual literacy studies are a means to critique discourses that codify language standardization, privileging monolingualism and Whiteness. De-linking from such ideologies and practices demands that language and literacy researchers focus on struggles for language legitimacy across different contexts to understand how monolingualized orientations to standardization and concentrating power have constituted racially minoritized populations.

"WE SPEAK ENGLISH IN AMERICA"

To illustrate a potential text that could examine the racialized elements of translingualism for students, I offer a discussion of a viral video depicting a confrontation at a breakfast restaurant (Daily Picks and Flicks 2015). On July 31, 2015, Carlos Vasquez and his mother were harassed by an elderly White woman at an IHOP in Los Angeles. The video takes place in the line awaiting entrance to the restaurant and captures a racialized encounter about speaking Spanish in public. After a few moments of being insulted for speaking Spanish in public, Vasquez began to record the interaction on his cell phone where he confronts the racist English-only ideologies voiced by the woman. Vasquez shared the video on Facebook, and it went viral.

In the video, the woman verbally attacked Ms. Vasquez, saying:

- "We want English. We don't want the Nazis back. We don't want the fascists back. We don't want Castro back."
- "You go back to Spain!"
- "Spanish is from Spain."
- "I don't want Spanish, I've been to Spain."

Whether the woman harassing the Vasquezes spoke English in Spain is another question altogether. The arguments the woman makes equating linguistic diversity with fascism ring hollow in her own fascist attempts to publicly police the languages of People of Color. The use of "go back" reinforces the argument that immigrants are outsiders and perpetual threats to the White status quo. The racist undertones to the woman's rhetoric are clear, as is the way she masks what she says in language policing. Ms. Vasquez defends herself from the racist attacks by speaking in English to the woman, speaking to the dignity of her language, her work, and her life. It is painful to watch, as Ms. Vasquez becomes emotional; in tears she chimes back at the woman who has just called her "trash": "I speak English too! Not good, but I speak English. I have a job in this country, I have a job in this country! I clean offices, I clean restrooms. I speak English!"

This painful episode directly illustrates how monolingualism and race are bound together in the lived experiences of People of Color and also how their languages are policed. As I watch this video, I marvel at how such a racist assumption about the illegitimacy of speaking Spanish in public could be defended by a woman who was ordering pancakes at a Koreatown location of IHOP in Los Angeles. Further, how could this racist woman assume linguistic superiority when the woman she attacked was bilingual?

Videos such as this one naturally elicit discussions from students that open classes to debates about how race, language, and power are observable in everyday instances. Raciolinguistics gives a lens to these types of translingual "negotiations" in which bilingualism, power, racism, and history are overwhelming. Yes, we can use translingualism to study how the speakers moved across languages in the interaction and also the language ideology inherent in the dehumanizing rhetoric of the attacker. But not examining race, language, power, and, in this case, social media would limit the possibilities for potentially transforming situations like this in the future—and there will be more, unfortunately. The confrontation in this viral video dramatizes raciolinguistic struggles in illustrative ways but also leads students to ask how they can prevent such injustices and how they could read the situation and potentially rewrite it. The demystification of the White gaze, therefore, becomes the first project of interpretation, which, again, is the basis for a raciolinguistics approach. Layered on the policing of languages, we can see how a critical translingual orientation to raciolinguistics can be a useful set of tools.

CLASSROOM PRAXIS AND ETHNOGRAPHY

Raciolinguistics and translingual literacy research begins with a method of demystifying standardized notions of official literacies linked to Whiteness to challenge the policing and reproduction of such social inequalities. The demystification happens at multiple levels, from micro-, individualized experiences with language and race and resonating further in macro-waves into the larger social order. Thinking of research in this frame honors the lived experiences of all, and a teaching praxis can develop from the theorizations community as local narratives become participatory action research when writing about the self as researcher connects the self to research projects as participant and informant. The significance of educators' self-understanding requires inquiry into false beliefs and mis-recognitions in maintaining power in privilege (Bourdieu 2000). This realistic turn to race in everyday experience is of primary importance to decode. Raciolinguistics asks us to consider our students' lived experiences from the way they understand the situation. That said, educators feel a certain pressure to steer away from critically probing deeper into structural aspects of race that affect students as well as teaching colleagues. A raciolinguistics framework analyzes what is appropriate but also the ways voices are appropriated and how the racializing White gaze projects deviance onto the linguistic productions of marginalized students. Layered with a critical translingual orientation, raciolinguistics as pedagogy will open up new avenues of assessment, new strategies to understand intelligence, and writing projects that ask students to research their lived experiences of race and language in their communities.

To accomplish much of this, I suggest that educators adopt ethnographic methodologies that position students as researchers conducting fieldwork in their communities. Maisha T. Winn and Latrise Johnson (2011, 71) build on the literacy research of Valerie Kinloch (2009), offering two ideas about students becoming ethnographers: "Students can be involved in participatory action projects such as examining 'spatial location and demographic trends' in their community . . . and study the linguistic practices of others through close listening." Creative writing genres such as memoirs, poetry, and fiction can also become expressive outlets, especially when students research, listen to, and learn with and from communities. This kind of work leads students to share uncovered research about local demographics and represent the voices of communities, in particular racially and linguistically minoritized communities. The ethnographer-student thus mediates between community audiences and participants, between representations and stories with subjective experiences, while being attuned to the affordance of different genres. This ethnographic stance fits perfectly with a raciolinguistics pedagogy in which students-as-researchers pose arguments about themselves, their intentions in their research, and their research questions. As a methodology, this kind of ethnographic approach entails students doing a great deal of informal writing, such as taking field notes and conducting and transcribing interviews. It also contributes to students' increasing awareness of social and cultural contexts and works to build confidence, voice, and valuable research experience. This requires listening, sharing stories, and time—lots of time. Writing courses at all levels stand to gain by incorporating ethnography and ethnography projects that take students into communities to conduct field research as homework. To further gain social perspectives, students can engage in ethnographic homework projects involving groups of students of different backgrounds, each taking part in researching classmates' homes and languages for writing. Students would thereby practice reflexive critical thinking skills, resulting in relevant language arts homework projects rooted in students' lived experiences.

Writing projects that ask students to gather field notes on language uses in their homes and communities can invite diverse participants as informants, including individuals who speak, read, and write different languages and who experience race differently. Teams of students taking on projects in which they explore their classmates' languages and literacies have much to offer when sharing language differences within the classroom community. Students called upon to translanguage fieldwork data in discussion workshops demonstrate to fellow fieldworkers how tactics to interpret language are enhanced with theoretical frameworks, such as raciolinguistics. Supplementing research that involves local perspectives as well as student research would lead to ethnographic projects that extend over time for increased complexity. In addition, transmodal projects that combine texts, translations, and images for both research sources and student-led publications would invite dynamic ways of synthesizing and communicating information. For those with the luxury of time, a portfolio project of student work—perhaps the author's self-published volume, a series of books by students, or an anthology—could become a text to share with students and members of the community. Projects that relate directly to communities could also become shared spaces for dialogues with students' work, showcasing direct community research. The collecting and sharing of stories quickly becomes a literacy project that has the potential to tap into the local community and engage students with their lived experiences as they become critically aware of their lives as topics for research. In other words, when students begin to research their own local positioning, they do so from a research stance, trying to make strange their sense of the everyday. This reorientation of participant observation and action results in the narrating of their own and others' stories in a new way, as students learn to negotiate their voice and their authority and gain confidence in representing elements of the communities and expertise from their lives. Such projects engage parents and local communities in conversations about race, language, educational goals, motivations, and the ways reading and writing are used expressively in community literacy projects.

REFERENCES

Alim, H. Samy, John R. Rickford, and Arnetha F. Ball, eds. 2016. *Raciolinguistics: How Language Shapes Our Ideas about Race.* New York: Oxford University Press.

Baker-Bell, April. 2017. "'I Can Switch My Language, but I Can't Switch My Skin': What Teachers Must Understand about Linguistic Racism." In *The Guide for White Women Who Teach Black Boys: Understanding, Respecting, Connecting,* ed. Eddie Moore, Ali Michael, and Marguerite W. Penick-Parks, 97–107. Thousand Oaks, CA: Corwin.

Bourdieu, Pierre. 2000. *Pascalian Meditations.* Translated by Richard Nice. Stanford, CA: Stanford University Press.

Canagarajah, Suresh. 2013a. "Negotiating Translingual Literacy: An Enactment." *Research in the Teaching of English* 48 (1): 40–67.

Canagarajah, Suresh. 2013b. *Translingual Practice: Global Englishes and Cosmopolitan Relations.* New York: Routledge.

Canagarajah, Suresh, and Xuesong Gao. 2019. "Taking Translingual Scholarship Further." *English Teaching and Learning* 43 (1): 1–3.

Daily Picks and Flicks. 2015. "Racist Lady Orders Hispanic Woman to Speak English." YouTube video, 3:22. August 4. https://www.youtube.com/watch?v=X2rKv-IDhJ8. Accessed April 18, 2022.

Flores, Nelson, and Jonathan Rosa. 2015. "Undoing Appropriateness: Raciolinguistic Ideologies and Language Diversity in Education." *Harvard Education Review* 85 (2): 149–71.

García, Ofelia, and Tatyana Kleyn, eds. 2016. *Translanguaging with Multilingual Students: Learning from Classroom Moments.* New York: Routledge.

García, Ofelia, Heather H. Woodley, Nelson Flores, and Haiwen Chu. 2013. "Latino Emergent Bilingual Youth in High Schools: Transcaring Strategies for Academic Success." *Urban Education* 48 (6): 798–827.

Gilyard, Keith. 2016. "The Rhetoric of Translingualism." *College English* 78 (3): 284–89.

Horner, Bruce, Min-Zhan Lu, Jacqueline Jones Royster, and John Trimbur. 2011. "Language Difference in Writing: Toward a Translingual Approach." *College English* 73 (3): 303–21.

Kinloch, Valerie. 2009. *Harlem on Our Minds: Place, Race and the Literacies of Urban Youth.* New York: Teachers College Press.

Lu, Min-Zhan, and Bruce Horner. 2013. "Translingual Literacy, Language Difference, and Matters of Agency." *College English* 75 (6): 582–607.

Otsuji, Emi, and Alastair Pennycook. 2018. "The Translingual Advantage: Metrolingual Student Repertoires." In *Plurilingualism in Teaching and Learning: Complexities across Contexts*, ed. Julie Choi and Sue Ollerhead, 71–88. New York: Routledge.

Pennycook, Alastair. 2019. "From Translanguaging to Translingual Activism." In *Decolonizing Foreign Language Education: The Miseducation of English and Other Colonial Languages*, ed. Donaldo Macedo, 169–85. New York: Routledge.

Rosa, Jonathan. 2019. *Looking Like a Language, Sounding Like a Race: Raciolinguistic Ideologies and the Learning of Latinidad.* New York: Oxford University Press.

Seltzer, Kate. 2017. " 'Resisting from Within': (Re)imagining a Critical Translingual English Classroom." PhD diss., CUNY Graduate Center, New York, NY.

Seltzer, Kate, and Cati V. de los Ríos. 2018. "Translating Theory to Practice: Exploring Teachers' Raciolinguistic Literacies in Secondary English Classrooms." *English Education* 51 (1): 49–79.

Smitherman, Geneva. 2017. "Raciolinguistics, 'Mis-Education,' and Language Arts Teaching in the 21st Century." *Language Arts Journal of Michigan* 32 (2): 4–14.

What's Trending Now. 2015, August 3. *Woman Goes on Racist Rant at IHOP* [video]. YouTube. https://www.youtube.com/watch?v=qgpqo_doz5c. Accessed May 12, 2022.

Winn, Maisha T., and Latrise Johnson. 2011. *Writing Instruction in the Culturally Relevant Classroom.* Urbana, IL: NCTE.

Zentella, Ana Celia. 1997. *Growing up Bilingual: Puerto Rican Children in New York.* New York: Wiley-Blackwell.

12
PARTICIPATORY RESEARCH, HOME LANGUAGE, AND RACE-CONSCIOUS TRANSLINGUALISM

Shawanda Stewart and Brian Stone

For racial groups who are regularly marginalized, the constant reminder of race and racism persists in their everyday experience. It is not a theoretical construct or concept; it is real. It is alive and material, and it extends beyond theories and best practices. When misunderstood or denied, it has the ability to steal a person's livelihood; and to reframe translingual theory, practice, and pedagogy to better engage with questions of race and racism, we must first acknowledge the ways language ideologies that privilege certain language use over others are closely tied to racist ideologies that perpetuate racism in our classrooms. In this chapter, we will use critical race theory (CRT) as a framework to attend to issues of race and racism in college composition classrooms and make a case for participatory action research (PAR) of language practices in students' own communities (or communities of interest) as one way to conceptualize a race-conscious translingualism in the composition classroom. We share findings from a Conference on College Composition and Communication Research Initiative Grant–funded study of a piloted composition curriculum and pedagogy we call "Critical Hip Hop Rhetoric Pedagogy," and we share the successes and challenges of the study in light of translingual work.

We define a race-conscious translingualism as an orientation to linguistic practices that centers racialized linguistic experience and the fluid, dynamic nature of language and language users. However, translingualism is an "unsettled term" (Horner and Tetreault 2017, 4), and scholars still debate its definition. Yet Bruce Horner and Laura Tetreault (2017) have identified shared alignments in the various theoretical and pedagogical translingual approaches in composition studies. They summarize the situation:

First, they [translingual approaches] signal the acceptance of the copresence of more than one language as the norm of communicative situations rather than a deviation from that norm. Second, they signal the fluidity of the defining boundaries between these languages. Third, and relatedly, they position language use as entailing the mixing and changing of different languages, and fourth, and also relatedly, they grant agency to language users to do so rather than seeing such mixing and changing as evidence of linguistic failure, cognitive incompetence, or cultural threat. (4–5).

In contemporary translingual work, language is also considered within material social history and not as a static entity unrelated to states of affairs; which is to say, translingualism pushes us beyond a Saussurean view of language as a system of codes. A translingual orientation should also take into consideration racial identity and history, as well as agency and fluidity. As Asao Inoue (2017, 119–20) explains, "Translingual approaches understand language is not static and see variation in language use by individuals and groups as both naturally occurring and a strength in the writing classroom . . . translingual approaches to language attempt to use difference and diversity in language practices as the materials for comparing and questioning all language norms and practices." Thus, a raced translingualism considers the norms and commonalities within racial groups while also acknowledging linguistic practices as local, situated, and continuously in flux; each individual student has a unique language practice and history.

Hip-Hop offers an ideal source of investigation and reflection on the nature of linguistic practices that allows us to encourage student critical engagement. As Geneva Smitherman (1997) writes, rap has its origins in the Black oral tradition and its foundation in the response to the day's social concerns. The same holds true today. Before we go further into this, we will situate raced translingualism within the greater context of critical approaches to language education in composition.

LARGER CONTEXT: LANGUAGE AND RACE IN COMPOSITION STUDIES

Since 1974, numerous efforts in composition have attempted to counter deficit notions of linguistic practices of minoritized students. Students' Right to Their Own Language forerunners Geneva Smitherman, Arnetha Ball, and Keith Gilyard have long advocated for language rights for African American students; and many scholars have written about their own personal racialized linguistic experiences, demonstrating how their *race* identity is closely linked to their *language* identity.

For example, in his autobiographical narrative *Voices of the Self*, Gilyard (1991, 27) identifies Black English as his native tongue and writes that it is "the language variety I first acquired and the one I have always been able to use with the greatest facility." He later proclaims that "my proficiency in language use, therefore, was inextricably bound up with my emerging self" (105). Vershawn Ashanti Young (2007) has written about the intersection of race, language, and identity in *Your Average Nigga*, where he offers code meshing as a solution to the linguistic dualism he experienced as a child and as an adult. In his literacy narrative, Young writes that "language is often a touchstone for racial performance" (7) and explains that although he was good at situational code switching and was "embraced and rewarded" (7) at school for it, he "never quite mastered it" (7). Young considers such instruction "racially biased, requiring blacks to separate the codes that bespeak their identities from those they use at school" (7). The complexities of the relationship of race and language have more recently been elucidated in H. Samy Alim, John R. Rickford, and Arnetha F. Ball's (2016) interdisciplinary edited collection of essays, *Raciolinguistics: How Language Shapes Our Ideas about Race*, which includes essays about racing language and languaging race from a sociolinguistic and anthropological perspective. Essays in this collection explore the way language constructs race and how ideas about race influence language use. Sara Alvarez and her colleagues (2017, 32) have challenged the validity of theories of code meshing and code switching—such as Young's (2007)—as linguistic categories, arguing that scholars "must move beyond Saussurean language ideologies" and that such categories "reinforce the view of languages as discrete and bounded objects." Translingualism, in contrast, "is an ongoing effort to disabuse any analysis of such distinctions and sheds light on processes and practices people engage in during their signifying moments beyond the product or form of their language use" (32–33).

This conversation is ongoing. Several composition scholars have drawn attention to the pervasiveness of language ideologies not only in instructional practices that privilege Standard American English (SAE) but also in curriculum design and assessment of both student writing and first-year writing programs. An element of this scholarship that is enduring is the affective, personal dimension of the experience of linguistic discrimination. In his "Foreword: On Antiracist Agendas" in *Performing Antiracist Pedagogy in Rhetoric, Writing, and Communication*, Asao Inoue (2016) describes an encounter he had in school at age seven that occurred among a White teacher, a Black student, and himself. The teacher overheard the Black student refer to Inoue as *honkey* and immediately handled the situation by asking the Black student how he'd feel about being called *nigger*. Making it clear that he is not defending the use of *any* racial slur, Inoue goes on to show how "her [the teacher's] attempt to be antiracist in her classroom practice ended up being racist through the strict enforcement of a rule about racial slurs with no regard to who said what to whom or what racial slur was used, and no regard to our linguistic privacy" (xii). Inoue concludes his narrative with an explanation of how racism works in the classroom:

> So when a teacher treats race as if it is a system of politically equal categories that people fit or place themselves into and see racism as when people associated to one category are slighted or treated differently than those in another, then the method is unfair. That's not how racism works. It works by hierarchical categories, not equal ones. It works by vertically uneven relations to power, not laterally even ones. These things affect rewards and punishments, and in the academy, rewards and punishments mean assessment and grading, opportunities and chances, policies and their methods. (xiii)

Similar to Inoue's caution against viewing race simply as politically equal categories in which people fit is Gilyard's (2016) concern that translingualism risks engaging a "sameness-of-difference model" (287) that can lead to the "flattening of language differences" (284). It is this risked flattening that if persisted can deny the racialized material realities of language and the ways language and race intersect in a manner that defines and shapes one's identity. Alim (2016b, 35) reminds readers that identity is not static, and he theorizes about the intersection of language and race, "paying particular attention to how both social processes mediate and mutually constitute each other." It is Alim's contention—and is indeed the thrust of this entire collection—that language is central in the ways ideas of race are shaped and how race shapes ideas about language.

It is clear that there are a variety of theoretical and pedagogical approaches to race and language in the composition classroom, and the scholarship points to renewed vigor in these areas of inquiry and practice.

LOCAL CONTEXT: CRITICAL HIP-HOP RHETORIC PEDAGOGY AT AN HBU

Huston-Tillotson University (HT) is a private, liberal arts, Historically Black University (HBU) in Austin, Texas, composed of a tight-knit community with a diverse culture. HT has served the African American community in

Austin since the late nineteenth century and was created from a merger of two historically black colleges: Tillotson College and Samuel Huston College. The two colleges merged in 1952 and remained the sole institution of higher education for African Americans in central Texas until the *Brown v. Board of Education* decision in 1954. Huston-Tillotson College achieved university status in 2005. The history of the university is not only alive in lore and institutional ethos but can be witnessed materially in several of the buildings that were named after university presidents and faculty who were active in the struggle for racial equality, including Karl Everette Downs and Reuben Shannon Lovinggood.

As of spring 2018, 62 percent of HT students identified as Black, and 27 percent identified as Hispanic/Latino (Office of Institutional Planning, Research, and Assessment 2018, 2). The school is located on the east side of Austin in a formerly segregated (due to Jim Crow segregation laws)—and rapidly gentrifying—African American neighborhood, so racial identity is central to student life and the general education curriculum at HT. At our university, students want an opportunity to speak openly and regularly about race and their racialized experiences, and student activities often deal with race-related community concerns—many of which have affected students personally in some way or another. In addition, students' interests in race-related topics and experiences present themselves in their chosen essay topics and shared experiences and examples during class discussions. It is within this institutional context that the present study was set.

In the fall semester of 2015, just two weeks after the one-year anniversary of the police shooting death of unarmed teenager Michael Brown in St. Louis and in the midst of the rise of the Black Lives Matter movement—a movement felt strongly on the HT campus—we piloted a first-year writing course based on Hip-Hop and language. In this course, we synthesized multidisciplinary perspectives on race, language, and pedagogy—especially participatory action research—to create a curricular intervention that prioritized student linguistic experience in the curriculum and acknowledged student experience and knowledge. The curriculum and pedagogy embraced translingual practices as a means of gaining academic confidence and developing a positive identity as a student writer.

Drawing from H. Samy Alim's phraseology and scholarship, we developed a critical pedagogy we termed "Critical Hip Hop *Rhetoric* Pedagogy" (CHHRP) designed to *center* students and their language practices and preferences in the course. This was realized curricularly through a high-stakes writing assignment, a "linguistic profile essay," in which students wrote about language use in a particular community to which they belong, are familiar with, and/or have an interest in learning about. In this chapter we share our analysis of students' essays, as well as examples of a typical case (Mitchell 1984). Below, we explain how this assignment, which includes participatory action research, enables students to engage in the translingual practice of constructing and negotiating meaning in and across various rhetorical, spatial, and temporal contexts and making greater meaning of language ideologies in relation to their personal language choices by "directly confronting English monolingualist expectations" (Horner et al. 2011, 306) through personal interviews.

CRITICAL RACE THEORY

The movement toward a race-conscious composition pedagogy is indebted to the movement for social justice writ large. As such, we offer critical race theory as a framework by dispelling the myth of a post-racial America and the myth of meritocracy by engaging counter-stories to master narratives. Working from a CRT framework includes considering how macro- and micro-level practices and decisions about pedagogy support or deny racism in our classrooms. As Margaret Zamudio and her colleagues (2011, 7) note, "Critical race theory provided educators and students alike with a basis for critical action (i.e., praxis, understood as critically informed action in service of social justice) intended to transform education to better serve the needs of all students." For example, the argument that students *need* SAE for professional success persists in writing departments and classrooms because it is a master narrative that requires countering. In our field, there is common agreement that there is no *standard* written (or spoken) English, yet the rules written in our textbooks are those of SAE. Some argue that there is a need for a *standard* for communication purposes—all of us have had these conversations with our colleagues. As an example, Allen N. Smith (1976, 168) vehemently exclaims in "No One Has a Right to His Own Language": "We teach English as it has come down to us over many centuries of thought and effort." This is a naive conception of language change, and as Thomas Lavelle (2017, 190) has written, such a monolingual language ideology is a "deeply flawed" theory of language that "portrays languages as largely autonomous, largely stable systems" and is indefensible intellectually.

Asao Inoue (2015) has eloquently articulated the significance of racial identity in college opportunities, especially relevant to writing assessment, writing that Hunter Breland " . . . found differences in mean scores on the SAT essay among Asian-American, African-American,

Hispanic, and White racial formations, with African-Americans rated lowest (more than a full point on an 8 point scale) and Hispanic students rated slightly higher (5), yet when looking for differences in mean SAT essay scores of 'English first' (native speakers) or 'English not first' (multilingual) students, they found no statistically significant differences (6)—the mean scores were virtually identical in these two groups" (Inoue 2014, 34). The picture is similar when one looks to academic success at the secondary level, as well as success in first-year writing. H. Samy Alim (2007, 16) has made clear that the further into their education Black students advance, the further behind their White classmates they fall, and language is a crucial factor in this phenomenon. The primacy of SAE has been to the detriment of "cultural and personal identity, education and linguistic ideologies, and diverse language practices" (17); and it supports the myth of meritocracy that "assumes a level playing field where all individuals in society have an equal opportunity to succeed" (Zamudio et al. 2011, 11–12). Like Alim, Young and his coauthors (2014, 56) have called for a writing pedagogy that "presents an alternative vision of language to teachers, one that offers the 'disempowered' a more egalitarian path into Standard English, a route that integrates academic English with their own dialects and that simultaneously seeks to end discrimination"—a counter-story to the meritocracy master narrative. While the approaches of Inoue, Alim, and Young may differ, their work has been critical in drawing attention to the significance of language in the academic success of students from diverse and racialized linguistic backgrounds.

This work to undo the perpetuation of social injustice in the language arts classroom has its foundations in the movement to desegregate America's classrooms. Indeed, an understanding of such educational movements as part of the ongoing process of desegregation is essential. Alim and colleagues (2016a, 3) argue that in the years following the Obama presidency, America has become more segregated (resegregated) since supposed integration and that we are living in a "hyperracial" society. Therefore, such critical writing pedagogies should have a renewed significance and compositionists a renewed responsibility.

Inoue (2015, 26) argues that, in fact, translingualism and multilingual pedagogies can be used as ways of getting around conversations about race in writing studies. However, race is a significant and much needed angle from which to examine expectations in our composition classrooms, and it is our belief that discourses on race and translingualism can work together to productive ends. Alim (2016a, 2) has argued that as scholars "come into a new understanding that language varieties are not just lists of features that belong to a given 'race,' even questioning the very notion of a fixed 'language variety,' we can move toward speaking in terms of the more fluid sense of 'linguistic resources' [and] can now view linguistic resources as being employed by speakers as they shape and engage in processes and projects of identification." Alim is describing a racialized translanguaging. The response to these important theories in composition studies has been persistent, and yet there is still much ground to be gained.

CRITICAL HIP-HOP *RHETORIC* PEDAGOGY

When developing our pedagogical and curricular intervention for our piloted first-year composition course, CHHRP, we wanted students to engage with various speech communities to learn how different communities use language in a variety of contexts, for a variety of purposes, and in a range of genres. We wanted students to come to see language as a dynamic process intimately related to individual identity. More specifically, we wanted students to explore the racial dimensions of translingual practices, such as Hip-Hop. We also believed it was essential to center student language histories and experiences but to avoid essentializing the linguistic experiences of any one group. We used Hip-Hop for the course content and centered students themselves as sources of knowledge in the course. In this way, students analyzed the nuanced meanings, practices, and attributes of Hip-Hop language, culture, and identity—drawing from both course materials and lived experiences.

Students were asked to read and watch a variety of texts, as well as engage with Hip-Hop lyrics and performances. Primary examples included "A Hybrid Tongue or Slanguage?" by Daniel Hernandez and "Hip Hop's Phenomenal Rise" by Laurie Fourquet, balanced with "What Is Academic Writing?" by L. Lennie Irvin. Our goal was to get students to think about the ways language use varies by individual and context and to understand academic language as one language among many rather than *the* correct language. Students analyzed classic rap songs, such as "Dear Mama" by Tupac and "Close Edge" by Mos Def, songs that speak to larger societal and racial issues. Most important, we turned to students as content-area experts and asked them to bring their own playlists to class. Several class periods were dedicated to analyzing Hip-Hop lyrics with which they were familiar and to which they related. This led to conversations about rhetorical and stylistic choices the artists made, as well as a Hip-Hop vocabulary that only those with access to that speech community would fully understand.

In class, some students resisted the idea of a Hip-Hop course because they didn't see how such a course would benefit them. This demonstrated to us the extent to which dominant language ideologies shaped our students' identities. In his reflection of the course, one student, who we will call Sam, wrote about his initial resistance: "English 1301 wasn't like any other English class. This course was all based in language, particularly in Hip-Hop. This gave me doubts of actually attending to the class. Why would I need to take a class that has language and hip hop as the backbone of the course?" Sam's initial reaction to the course (and conversations with him throughout the term) demonstrates the influence of language ideologies. Rusty Barrett explains in *Other People's English* that language ideologies are "the dominant set of commonly held folk beliefs concerning language . . . [that are] primarily forms of social prejudice" (Young, Barrett, and Lovejoy 2014, 17). While having conversations with Sam and other students in the class, it became apparent to us that many of them did not consider Hip-Hop to be *academic*, and they wanted to make sure they were receiving from the course *acceptable* academic instruction—instruction that emphasized what they knew to be appropriate for the academy; that is, pedagogy that included SAE.

However, Sam noted that after he became more familiar with the course and after completing the assignments, not only did he enjoy the course, but he was more confident as a writer. In addition, he learned more about local language use in different communities: "Most of the essays we did all were based on language yes, but it was current language, language we as students either were raised with or interacted with for the most part. Language in our communities, in the social media we were raised with, etc." As Sam came to realize, Hip-Hop grew out of the African American oral tradition, as reflected by many of its distinctive forms such as call and response and signifying (Richardson 2006). Further, as Marcyliena H. Morgan (2014, 68) explains in *Speech Communities*, "Because Hiphop doesn't privilege one dialect over another, Hiphop culture enables all citizens of the Hiphop Nation to reclaim a range of contested languages, identities and powers." Therefore, Hip-Hop is an ideal medium through which to engage students with the precepts of translanguaging and the complexities of race and identity. Making Hip-Hop the primary discourse for this course was a means of making students feel comfortable discussing their own language practices without fear of marginalization while introducing them to the fluid, dynamic nature of both language and identity. The resistance to such a pedagogy and curriculum raises questions and issues we did not anticipate, and this element of student experience in such a course at an HBU—a space where race and identity is central to every element of student life—calls for further research. Though some students were initially resistant to the Hip-Hop curriculum, this was an essential step in introducing them to academic discourse communities and their own fluid and dynamic nature.

TRANSLINGUAL CURRICULUM AND THE LINGUISTIC PROFILE ESSAY

As elaborated above, central to our CHHRP first-year writing course was developing in students an awareness of linguistic practices and their relationship to identity. To achieve this, we created a curriculum that asked students to take on the role of language researchers. The first assignment of the semester was a low-stakes "literacy letter" in which students wrote earnestly about their previous experiences in language arts classes. This was an essential data set for our study and revealed the anxiety students had about writing and writing classes. It also revealed the extent to which the culture of standardized testing and assessment in secondary education had not only instilled anxiety but had shaped language ideology. After this, students composed a "multimodal literacy narrative" in which they narrated their experiences by developing a literacy—alphabetic or otherwise—using a variety of modes, including rap lyrics, performance, images, videos, and other media. Our goal with this assignment was to foster further reflection on linguistic experience and the development of literacies beyond SAE. We encouraged students to write about Hip-Hop and vernacular literacies, but as with the course in general, students were reticent to disclose such narratives.

After this, we introduced the "linguistic profile essay." For this essay, students did primary research and collected data through ethnographic interviews in a speech community of their choice, including friends, family, and/or classmates. We then asked students to reflect on their experience. This assignment responds to Alim's (2007, 17) call to make students "the sources, investigators, and archivers of varied and rich bodies of knowledge rooted in their cultural-linguistic reality." Students were trained in the construction of interview questions, and central to discussion in this unit was the concept of "speech community." Morgan (2014) writes that speech communities are not necessarily groups of people who speak the same language; rather, they are "groups that share values and attitudes about language use, varieties and practices" (1) and "are one way that language ideologies and social identities are formed" (2). Once again, not all students conducted interviews that engaged with linguistic and racial identities. Though we could have required this of students, we wanted to give them agency in choosing their research subjects. Their reticence to do so speaks to the pervasiveness of language ideologies and the challenge composition instructors face in overcoming it. HBUs are, of course, institutions that center experiences of race and racism. Yet even in this context, students were resistant to a raced, translingual pedagogy and curriculum. However, all students did research the intersections of language and identity, whether community, individual, or both. As Alim, Rickford, and Ball (2016, 5) write, "Rather than fixed and pre-determined, racial and ethnic identities are (re)created through continuous and repeated language use"; and so by creating a space where students and faculty could talk openly about their language varieties, race, too, became a part of the conversation (as seen in the examples below). To us, this shows how important it is that theorists and practitioners do not essentialize the linguistic experience of any one group, as each of our students has a unique linguistic experience and identity.

The "linguistic profile" assignment guidelines state:

> To write your essay, you must conduct an interview with someone who is a part of this chosen community and whose language is representative of this place. Please be sure to observe your subject (place and language) closely, and then present what you have learned in a way that both informs and engages readers. You will be a guide for your readers, providing them with valuable details and persuading them of the relevance of language in relation to this place.

Students interviewed individuals from a chosen speech community and reflected on the linguistic practices and identities their respondents revealed. To demonstrate the potential of such participatory action research in an anti-racist, translingual curriculum, we share excerpts from essays written by two students we will call Tonya and James. Tonya interviewed her uncle, who had spent time in jail, and wrote about what she called "jail community language." James interviewed a friend from Jamaica to learn more about the unique attributes of his friend's Patois language and culture.

James interviewed a classmate from Kingston, Jamaica, about his experiences with Jamaican speech communities. This line of inquiry led James to understand regional variation and the ways place—and the history of a place—affects dialect and its close relationship to identity:

> I asked Nathanael if the accent of most Jamaicans is stronger in Kingston compared to being from other places in Jamaica and he said "yes! Kingston is the one place that really cares about the language and tries to

stay with the origin and how they speak." This was very interesting because, I compared it to someone who is from east Texas versus south Texas and it makes sense. People who aren't from texas [*sic*] think that everyone from Texas has the same accent but they don't. Dallas compared to San Antonio is a big difference when it comes to having a southern accent.

Perhaps of greatest importance in this example is the way James connected Nathanael's experience to his own. Nathanael's response also made it clear to James that the way one speaks is closely connected to one's identity. Michael J. Kral and James Allen (2016) state that relationship development is important to participatory action research. They write, "Participatory research emphasizes reciprocity in a respect for local knowledge, belief in democratic principles, and commitment to social justice that leads to positive change" (255). We argue that this type of relationship building is necessary for racing translingualism, which involves students and instructors accepting and acknowledging the ways by which "ethnoracial identities are styled, performed and constructed through minute features of language" (Alim 2016a, 5).

Further, when asking about Creole and its place in education in Jamaica, James discovered the historical and cultural implications of language education:

> He said no country uses creole as an official language in education yet what makes it special is its history. The combination of English and African languages is not unusual and Nathanael gave me several examples of how it isn't. This blend of language is referred to in many different names but Nathanael said for this essay it will be referred to as Patois. "The language reflects the struggles of slavery" Nathanael says and ancestry from Africa as well as the European influences throughout history on the island of Jamaica. Even though it might not be the official language, [it] has come to represent the people, the culture, history and struggles of the lives of many Jamaicans. Even though the worldwide use of English is common, Patois continues to remain important in preserving traditions in Jamaica.

In this paragraph, James demonstrates profound insight into the societal dimensions of language relevant to colonial matrices of power. In his statement "Even though it might not be the official language, [it] has come to represent the people, the culture, history and struggles of the lives of many Jamaicans," James shows both how significant Patois is to his identity and his recognition of its historical and cultural relevance, despite it not being considered the official language. Just as James saw a parallel with his own linguistic experience in Texas, this insight demonstrates the ability of such primary research to bring students to understand the ways language ideologies work and the prevalence of Standard English in his everyday life. In class we can teach students about the relationship between language and power, but in this instance James was able to discover on his own how such relationships affect individuals the world over.

In this example, we see the powerful potential of translingual pedagogies when combined with a raciolinguistic orientation. While scholars and teachers turn to theory and academic publications to elucidate these issues in classrooms, our students are an essential resource for knowledge of language and identity. We must set aside our own presuppositions and allow students to speak to their own linguistic experiences. Also, when James mentions the "blend" of languages, he is shedding light on translingual practices and examining the very nature of language while also considering the role racism plays in marginalizing a language that holds rich historical value. Accordingly, we see here that James's subject, Nathanael, is quite aware of language ideologies and linguistic discrimination. When he writes that "no country uses creole as an official language in education yet what makes it special is its history," Nathanael demonstrates how systemic racism is so commonplace that it disguises itself as *ordinary*. Nathanael's response makes clear that it is the African ancestry of Patois that excludes it from the educational system, an important point for James to reflect on.

Much like James, Tonya's research led her to investigate matrices of power. Her insights go beyond the scope of this chapter, but her choice to interview her uncle who had done time in prison for armed robbery led to intense reflection on criminality and the ways socioeconomics and institutionalized racism relate to high rates of incarceration in Black communities. As for language, Tonya found that even within a prison's walls it is always changing and evolving:

> "In those 27 years did the language in prison change from when you got there to when you were almost done serving your sentence?" nodding his head "Yes, absolutely. Think of jail as being Austin. People come in and out of Austin just like people come in and out of jail. Leaving behind their culture, language that's spoken in their community and also people come in with different personalities. I was gone for a very long time; everything that was going on in the real world was brought to jail but to a certain extent. But language was something that was available and could be passed in and out of jail."

Tonya's uncle reflects on the fluidity and ever changing nature of language, an essential insight. This response prompted Tonya to inquire further into the types of prison discourse that are distinct from those used on the outside:

> Just like slang used on the street, prison language is primarily a spoken language; it can be written down but is not intended to be used for

writing. I asked my uncle about it and he agrees to a certain extent. He says, "In prison you can't just chit chat on the phone whenever and however long you want to. However, you can write letters as much as you want to. In those letters depending on what another inmate and a [sic] outsider is discussing, you have no choice but to write in slang so the mail senders that read it can pass through your letter without rejecting it or reporting you, which could cause more time to be added to your sentence."

From a colonial, historical perspective, such use of language is similar to the coded messages used by slaves to avoid detection by the slave master. While an instructor can discuss these things in class, based on a textbook reading, Tonya was able to realize this function of language as a continuation of these practices that are relevant to her family and thus to her life. As scholars of language with an awareness of the linguistic inheritance of the transatlantic slave trade, we turn such phenomena into objects of inquiry and critique. For a young student, to see firsthand how language reflects and refracts colonial histories and matrices of power and how critical race theory and translingualism is witnessed at home is a profound educational moment because "categories and subgroups, then, are not just matters of theoretical interest. How we frame them determines who has power, voice, and representation, and who does not" (Delgado and Stefancic 2012, 61).

Tonya's final reflection is a fitting place to conclude this chapter:

A lot of African Americans that are in jail share a common ground. Most of them came from the streets or been in the streets, so the language is very much understood between them . . . Slang is a language that will never goes away. It will spread and spread throughout the world. Prison language is nothing but slang and English that is put together . . . Bringing your own slang that no one ever heard of to a prison is very benefited to inmates because it's best to keep from officers. Language is something that brings people together because there are different languages but in every community and every language you will find a lot of similarities. Some words just may have different meaning than the other. Gaining information about another language can be beneficial and helpful *because you never know where life may take you* (emphasis added).

Tonya describes translingualism and linguistic identity with more astuteness than some academics could muster. "Prison language" is an instance of translingualism so clearly caught up in the matrices of colonial power, embodiment, and race that it deserves more attention from scholars. Tonya's final sentiment illuminates the high stakes of academic success for our student body and the reality of which so many of our students are keenly aware. Tonya's insight into the embodiment of linguistic experience—the Black prisoner as opposed to the prison guard or the Black student as opposed to the English teacher—speaks to the savvy awareness our students have of the relationship of language and power.

CONCLUSION

This curriculum and pedagogy, designed for the ends of social justice, had a positive impact on our students. In the quantitative part of our study, we found that there was a statistically significant decrease in the number of students who failed due to not completing high-stakes assignments (Stone and Stewart 2016, 185); students were more likely to engage with and complete these writing tasks. We see PAR and translingual elements of the curriculum as an essential factor in this achievement. Enabling first-year students to actively participate in primary research on language and language use and encouraging them to think about the sociopolitical and historical positioning of language through a critical race lens is important for their coming to an understanding of the ways language and identity intersect. In addition, it is important that researchers continue to listen to student voices at historically Black colleges and universities and that student linguistic experience remains primary in such a course. We must not essentialize student linguistic experience based on race, social class, or any other factor; to do so is to perpetuate the linguistic violence that has led our students to be wary of writing classes.

For example, for the "linguistic profile," we did not require students to profile language use in the communities where they grew up or in Hip-Hop communities. Rather, because we wanted students to conduct research in communities in which they were most interested and comfortable, we left their chosen speech community up to them. And although the pilot was indeed a success, the results were mixed. Such mixed results are not uncommon in translingual interventions. In his response to the collection of essays in *Crossing Divides: Exploring Translingual Writing Pedagogies and Programs*, Lavelle (2017, 193) writes that each chapter "chronicles mixed results, and local conditions—material and ideological—unquestionably influence the outcomes, but those conditions are the starting point for translingual efforts, the dominant givens against which translingual work works." An influential local factor that worked against some students embracing a raced translingual orientation is the belief at HT that SAE is an essential vehicle for academic and professional success for our student body.

As stated earlier, our classrooms, which reflect campus demographics, are composed mostly of Black and Latinx students; although we hoped that more students would want to research communities distinctly distinguishable by race, most did not. Why not? It is our contention that student linguistic identity and experience is unique, and whereas some students may have been interested in examining further language use unique to their speech communities, others were not. Our course content and discussions centered around Hip-Hop acted as the conduit for students to consider a non-SAE language and culture as important, accessible, and completely acceptable in an academic setting. We consider race-conscious translingualism to not only center race but to also offer students the opportunity to choose their racial identities; anything to the contrary risks falling under the sameness-of-difference model mentioned above, even within racial groups. If we are to truly center our students' linguistic experiences, then we should make a space for students to feel comfortable bringing in their vernacular choices, regardless of whether they represent a more standard variety. Linguistic identity is complex, embodied, and caught up in power relations. A student's choice to perform their own identity linguistically is their choice, born of their experience; student agency is essential.

REFERENCES

Alim, H. Samy. 2007. " 'The Whig Party Don't Exist in My Hood': Knowledge, Reality, and Education in the Hip Hop Nation." In *Talkin Black Talk: Language, Education, and Social Change*, ed. H. Samy Alim and John Baugh, 15–29. New York: Teachers College Press.

Alim, H. Samy. 2016a. "Introducing Raciolinguistics: Racing Language and Languaging Race in Hyperracial Times." In *How Language Shapes Our Ideas about Race*, ed. H. Samy Alim, John R. Rickford, and Arnetha F. Ball, 1–30. New York: Oxford University Press.

Alim, H. Samy. 2016b. "Who's Afraid of the Transracial Subject? Raciolinguistics and the Political Project of Transracialization." In *Raciolinguistics: How Language Shapes Our Ideas about Race*, ed. H. Samy Alim, John R. Rickford, and Arnetha F. Ball, 33–50. New York: Oxford University Press.

Alim, H. Samy, John R. Rickford, and Arnetha F. Ball, eds. 2016. *Raciolinguistics: How Language Shapes Our Ideas about Race*. New York: Oxford University Press.

Alvarez, Sara, Suresh Canagarajah, Eunjeong Lee, Jerry Won Lee, and Shakil Rabbi. 2017. "Translingual Practice, Ethnic Identities, and Voice in Writing." In *Crossing Divides: Exploring Translingual Writing Pedagogies and Programs*, ed. Bruce Horner and Laura Tetrault, 31–47. Logan: Utah State University Press.

Def, Mos. 2004. "Close Edge." Track 9 on *The New Danger*. Rawkus and Geffen Records.

Delgado, Richard, and Jean Stefancic. 2012. *Critical Race Theory: An Introduction*. New York: New York University Press.

Fourquet, Laurie. 2015. "Tracing Hip-Hop's Phenomenal Rise." *New York Times*, July 23. https://www.nytimes.com/2015/07/24/arts/international/tracing-hip-hops-phenomenal-rise.html. Accessed April 25, 2022.

Gilyard, Keith. 1991. *Voices of the Self: A Study of Language Competence*. Detroit: Wayne State University Press.

Gilyard, Keith. 2016. "The Rhetoric of Translingualism." *College English* 78 (3): 284–89.

Hernandez, Daniel. 2003. "A Hybrid Tongue or Slanguage?" *Los Angeles Times*, December 27. https://www.latimes.com/archives/la-xpm-2003-dec-27-me-spanglish27-story.html. Accessed April 22, 2022.

Horner, Bruce, Min-Zhan Lu, Jacqueline Jones Royster, and John Trimbur. 2011. "Language Difference in Writing: Toward a Translingual Approach." *College English* 73 (3): 303–21.

Horner, Bruce, and Laura Tetrault, eds. 2017. *Crossing Divides: Exploring Translingual Writing Pedagogies and Programs*. Logan: Utah State University Press.

Inoue, Asao. 2015. *Antiracist Writing Assessment Ecologies: Teaching and Assessing Writing for a Socially Just Future*. Fort Collins, CO, and Anderson, SC: WAC Clearinghouse and Parlor Press.

Inoue, Asao. 2016. "Foreword: On Antiracist Agendas." In *Performing Antiracist Pedagogy in Rhetoric, Writing, and Communication*, ed. Frankie Condon and Vershawn Ashanti Young, xi–xx. Fort Collins, CO, and Anderson, SC: WAC Clearinghouse and Parlor Press. https://wac.colostate.edu/books/antiracist/. Accessed February 26, 2018.

Inoue, Asao. 2017. "Writing Assessment as the Conditions for Translingual Approaches." In *Crossing Divides: Exploring Translingual Writing Pedagogies and Programs*, ed. Bruce Horner and Laura Tetrault, 119–34. Logan: Utah State University Press.

Irvin, L. Lennie. 2010. "What Is 'Academic' Writing?" *Writing Spaces: Readings on Writing* 1: 3–17. https://wac.colostate.edu/docs/books/writingspaces1/irvin–what-is-academic-writing.pdf. Accessed March 1, 2018.

Kral, Michael J., and James Allen. 2016. "Community-Based Participatory Action Research." In *Handbook of Methodological Approaches to Community-Based Research: Qualitative, Quantitative, and Mixed Methods*, ed. Leonard A. Jason and David S. Glenwick, 253–62. New York: Oxford University Press.

Lavelle, Thomas. 2017. "The Ins and Outs of Translingual Work." In *Crossing Divides: Exploring Translingual Writing Pedagogies and Programs*, ed. Bruce Horner and Laura Tetrault, 190–98. Logan: Utah State University Press.

Mitchell, C. J. 1984. "Case Studies." In *Ethnographic Research: A Guide to General Conduct*, ed. Roy F. Ellen, 237–41. London: Academic Press.

Morgan, Marcyliena H. 2014. *Speech Communities*. New York: Cambridge University Press.

Office of Institutional Planning, Research, and Assessment. 2018. *Huston-Tillotson University Fact Book for 2014–2015*. Austin: Huston-Tillotson University.

Richardson, Elaine. 2006. *Hiphop Literacies*. New York: Routledge.

Shakur, Tupac. 1995. "Dear Mama." Track 9 on *Me against the World*. Interscope Records and Jive Records.

Smith, Allen N. 1976. "No One Has a Right to His Own Language." In *Students' Right to Their Own Language: A Critical Sourcebook*, ed. Staci Perryman-Clark, David E. Kirkland, and Austin Jackson, 163–68. Boston: Bedford/St. Martin's.

Smitherman, Geneva. 1997. "'The Chain Remain the Same': Communicative Practices in the Hip Hop Nation." *Journal of Black Studies* 28 (1): 3–25.

Stone, Brian J., and Shawanda Stewart. 2016. "HBCUs and Writing Programs: Critical Hip Hop Language Pedagogy and First-Year Student Success." *Composition Studies* 44 (2): 183–86.

Young, Vershawn Ashanti. 2007. *Your Average Nigga: Performing Race, Literacy, and Masculinity*. Detroit: Wayne State University Press.

Young, Vershawn Ashanti, Rusty Barrett, and Kim Brian Lovejoy. 2014. *Other People's English: Code-Meshing, Code-Switching, and African American Literacy*. New York: Teachers College Press.

Zamudio, Margaret, Christopher Russell, Francisco Rios, and Jacquelyn L. Bridgeman. 2011. *Critical Race Theory Matters: Education and Ideology*. New York: Routledge.

PART III

Responses

Afterword
REWRITING RACING TRANSLINGUALISM
Difference, Labor, Opacity

Bruce Horner

I'll use this afterword to sketch some of the challenges in efforts like this collection's to advance the field of rhetoric and composition's "professed commitment to . . . racial and social justice" (Do and Rowan, introduction, this volume) and to "hold translingual theory and practice accountable" "about the links among language diversity, race, and racism" (Do and Rowan, this volume), drawing on Édouard Glissant's (1990) concept of opacity as counter and alternative to many of the efforts exemplified in this collection to meet those challenges. In doing so, I will simultaneously be arguing for and defending a particular inflection of translingualism and its raciolinguistic politics and against other inflections of translingualism that, from my perspective, conflate translingualism with the discourse of multilingualism complicit with the language ideology of monolingualism.

Among the many challenges facing efforts to race translingualism, I single out two: first, the difficulty of identifying the relationship between race and translingualism, given the morass of conflicting definitions of "translinguality" (see Horner and Alvarez 2019) and, in parallel, what H. Samy Alim (2016, 9) highlights as the ever emergent character of the meaning of "race," as well as the ideological character of both, particularly in their relationship to one another (see also Alim, Rickford, and Ball 2016; Rosa and Flores 2017). Second and conversely, there is the politically and ethically precarious danger Glissant warns against of alleging and demanding the transparency of "absolute truths" about difference versus acknowledging and engaging opacity. As Glissant (1997, 189–90) puts it:

> Difference itself can still contrive to reduce things to the Transparent. If we examine the process of "understanding" people and ideas from the perspective of Western thought, we discover that its basis is this requirement for transparency. In order to understand and thus accept you, I have to measure your solidity with the ideal scale providing me with grounds to make comparisons and, perhaps, judgments. I have to reduce.
>
> Accepting differences does, of course, upset the hierarchy of this scale. I understand your difference, or in other words, without creating a hierarchy, I relate it to my norm. I admit you to existence, within my system. I create you afresh. But perhaps we need to bring an end to the very notion of a scale. Displace all reduction. Agree not merely to the right to difference but, carrying this further, agree also to the right to opacity that is not enclosure within an impenetrable autarchy but subsistence within an irreducible singularity.

Anyone attempting to race translingualism who takes these challenges into account is likely to see their task as a project that entails posing questions about and rethinking dominant presuppositions about both race and translingualism by bringing discourses on either into conversation. To do otherwise would require presupposing fixed notions of both race and translingualism that do not obtain (cf. Shim 2020). However, that amplitude sits well with neither the justifiable sense of urgency surrounding issues of race nor the demand, often accompanying that sense of urgency, for what Glissant (1997) refers to as "transparency"—for what is understandable, graspable—versus what he terms "opacity." Hence the frequent reversion to more understandable—because common—ways of thinking about language, race, and their relations, however limited and limiting those ways of thinking about these issues may be.

We can see the chapters in this collection sometimes vacillating between the pulls of either approach. As several chapter authors complain, there is often a conflation of translingualism with these more familiar ways of thinking about language, race, and their relations. But it is that conflation that has been taken up most enthusiastically in scholarship on translingualism. Thus, whereas the editors, in their introduction, suggest that translingualism has been taken up enthusiastically because of its erasure of race, I would suggest instead that it is this familiar discourse on language, not translingualism per se, that has been taken up; and it has been taken up enthusiastically because of its rehearsal of common tropes of racial and linguistic difference, diversity, inclusivity, rights, and the like, to which the responses of much translingual theory can seem opaque, even deliberately obtuse. As a way of sorting out both the difficulties presented by competing discourses on race and language for those committed to working to race translingualism and alternative strategies by which to take up such work, I'll focus on two terms on which arguments about race, translingualism, and their relations hinge—difference and labor.

DIFFERENCE

The languages used to debate language difference and its relation to race posit quite different forms of that difference. We can see these competing views of difference in the ways several of this collection's chapters take up translingual theory's insistence on difference as "the norm" rather than the exception to a norm of sameness in language. Often this is taken to mean merely that the presence of multiple named languages and language varieties, rather than one, is the common and increasingly undeniable condition that obtains, partly as a consequence of shifts in global migration. The response then advocated is to embrace this difference, defined and coded as diversity, in an effort to be inclusive. But this argument maintains the kind of language difference the language ideology of monolingualism posits even while the attitude toward such difference is changed from one of intolerance to one of tolerance—what Glissant (1997) describes as "accepting differences." This is the argument for multilingualism, multiculturalism, diversity, and inclusion—to allow for and even encourage what monolingualism itself identifies as difference. To that argument, I would say, translingualism has little to add. Translingualism, instead, follows from skepticism about that difference, so defined.

Against such an approach to difference, Glissant (1990, 1997) and those following him pose the right to opacity (*le droit à l'opacité*) (see Bernabé, Chamoiseau, and Confiant 1989, 52; 1990, 113) and against the cloisonné approach to language and culture signaled by *diversité* (diversity) in favor of *diversalité* (a neologism for which currently there is no English language cognate) to acknowledge the fluid and contingent character of any demarcation of a particular language or variety and the inevitability and fact of continual mixing and sharing among such demarcations (1989, 48; cf. Pennycook 2008, 37–38). Otherwise, as David Gramling (2016) has argued, the difference for which tolerance is pleaded is inseparable from an insistence on a reductive notion of friction-free translation among those identified as different—neoliberalism's claim to speak every language and to include, in order to exploit, every market (see Horner and Tetreault 2016, 14–15).

It is that difference that Keith Gilyard (2016, 284) appears to have in mind, in a passage on which many of this collection's chapters rely, when he warns about the need to highlight differences in the distance in language from a language standard and the danger of positing a "linguistic everyperson" composed purely of individuals, in line with warnings issued by others about a "pluri'" turn (see, for example, Flores 2013; Kubota 2016). Gilyard (2016, 285) himself notes that while translingual theorists don't posit this kind of "sameness-of-difference" tenet, it's often "heard" as such. But to add to this, translinguality, at least as I understand it as a language ideology, rejects the very terms of the kinds of arguments to which Gilyard points. Whereas arguments for multilingualism are meant to redress the unequal status accorded specific named languages and language varieties—in Glissant's (1990, 1997) terms, to reject the established "hierarchy" among them—translingualism rejects the ontological status monolingualism assigns all such languages and language varieties. Translingualism as language ideology thus conflicts with the conceptual framework within which arguments like those for as well as against language rights operate, which may be why there is a strong tendency to conflate translingualism instead with multilingualism and arguments for language diversity and inclusion, despite the rare appearance of such terms in documents advancing a translingual perspective.[1]

In that sense, those committed to arguing for language rights are justified in seeing translingual ideology as a threat, as Tom Do argues (chapter 4, this volume), since it calls into question the terms of argument for as well as against language rights—terms that lead those involved to ask which language(s) should be allowed, where, when, and for what purposes. Alternatively, from a translingual perspective, the question to be asked is how language is and might be (re)worked, and why, in every utterance, given the inevitability of its being so reworked. Rather than debating established hierarchies among languages and language varieties, it rejects the ontological status monolingualism claims for any and all languages and varieties: a status that denies their emergent character as the product of the ongoing concrete labor of speakers and writers (Horner and Alvarez 2019). For, *pace* Gilyard's (2016) other expressed concern about the abstraction of languages, translingualism does not deny the existence of languages but the way monolingualism defines the character of their existence.[2] It defines the character of that existence differently, as the always emergent product of human labor. Difference in this sense is not something to be tolerated (or not); it is an unavoidable feature of all utterances—even those that appear merely to repeat what has appeared before—insofar as every utterance differs in spatiotemporal location from every other.

LABOR

To deny the kind of ontological status monolingualism assigns languages and language varieties might well seem to have very little to do with racial justice and to be highly unpromising as a strategy by which to advance such justice, if not a threat to those efforts. Further, insofar as it is mistakenly taken to mean simply that "languages don't exist" in any way, then, at least by analogy, it might well be mistakenly understood to be implying that "races don't exist" and thus to be advancing a suspect "colorblind" racism by which the realities of racism and its effects are denied. Monolingualist ideology makes us all prone to such gross misreadings. For monolingualism grants only one possible form of existence for languages and their varieties as stable, internally uniform, discrete entities that are simply "there" for people to use—well or poorly, appropriately or not, correctly or not—and to "own" as rightfully "theirs" (or not). The alternative to viewing language this way, monolingualism claims, is to believe that languages don't exist at all.

But translingual theory posits not the nonexistence of languages but a different kind of existence for them as always emergent. This is akin to the notion of races as social constructs. To say that races are social constructs is, of course, not to deny their reality; it is instead to assign them a different kind of reality, fully powerful, demonstrable, and demonstrated, with demonstrated demonstrably hideous effects (Alim and Reyes 2011). As Carmen Kynard (2015, 2) has explained, we can "dutifully acknowledge that race is socially constructed and, therefore, a product of social relations and not biological/genetic difference" without then assuming "that race is illusory or peripheral to social organization, past or present, or that our identities are so multiple and complex that race can evaporate as a social category." Moreover, acknowledging language and race as an ever emerging result of social processes is to insist on the contribution of human labor, for good or ill, and the necessity of that contribution to the ongoing project of language (re)production and revision, as well as to the project of race (as Rowan discusses in chapter 1, this volume). Such labor contributes to the production of all utterances, not only utterances that monolingualism disposes us to recognize as different in language (whether deemed artful or deficient). Thus, as several of the chapter authors here remind us, translingualism's concern with labor leads it to insist not on what monolingualism disposes us to recognize as language "play" or "creativity," as in code-meshing or other stylings, but on the difference all utterances make in renewing language—to recognize the production in language reproduction as well as revision.

The recognition of opacity as a precondition of all languaging brings that labor, and thus the historically contingent (and inherently different) character of its effects, to the foreground. By opacity, Glissant (1990, 1997) refers not to deliberate obfuscation but, rather, as Nicole Simek (2015, 369–70) observes, to "an impetus to open-ended interpretation [that] counters the impulses animating both colonialist reductions of the other to transparent, knowable object, and contemporary neoliberal, technocratic applications of transparency." Thus, what the right to opacity entails is a willingness to "enter into the penetrable opacity of a world in which one exists, or agrees to exist, with and among others" (Glissant 1997, 114; see Simek 2015, 369); it impels us to engage while recognizing that "absolute knowledge still remains unavailable" (369). In short, opacity is "inextricable from interpretation" (369). Acknowledging the right to opacity entails acknowledging the necessity and inevitability of labor to communication, not as an index of difference from the norm but as itself the norm of communicative activity: labor that, Simek (372) argues, "is unavoidably political and that must go on, that must be undertaken not in spite of but in light of that fact that absolute transparency is unattainable and undesirable."

Thus, whereas Gilyard (2016, 286), in alignment with monolingualism's demand for transparency, laments not being able to comprehend "people who speak a language foreign to me," a translingual perspective would acknowledge such experiences of incomprehension as, in fact, the norm, including for those situations involving people who are all speaking what is ostensibly the "same" language. It thus restores opacity (and the inevitability of concrete labor to engage with opacity) to its rightful place as part of the norm of all communicative processes (Bernabé, Chamoiseau, and Confiant 1989, 52; 1990, 113). There is, of course, a clear difference in the degrees of difficulty we may experience in our engagements in such communicative efforts (again, as Gilyard's lament illustrates). But monolingualism's claims notwithstanding, it is a difference not in kind but in degree, being neither purely linguistic (if one can imagine any such encounter) nor purely affective or cognitive or political but always all of these and more in intersection.

RACIOLINGUISTIC POLITICS AND OPACITY

I have been arguing that despite their opposition to the insistence on policies such as "English only" and to prejudice against users of specific languages, efforts to advocate for and defend language diversity operate within and thereby reinforce the language ideology of monolingualism.

For they maintain its assumption of a linguistic norm of sameness against which language difference and those exhibiting such difference are set rather than claiming difference in what monolingualism identifies as "the same." While rejecting the hierarchy that explicitly monolingual policies such as "English only" demand, monolingualism's defining terms of language difference are reinforced.

This is not to abandon long-standing efforts to pursue social justice by redressing the asymmetrical power relations among groups demarcated by race, the established dominant hierarchies among the languages and language varieties identified with these groups, and the unjust effects the established hierarchy imposes. Such efforts are aimed at redressing the injustices perpetrated daily by language policies, explicit or tacit, bequeathed to us by the language ideology of monolingualism, whereby racism is expressed through attacks on language as proxy for race.

But as I've been at pains to suggest, those efforts are simultaneously at risk of reinforcing that ideology by working within its terms and conceptual frameworks, thereby leaving them intact. Toni Morrison (1975, 7, original emphases) cautions:

> It's important . . . to know who the real enemy is, and to know the function, the very serious function of racism, which is distraction. *It keeps you from doing your work.* It keeps you explaining over and over again, your reason for being. Somebody says you have no language and so you spend 20 years proving that you do. Somebody says your head isn't shaped properly so you have scientists working on the fact that it is. Somebody says that you have no art so you dredge that up. Somebody says that you have no kingdoms and so you dredge that up.
> *None of that is necessary.*
> There will always be *one more thing* . . .
> For there is a deadly prison: the prison that is erected when one spends one's life fighting phantoms, concentrating on myths, and explaining over and over to the conqueror your language, your lifestyle, your history, your habits.

The strategy of the translingualism I have argued for works differently. Rather than defending the legitimacy of the languaging of minoritized racial groups, it refuses the distraction of the demand for such a defense by rejecting the legitimacy of the very terms that monolingualism and the racism it manifests and contributes to demand. It pursues a strategy of insidious subversion by identifying difference—albeit a different kind of difference—in what is claimed to be the same rather than accepting what monolingualism identifies as either sameness or difference. It does not wear its raciolinguistic politics on its sleeve, as it were, because it rejects the terms monolingualism prescribes for identifying, defining, recognizing, understanding, and carrying out such politics. It thus can be seen as and accused of having no such politics: to be "opaque" in relation to raciolinguistics. But we should be wary of limiting ourselves to strategies that accept and fight on terms that monolingualism itself and its raciolinguistic politics demand as the only possible terms one may use. We need not accede to monolingualism's demand for transparency in response to the opacity on which translingualism insists.

NOTES

1. For example, the word *diversity* appears only twice in what the introduction to this volume describes as the "manifesto" of translingualism (Horner et al. 2011): a reference to human "linguistic diversity" (308) and a reference to the diversity in the corpus of writing identified as exemplifying edited American English (315n4). "Inclusive" appears only in an endnote, in which the authors demur, "Our essay is neither all-inclusive on the issues it does address, nor the final word" (315n1). For a summary of critiques of valorizations of linguistic diversity, see Pennycook (2010, 92–109).
2. In critiquing Louis-Jean Calvet's (1999, 2006) emphasis on language as abstraction, Gilyard (2016) neglects Calvet's insistent concern with "*representations*—what people think about languages and the way they are spoken—representations that act on [language] practices and are one of the factors of change" and hence that "constitute an intervention in and modify the ecolinguistic niche" (Calvet 1999, 241; 2006, 248, original emphasis).

REFERENCES

Alim, H. Samy. 2016. "Introducing Raciolinguistics: Racing Language and Languaging Race in Hyperracial Times." In *Raciolinguistics: How Language Shapes Our Ideas about Race*, ed. H. Samy Alim, John R. Rickford and Arnetha F. Ball, 1–30. New York: Oxford University Press.

Alim, H. Samy, and Angela Reyes. 2011. "Complicating Race: Articulating Race across Multiple Social Dimensions." *Discourse and Society* 22 (4): 379–84.

Alim, H. Samy, John B. Rickford, and Arnetha F. Ball, eds. 2016. *Raciolinguistics: How Language Shapes Our Ideas about Race*. New York: Oxford University Press.

Bernabé, Jean, Patrick Chamoiseau, and Raphaël Confiant. 1989. *Éloge de la créolité*. Paris: Gallimard.

Bernabé, Jean, Patrick Chamoiseau, and Raphaël Confiant. 1990. *Éloge de la créolité / In Praise of Creoleness*, translated by Mohamed Bouya Taleb-Khyar. Baltimore: Johns Hopkins University Press.

Calvet, Louis-Jean. 1999. *Pour une ecologie des langues du monde*. Paris: Plon.

Calvet, Louis-Jean. 2006. *Towards an Ecology of World Languages*, translated by Andrew Brown. London: Polity.

Flores, Nelson. 2013. "The Unexamined Relationship between Neoliberalism and Plurilingualism: A Cautionary Tale." *TESOL Quarterly* 47 (3): 500–520.

Gilyard, Keith. 2016. "The Rhetoric of Translingualism." *College English* 78 (3): 284–89.

Glissant, Édouard. 1990. *Poétique de la Relation*. Paris: Gallimard.

Glissant, Édouard. 1997. *Poetics of Relation*, translated by Betsy Wing. Ann Arbor: University of Michigan Press.

Gramling, David. 2016. *The Invention of Monolingualism.* New York: Bloomsbury.
Horner, Bruce, and Sara P. Alvarez. 2019. "Defining Translinguality." *Literacy in Composition Studies* 7 (2): 1–30.
Horner, Bruce, Min-Zhan Lu, Jacqueline Jones Royster, and John Trimbur. 2011. "Language Difference in Writing: Toward a Translingual Approach." *College English* 73 (3): 303–21.
Horner, Bruce, and Laura Tetreault. 2016. "Translation as (Global) Writing." *Composition Studies* 44 (1): 13–30.
Kubota, Ryuko. 2016. "The Multi/Plural Turn, Postcolonial Theory, and Neoliberal Multiculturalism: Complicities and Implications for Applied Linguistics." *Applied Linguistics* 37 (4): 474–94.
Kynard, Carmen. 2015. "Teaching while Black: Witnessing and Countering Disciplinary Whiteness, Racial Violence, and University Race-Management." *Literacy in Composition Studies* 3 (1): 1–20.
Morrison, Toni. 1975. "A Humanist View." Speech delivered at Portland State University. Transcription from Portland State University's Oregon Public Speakers Collection: "Black Studies Center Public Dialogue: Pt. 2." https://www.mackenzian.com/wp-content/uploads/2014/07/Transcript_PortlandState_TMorrison.pdf. Accessed May 5, 2020.
Pennycook, Alastair. 2008. "English as a Language Always in Translation." *European Journal of English Studies* 12: 33–47.
Pennycook, Alastair. 2010. *Language as a Local Practice.* New York: Routledge.
Rosa, Jonathan, and Nelson Flores. 2017. "Unsettling Race and Language: Toward a Raciolinguistic Perspective." *Language in Society* 46 (5): 621–47.
Shim, Jenna Min. 2020. "Meaningful Ambivalence, Incommensurability, and Vulnerability in an Antiracist Project: Answers to Unasked Questions." *Journal of Teacher Education* 71 (3): 345–56.
Simek, Nicole. 2015. "Stubborn Shadows." *symploke* 23 (1–2): 363–73.

AN AFTERWORD
Some Thoughts

Victor Villanueva

> *Everybody want to go up to heaven but none o' them, none o' them, want to die.*
> —Peter Tosh, "Equal Rights"

I'll get to that epigraph in a moment.

As I read, I learned and thought. I thought I'd address the authors' comments. But why would I do that, since they had—all of them—said it all so well? Then I thought that commenting on each author would be more a review than a response. And maybe it'd be better to respond to the concepts—language, translanguage, racism.

The translingual-as-raciolinguistic (to quote Bethany Davila, chapter 5, this volume) can get pretty webby, all meshed up. Been all meshed up since the colony (in this case, the colony that became the empire) gathered us all together. When we melted (or not fully). The context for the upcoming quote is the introduction to *Language Diversity in the Classroom*, edited by Geneva Smitherman and me in 2003 (and this isn't just self-promotion; there's more to the connection between this collection and my response that I'll get to).

> Victor gets an e-mail question from a graduate student:
> A question from a graduate student:
> Why do you call yourself an "American" academic of color in the title of your book? Why not a Puerto Rican in the US academy? Or an AmeRican academic? Or something a little less . . . "American?"
> Language and racism. Language and nationalism.
> A response:
> This is not an unreasonable question from a Rican. And *Bootstraps* does address this in any number of ways. But I'll answer it this way. I was born in Brooklyn. Raised there with Black kids and Asian kids and one Mexican kid and Boricuas. When I was 16, the family moved to California. I've been in the West (except for two years in Kansas City and trips abroad) ever

since—with Mexican kids, Chicano kids, vato kids, pachuco kids, Indian kids, Asian kids, Black kids, and White kids. And the nonsense that Ricans have to endure in New York is the same nonsense that all the other kids of color endure. And I wanted that understood ("ethno-nation" is Ramón Grosfoguel's language). Or let me do a variation of Tato Laviera:
My tongue is Boricua
My ear is Boricua and Black
My being in this country is Color
even though
My skin is White.
I'm a Puerto Rican and a portorican (the way we used to say it in New York) but with all those crazy mixes of the ghetto. I can never be just simply American, even though Borinquen Arawak Taíno is America. For here, this place where I have lived my life, I am a person of color. And you are too while you're here, but you have a home to go to—Puerto Rico—and in a very real sense, I do not. My parents do—Río Piedras y Caguas. But I don't. I'm a Nuyorican. But to get the point across, an Academic Nuyorican wouldn't have drawn the same number of readers, and my last 53 years have been all of it but White—color, Latino, Nuyorican with a mythic homeland I've visited but have never really known—Puerto Rico.
How's that?
victor. (Smitherman and Villanueva 2003, 1–2)

My very existence is translingual. And I'm hardly alone, as some of the chapters we've just read tell. If anything, I would guess that I'm more typical for an American of color, for the child of immigrants, immigrants from the world's oldest continual colony.

Colony, as Rachel Shapiro and Missy Watson (chapter 2, this volume), Aja Martinez (chapter 3, this volume), Esther Milu (chapter 7, this volume), and others pointed out, is inextricably linked to language and power. For Peruvian sociolinguist Aníbal Quijano (1992) (and others, like Ramón Grosfoguel and Walter D. Mignolo [2007]), the imperial project of Europe necessitated the creation of "races" through what Quijano termed the "coloniality of power." At another point, Quijano (1992) called it "el patron colonial de poder" (the colonial pattern of power). Walter Mignolo (2007) will call it the "colonial matrix of power." For now, what matters is that Quijano wrote that for the Europeans to maintain power, they had to create the races (though there will be others who do so "scientifically"), and as María Lugones (2007) points out, the imperial powers had to maintain the division of genders. And Ana Mariella Bacigalupo (2003) demonstrates in "Mapuche Shamanic Bodies and the Chilean State" the power needed to normalize the genders, to create a clear heteronormativity, even when the Indigenous peoples the Europeans discovered were not so rigid. So the coloniality of power established the superiority of European men. But it was (is) racism that formed (forms) "the darker side" of modernity. Modernity is dependent on racism. And how that coloniality of power takes shape is through hierarchical systems, systems of knowledge, and cultural systems. Here's how Anibal Quijano (2000, 533) puts it: "One of the fundamental axes of this model of power is the social classification of the world's population around the idea of race, a mental construction that expresses the basic experience of colonial domination and pervades the more important dimensions of global power, including its specific rationality: Eurocentrism. The racial axis has a colonial origin and character, but it has proven to be more durable and stable than the colonialism in whose matrix it was established. Therefore, the model of power that is globally hegemonic today presupposes an element of coloniality."

And, like I have written before, this adherence to the colonial remains tied to composition studies (Villanueva 1997) and, until very recently, tied to the history of rhetoric (Villanueva 1999). None of us is immune. So there is no doubt that when we say "structural racism," we're trying to say that racism is larger than any one individual. But here's the thing. We know that hegemony is carried through most often unrecognized consent. We intuitively abide by the power unless its abuse is so abhorrent that we revolt (but we do not enter into true revolutions until there's nothing left to lose; and America is great at avoiding those circumstances through revolution-restoration, a term from Gramsci). And we know that consent is gained and maintained more through the ideological than through coercion, that consent is carried in the rhetoric of the everyday. The metaphor of a structure distances us all from admitting that we are consenting to racism's ongoing existence. Racism is not a structure *out there*; it's an ideology we carry *in here*, a continuing aftermath of European and American imperialism and its matrix of power. Some of the empirical studies in this collection especially point that out.

You see, we're all believers to a great extent. We make rational arguments and provide rational proofs. But if the rational were sufficient, we would have stamped out racism and sexism and heterosexism long ago. Sure, there's the percentage of those who continue to believe firmly in White superiority, but folks who would pick up books like this one would not likely be among them. Yet here I am trying to make a rational argument.

At the heart of the collection edited by Geneva Smitherman and me is a chapter by Elaine Richardson (2003) in which she details the findings of the *CCCC Language Policy Committee Study* conducted in 1997. There were 983 respondents out of 2,970 professionals surveyed, English teachers from grades 9 through college, community college to megaversity. I'm going to cite the summary of the findings. Then I'll explain what I'm getting at.

> Statement 1: A student whose primary language is not English should be taught solely in English.
> *33.2% agreed; 66.8% disagreed*
>
> Statement 2: Students need to master standard English for upward mobility.
> *96.1 agreed; 3.9% disagreed*
>
> Statement 3: In the home, students should be exposed to standard English only.
> *13.2% agreed; 86.8% disagreed*
>
> Statement 4: Students who use nonstandard dialects should be taught in standard English.
> *89.1% agreed; 10.9 disagreed*
>
> Statement 5: There are valid reasons for using nonstandard dialects.
> *80.1% agreed; 19.9% disagreed*
>
> Statement 6: There are valid reasons for using languages other than English.
> *92.6% agreed; 7.4% disagreed*
>
> Statement 7: Students should learn grammar rules to improve their ability to understand and communicate concepts and information.
> *78.4% agreed; 21.6% disagreed. (45–46)*

For now, let's just say that the very principles that come out again in translingualism were agreed upon back then but that the perception that there must be the teaching of "the standard" for the sake of students' power was clear. It's an old argument. It remains the pervasive argument. And the grammar argument remains, despite so much research that has demonstrated that learning grammar is not learning to write more effectively. Yet WPAs continue to be chastised by faculty for not doing something about students' grammar or for students not knowing how to write (with the evidence based on students' writing—an infuriating contradiction).

The problem that the survey respondents tended to agree on clearly remains. The rest of the university, and even our co-workers in departments of English, often hold on to the idea that knowing how to write means following the discourse descended to us through Cicero, as Sharon Crowley (1990) makes clear. And even we believe it—not in what we have to say about students' linguistic rights, not in recognizing the legitimacy of the translingual, but in how we make our arguments. Our own need to be published, the need to keep a job, the need to be taken seriously, the need to be read and considered by others wins the day. That is, we not only believe in the power of rational argument (no matter how it continues to fail us, given ongoing racism, sexism, heterosexism, who maintains real state power despite outrageous irrationality), we also believe in the power of others who will judge and perhaps act on what we write. We are—all of us—subject to the colonial matrix of power. The hierarchy of power is alive and well. It's ingrained and not quite conscious.

Now, I don't say this to argue against translingualism. I don't say this to argue the need for teaching the standard. I say this to argue that change has to begin with us. We need to put ourselves at risk and help change the culture before we put students at greater risk from what already exists, given racism, sexism, heterosexism. It's odd to me that we continue to think of decolonial theory as something that pertains to the Othered alone when all of America was also the colony, all of Spain and the UK. Quijano (1992) argued that all knowledge is no less subject to the colonial, a matter also discussed by Enrique Dussel (1995) (and demonstrated in Villanueva 1999), that knowledge itself has been colonized so that "if knowledge is colonized one of the task [sic] ahead is to decolonize knowledge" (Mignolo 2007, 451). And here is how (well, here's a way to think about it that does bring in translingualism as something we must all do). Quijano writes:

> En primer término, la descolonización epistemológica, para dar paso luego a una nueva comunicación inter-cultural, a un intercambio de experiencias y de significaciones, como la base de otra racionalidad que pueda pretender, con legitimidad, a alguna universalidad. Pues nada menos racional, finalmente, que la pretension de que la específica cosmovisión de una etnia particular sea impuesta como la racionalidad universal, aunque tal etnia se llama Europa occidental. Porque eso, en verdad, es pretender para un provincianismo el título de universalidad. (quoted in Mignolo 2007, 453)

> In the first place, an epistemological decolonization, in order to give way to a new intercultural communication, an exchange of experiences and meanings, as the basis of another rationality that can claim, with legitimacy, to some universality. Well, nothing less rational, finally, than [to] claim that the specific worldview of a particular ethnic group is imposed as a universal rationality, [that] an ethnic group is called Western Europe. Because it is, in fact, a provincialism with the title of universality. (my translation)

In short, nobody gets away, a matter of degree, not kind. And so it is that we—the scholars, researchers, teachers—have to take part in an epistemic de-linking from the colonial matrix of power no less than others and Othered. Rather than ask our students to lead the way—and have them risk their fates in the hands of those who firmly believe in a nearly monolithic written standard (even as infinitives get split and singular nouns get plural pronouns, as prepositions get dangled, as *literally* can be used to mean *figuratively*—examples of changes during my career)—we must. We must be translingual first, de-linking the epistemic hold of our mutual and different colonial pasts.

REFERENCES

Bacigalupo, Ana Mariella. 2003. "Mapuche Shamanic Bodies and the Chilean State: Polemic Gendered Representations and Indigenous Responses." In *Violence and the Body: Race, Gender and the State*, ed. Arturo J. Aldama, 322–42. Bloomington: Indiana University Press.

Crowley, Sharon. 1990. *Methodical Memory: Invention in Current-Traditional Rhetoric*. Carbondale: Southern Illinois University Press.

Dussel, Enrique. 1995. *The Invention of the Americas: Eclipse of "the Other" and the Myth of Modernity*. Translated by Michael D. Barber. New York: Continuum.

Grosfoguel, Ramón. 2007. "The Epistemic Decolonial Turn." *Cultural Studies* 21 (2–3): 211–23.

Lugones, María. 2007. "Heterosexualism and the Colonial/Modern Gender System." *Hypatia* 22 (1): 186–209.

Mignolo, Walter D. 2007. "Delinking: The Rhetoric of Modernity, the Logic of Coloniality and the Grammar of De-Coloniality." *Cultural Studies* 21 (2–3): 449–514.

Quijano, Aníbal. 1992. "Colonialidad y Modernidad/Racionalidad." In *Los Conquistados: 1492 y la Población Indígena de las Américas*, ed. Heraclio Bonilla, 437–48. Bogotá: Tercer Mundo.

Quijano, Aníbal. 2000. "Coloniality of Power, Eurocentrism, and Latin America." *Nepantla: Views from the South* 1 (3): 533–90.

Richardson, Elaine. 2003. "Race, Class(es), Gender, and Age: The Making of Knowledge about Language Diversity." In *Language Diversity in the Classroom: From Intention to Practice*, ed. Geneva Smitherman and Victor Villanueva, 40–66. Carbondale: Southern Illinois University Press.

Smitherman, Geneva, and Victor Villanueva. 2003. "Introduction." In *Language Diversity in the Classroom: From Intention to Practice*, ed. Geneva Smitherman and Victor Villanueva, 1–6. Carbondale: Southern Illinois University Press.

Tosh, Peter. 1977. "Equal Rights." Track 5 on *Equal Rights*. Columbia Records.

Villanueva, Victor, Jr. 1997. "Maybe a Colony: And Still Another Critique of the Comp Community." *JAC* 17 (2): 183–90.

Villanueva, Victor, Jr. 1999. "On the Rhetoric and Precedents of Racism." *College Composition and Communication* 50 (5): 645–61.

INDEX

abstract liberalism, 21, 179
accents: accentless-ness, 160–63; discrimination against, 77; patterns of reading, 91–93; removing, 46; term, 76–77
Africa, 136, 237; African reserves, 123; European Scramble for, 123; indigenizing education system in, 132; racialization practices in, 128–37; and researcher positionality, 128–29; triple linguistic heritage, 129
African American English (AAE), 91, 93–95, 170–72, 175–76, 191, 193n4
Albracht, Lindsey, 99
Alexander v. Holmes, 202
Alim, H. Samy, 130, 139, 147, 230, 232
Allen, James, 237
Alvarez, Sara P., 49
Alvarez, Steven, 144
American Indians, 48
American Racial and Ethnic Experience. *See* first-year writing (FYW)
Americanness, 93
Anson, Chris M., 171
anti-racism, term, 20
anti-racist translingualism, 29–34
Anzaldúa, Gloria, 58, 60, 128
Arbery, Ahmaud, 3
assimilado, 131
Atkinson, Dwight, 27

Baker-Bell, April, 3, 219
Ball, Arnetha F., 170, 227
Banaji, Mahzarin R., 91
Barret, Rusty, 234
Bilge, Sirma, 29
Bismarck, Otto von, 123
Bizzell, Patricia, 199
Black and Puerto Rican Student Community (BPRSC), 105, 110–11; community partnership, 111–14; interrogating epistemic violence, 114–17; representation, 110–14
Black Dialect, 37
Black English, 3–4, 37, 47–48, 130, 228
Blacks: defining colorblind translingualism, 45–46; normative Black identity, 130–31; redefining collective subjectivity, 22–23; rhetorical education of, 19–20; University of Louisiana case study, 204–7
"Blind: Talking about the New Racism," 46
Bonilla-Silva, Eduardo, 18, 21–23, 28–29, 36, 41–43
Bootstraps (Villaneuva), 47
border thinking, framework, 57
borrowed eyes, 81
Bou Ayash, Nancy, 143, 145
Bourdieu, Pierre, 150
Brewer, Jan, 62
British, raciolinguistic experience, 129–31
Brodkey, Linda, 116
Browne, Kevin, 48
Brown II, 201
Brown v. Board of Education, 201
Buying into English (Prendergast), 46–47

Canagarajah, A. Suresh, 18, 27, 145, 200, 216–18
Capps, Lisa, 185
Carbado, Devon W., 30
Castillo, Ana, 61, 63
Chicanx language/identity, narrative, 56–57; affirming language, 60–62; dilemma, 58–60; literature courses, 62–66
Chrisx, La, 64–65
Citizenship Schools, 19
City University of New York (CUNY), 105, 199; community partnership at, 111–14; Newton Hall Statement, 118–19; representation at, 110–14; revisiting five demands, 110–11; translanguagers in, 106–7
Civil Rights Act, 201
Civil Rights movement, 21, 23
Civil Rights Project, UCLA, 203
Clarence-Smith, W. G., 131
Clary-Lemon, Jennifer, 148
colonization, 123–25. *See also* decolonial translingual pedagogy
colorblind racism. *See* colorblindness, translingualism
colorblindness, translingualism: averting, 35–55; contesting monolingualism,

262 INDEX

36–41; defining, 41–47; and rearticulation, 21–29; toward race-conscious translingualism, 50–55
communities of practice: and heritage language learning, 72–74; imagined communities, 79–85; marginalization, 75–79; non-participation, 75–79
community partnership, 111–14
composition: adopting translingual approach in studying, 125–27; contact zones, 198–200; language diversity in, 5–6; translingualism as racial project, 18–21; Whiteness in, 169–71
Conference on College Composition and Communication (CCCC), 4, 198
contact zones, 196–97; locating translingualism in, 198–200; segregated spaces in US literary education, 201–4; toward segregated-space translingual pedagogy, 207–12; University of Louisiana case study, 204–7
conventional multilingualism, 24–25
cooperative disposition, 145, 160
Corder, Jim W., 169
co-stories, 143–44; coding scheme, 155; locating, 153–56; major concepts, 144–52; study overview, 152–53; "Your English is Your English," 163–68
counter-narratives. *See* lived experience
Creole, 237–38
Critical Hip Hop Rhetoric Pedagogy, 226, 229–31, 233–35
critical race theory (CRT), 144, 149, 150, 226, 231–33
critical translingual approach, 214–15
critical transliteracies ecologies, 105–109; community partnership, 111–14; interrogating epistemic violence, 114–17; revisiting CUNY five demands, 110–11; student autonomy, 117–19; toward racialization-conscious translingualism, 119–22
cultural racism, 22, 178
cultural rhetorics, 56, 220
culturally based arguments, 178
Cushman, Ellen, 52

Davila, Bethany, 44
debt peonage, 46
decolonial translingual pedagogy, 123–25, 137–42; adopting translingual approach, 125–27; British raciolingusitic experience, 129–31; institutional/pedagogical context, 127–28; Portuguese raciolingusitic experience, 131–34; researcher positionality, 128–29; teaching language, 139–42

Decree number 77, 131
DeLoach, Khadija, 110
de los Ríos, Cati V., 57, 214
Delpit, Lisa, 44
Devos, Thierry, 91
discrimination, linguistic, 17, 42–43, 70, 80–81, 110, 228, 238
Do, Hein, 78
Do, Tom, 144
Dowell v. Oklahoma City, 202

English as a Second Language (ESL), 59, 107
English language learner (ELL), 106–107
English+, 218
epistemological racism, 149–50
ethnography, 222–25
experiential co-stories, 155

first-year writing (FYW), 127–28
Fish, Stanley, 148–49
Flores, Nelson, 39, 57, 96, 108, 213
Floyd, George, 3
Foucault, Michel, 150
Fourquet, Laurie, 233
French, raciolinguistic experience, 134–37

Gao, Xuesong, 218
genocide ideology. *See* raciolinguistics: French
Gidden, Anthony, 150
Gilyard, Keith, 7, 17, 27, 35, 47, 56, 67, 87, 126, 144, 145, 170, 199, 219, 227
Giroux, Henry A., 146
Glissant, Édouard, 245–47, 250
global contact zones, 200. *See also* contact zones
glossodiversity, 25
grading, perceived linguistic difference and, 93–94
Gramsci, Antonio, 21, 256
Grayson, Mara Lee, 147
Green v. New Kent County, 202
Greenfield, Laura, 35, 43
Grutter v. Bollinger, 204
Guerra, Juan C., 116, 126

Haque, Eve, 145–46
Harris, Joseph, 200
Harvard Civil Rights Project, 201, 202, 203
heritage language learning, 72–74
heritage language speakers, 67, 68, 82, 84; constraining, 69; de-legitimatizing, 76–77; embodied experiences of, 74; and imperialism, 125; material conse-

quences, 69; participation of, 72–74; Vietnamese, 10, 32, 70
Hernandez, Daniel, 233
Hing, Bill Ong, 92–93, 95
Hip-Hop. *See* Critical Hip Hop Rhetoric Pedagogy
Hispanic Serving Institutions (HSIs), 90
Historically Black University (HBU), 229–31
Horne, Tom, 62
Horner, Bruce, 6, 20, 68, 86, 105, 125, 148, 198
House Bill 2281, 62–63
Huston-Tillotson University (HT), 229–31

Ibrahim, Awad K., 130
identity: Chicanx, 60, 63; ethnic, 10, 32, 60, 68–69, 73–75, 79, 80, 83–84; linguistic, 50, 60, 137, 239, 241; national, 40, 91, 93; perceived, 89–91; Vietnamese, 70, 76–78, 81–82
imagined communities, 79–85
imperialism, English as past/present, 56–57. *See also* Chicanx language/identity, narrative
Inoue, Asao, 8, 35, 109, 228, 231–33
instructors: composition, 12, 44, 174, 197, 207, 209–10, 236; and narrative study, 169–95; surveying, 88–90; White, 175–76; writing, 94, 125–29, 169–70, 196
Inter-Territorial Language Committee, 130
intersectionality, 29–30, 33, 45–46, 50, 56, 144, 152–53, 165, 220
introspective co-stories, 155
Irvin, L. Lennie, 233

Jackson, Davena, 3
jail community language, 236
Jain, Rashi, 143
Janopolous, Michael, 94
Jeantel, Rachel, 48
Jefferson Community and Technical College (JCC), 205
Jefferson County Public Schools (JCPS), 205
Jefferson County, Kentucky, 204–7
Jenks, Christopher, 87, 145, 197
Johnson, Lamar, 3
Johnson, Latrise, 222

Kells, Michelle Hall, 68, 116
Kenyan Hip-Hop, 27
Kibria, Nazli, 81
Kigamwa, James, 124
King, Martin Luther, Jr., 41, 110
Kinloch, Valerie, 222

Kral, Michael J., 237
Kubota, Ryuko, 147
Kynard, Carmen, 3, 48, 105

labor, 249–50
Lamos, Steve, 105
language difference, 23–24, 247–48
"Language Difference in Writing: Toward a Translingual Approach," 6, 20, 67
language ideology, standard. *See* standard language ideology
Lardner, Ted, 172
Lave, Jean, 71, 73
Lavelle, Thomas, 231
leaning in, 174
Lee, Jerry Won, 87, 107, 145
legitimate peripheral participation, 71
Leonard, Rebecca Lorimer, 107, 145
Lin, Angel, 147
Lindquist, Julie, 128
linguistic everyperson, 8, 17, 67
linguistic innocence, 48
linguistic diversity, 8, 12, 28, 100, 125, 170; equating with fascism, 220–21; factoring into assessment, 191; inspiring interest in, 189, 193; and resisting race evasiveness, 98; and SLO, 99
linguistic profile essay, 235–42
linguistic tourism, 107–8
linguistic culture, 139
Lippi-Green, Rosina, 39–40, 43, 75, 162
literature courses, Chicanx, 62–66
lived experience, 144–46. *See also* co-stories
Lovejoy, Kim Brian, 170
Lu, Min-Zhan, 6, 48–49, 86, 105, 148, 198, 199–200
Luanda, 132
Lyons, Scott, 48–49, 68, 79, 126

marginality, 71–72
Martinez, Aja, 48, 93, 125
Matsuda, Paul Kei, 7, 87, 95, 107, 126, 145
Matsumomo, Yumi, 200
Mazrui, Ali, 129
McDade, Tony, 3
McMurty, Teaira, 3
mestiza consciousness, 64–66. *See also* Chicanx language/identity, narrative
metaphor, 98–102
metonymy, 98–102
microaggressions, challenging, 95–98; de-centering White monolingualism, 98–102; grading students, 93–95; perpetual foreignness, 91–93; surveying instructors, 88–90

Mills, Charles, 115
minimization, 22
Mlynarczyk, Rebecca Williams, 105
monolingual ideology, 24, 132, 170, 196, 198–99, 206–10
monolingualism: challenge to, 6–9; contesting all facets of, 36–42; de-centering White monolingualism, 98–102
Morgan, Brian, 145–46
Morgan, Marcyliena H., 234
Mos Def, 233
Mosher, Stephanie, 100
Motha, Suthanthie, 143, 147
Muhammad, Rashida Jaami', 170
multilingual language learners (MLL), 11; co-stories and, 151–52
multilingualism, 94–95, 138, 213–16, 245, 248; code meshing, 31; conventional, 24–25; engaging with, 27–28; perceived, 90–92; practice, 27–28, 123; reality, 145, 151, 165; speakers, 28, 38; students, 26, 107, 150, 164–65, 217, 232; writers, 27–28, 32, 144, 150–51, 156, 165

narratives, 169–71; analytical framework, 172–73; findings, 173–76; fitting new story into prior understanding, 176–86; learning about/exploring translingualism, 186–95; methodology, 171–72; study design, 171–72
narratives, importance of, 56–57. *See also* Chicanx language/identity, narrative
national languages, 132
naturalization, 22, 179
Ndemanu, Michael, 124
neighborhood schools, 202–203
Nelson, Cynthia D., 146
neo-liberalism, 30
new racism, 36; defining colorblind translingualism in, 41–47
non-participation, 71–72
norm, language difference as, 24–29
Norton, Bonny, 82

Oakland Ebonics, controversy, 176–78
Omi, Michael, 18, 21, 148
opacity, 245–47, 250, 252
Otsuji, Emi, 217
Otte, George, 105

participatory governance, 117–19. *See also* autonomy, students
Participatory Grounded Theory, 172
participatory research, 226–27; Critical Hip Hop Rhetoric Pedagogy, 229–31, 233–35; critical race theory, 231–33; language/race in composition studies, 227–29; linguistic profile essay, 235–42
participatory action research (PAR), 226
Passeron, Jean-Claude, 150
pedagogical co-stories, 155
Pennycook, Alastair, 217
People of Color, 40–41
peripheral participation, 71–72
peripherality, 71–72
Plessy v. Ferguson, 201
Portuguese, raciolinguistic experience in, 131–34
Pratt, Mary Louise, 196, 199–200
Prendergast, Catherine, 46
Prior, Matthew, 146
prison language, 238–40
"Professing Multiculturalism: The Politics of Style in the Contact Zone," 200

race: avoiding role of, 40–41; centering, 13, 68, 83, 98–100; in composition studies, 227–29; naming as signifier, 43; race-conscious translingualism, 10–13, 29–33, 50–52; term, 20
race consciousness, 29–34, 50–55
racial segregation. *See* University of Louisiana, case study
racialization, 147–48
racialization-conscious translingualism, 119–22
raciolinguistics: British, 129–31; French, 134–37; politics/opacity, 250–53; Portuguese, 131–34; translingual literacies, 140, 213–25
racism without racists, 21
racism: colorblind racism, 9–10, 17–18, 20–30, 36, 41–44, 48; cultural, 22, 178; as discourse, 149; on individual level, 149; institutionalized, 21, 34, 134, 137, 238; internalized, 134, 137; linguistic, 3, 12, 32, 219; new racism, 10, 36, 41–47; structural, 40–41, 99, 119, 149, 208, 210, 256; systemic, 3–4, 37, 44–45, 52, 204, 238; term, 20; White racism, 3
rearticulation, translingualism, 17–18; antiracist translingualism, 29–34; averting colorblindness, 35–55; colorblind racism, 21–29; contesting monolingualism, 36–41; possibilities for, 28–29; translingualism as racial project, 18–21; understanding difference as norm, 24–29
representation, 111–14
researchers, positionality of, 128–29
reverse racism, 21
"Rhetoric of Translingualism, The," 56–57, 199

rhetorical attunements, 107
Richardson, Elaine, 44
Rickford, John R., 228
Ríos, Cati V. de los. *See* de los Ríos, Cati V.
Roman Catholic Church, 131
Rosa, Jonathan, 39, 57, 96, 108, 213
Rowan, Karen, 41
Royster, Jacqueline Jones, 6, 86, 198
Rubin, Donald L., 94, 108
Rwanda, 134–37

sameness-of-difference model, 57, 75, 107, 229, 241; rethinking, 137–38
Schiffman, Harold F., 139
scholarship, translingual, 4, 7–8, 17, 30–33, 41, 45–48, 138, 143–51, 164–65, 218–19
Search for Education, Elevation, and Knowledge (SEEK), 105, 110–11
second generation, 70, 83, 110
second language writing, 5
segregation. *See* contact zones
Seltzer, Kate, 57, 139–40, 214
Shapiro, Rachael, 24
Smith, Allen N., 231
Smitherman, Geneva, 5, 37, 128, 139, 227
social practices, embodying culture/identities in, 67–70; heritage language learning, 72–74; imagined communities, 79–85; marginalization, 75–79; non-participation, 75–79; peripheral participation, 71–72; qualitative study, 70–71
Sohan, Vanessa Kraemer, 25
Solorzano, Daniel, 136
speech community, 233–36, 240
standard language ideology, contesting, 47–59
Standard American English (SAE), 5, 40, 59–60, 228
Standard English (SE), 3, 23, 31, 67, 169; challenging myth of, 97–98; defining, 96; new racism colluding with, 44–45
standard language ideology, 9, 27, 36, 39, 43–45, 69, 74–75, 179, 208, 221, 245, 247–48; contesting, 47–50; as deeply flawed theory, 231; and linguistic profile essay, 235; toward race-conscious translingualism, 50–52
standardized edited American English (SEAE), 86–87
stereotype lift, 95–98
strategic racialization, 160
student learning outcome (SLO), 99
Students for a Democratic Society (SDS), 105
"Students' Right to Their Own Language" (SRTOL), 5, 19, 198–99

Sue, Derald Wing, 93
Swann v. Charlotte-Mecklenburg, 202
Swords, Rachel, 5
synecdoche, 98–102

Tan, Amy, 128
Tashima, Wallace, 63
Taylor, Breonna, 3
teaching English to speakers of other languages (TESOL), 107
Tecle, Tsegga, 143
Tetrault, Laura, 27
Thiong'o, Ngũgĩ wa. *See* wa Thiong'o, Ngũgĩ
traditional multilingual model, 138
transcultural citizens, fostering, 116–17
translanguaging, 106
translingual dispositions, 107
translingual everyperson, 27
translingual literacies, raciolinguistics of, 213–16; classroom praxis, 222–25; racialized translingual literacies, 216–20; viral video analysis, 220–22
translingual text, defining, 26
translingual theory, 6–9
translingualism, racing, 3–14, 254–59; challenging Whiteness, 86–102; co-stories, 143–68; communities of practice, 67–85; contact zones, 196–212; critical transliteracies ecologies, 105–22; decolonial translingual pedagogy, 123–42; defining race-conscious translingualism, 226–27; English as past/present imperialism, 56–66; exposing microaggressions, 86–102; narratives, 169–95; participatory research, 226–42; rearticulation, 17–34; rewriting, 245–53; translingual literacies, 213–25
transliteracy, 108
Treaty of Guadalupe-Hidalgo, 58
Trimbur, John, 6, 68, 86, 105, 174, 198
Tuan, Mia, 83
Tupac, 233
two-way learning, 116

unfair inheritance, 109
United States, 65n1, 91, 117, 152; British spelling conventions in, 96; college-age gap in, 112; literary education in, 201–4; poverty in, 209; school segregation in, 201–204; sociopolitical upheavals in, 3
University of Louisiana (U of L), case study, 204–207
US Census, 88–90
US Supreme Court, 201
US-Mexico borderlands, 27, 58

Vietnamese Americans. *See* social practices, embodying culture/identities in
Villanueva, Victor, 35, 43, 46–47, 98, 147
violence, epistemic, 114–17
Voices of the Self (Gilyard), 47

wa Thiong'o, Ngũgĩ, 129–30
Wenger, Etienne, 71–73
Wheeler, Rebecca S., 5
White English, 26, 37, 44, 51, 53n3
white ignorance, 115
Whiteness, 28, 219; challenging, 86–87; in composition, 169–71; de-centering White monolingualism, 98–102; grading students, 93–95; and narrative study, 169–95; perpetual foreignness, 91–93; stereotype lift, 95–98; surveying instructors, 88–90
Williams-Farrier, Bonnie J., 3
Williams-James, Melanie, 94

Williams, Cen, 106
Winant, Howard, 18, 21, 148
Winn, Maisha T., 222
writing classrooms: as linguistic contact spaces, 196–212; race in, 147–48; racism in, 148–51
writing program administrator listserv (WPA-L), 4
writing program administrators (WPAs), 89

Yang, K. Wayne, 117
Yosso, Tara, 146
You, Xiaoye, 107
Young, Morris, 147
Young, Vershawn Ashanti, 3, 47, 147, 172, 228

Zamudio, Margaret, 231
Zepeda, Ofelia, 128

ABOUT THE CONTRIBUTORS

Lindsey Albracht (she/her/hers) works as a lecturer teaching undergraduate classes on writing at Queens College, CUNY. She also serves as one of several rotating administrators in the Queens College First-Year Writing Program. Lindsey recently earned a PhD from the Graduate Center at CUNY. For over a decade, Lindsey has worked as an instructor, a facilitator of interdisciplinary faculty education, and an administrator both within higher education and within the English Language Teaching (ELT) industry. Her recent work appears in *Journal of American Studies in Italy*, *Axis*, and *Visible Pedagogy*. She is inspired by CUNY student activists, past and present.

Steven Alvarez is associate professor of English at St. John's University. He is the author of *Brokering Tareas: Mexican Immigrant Families Translanguaging Homework Literacies* and *Community Literacies en Confianza: Learning from Bilingual After-School Programs*.

Bethany Davila is associate professor of rhetoric and writing at the University of New Mexico. Her research focuses on language and identity, particularly in relation to raciolinguistics, Whiteness, written standardness, and perceptions of student identities. She also publishes in the field of writing program administration, including a recent co-edited book on workplace bullying, *Defining, Locating, and Addressing Bullying in the WPA Workplace* (2019, Utah State University Press). Beth's teaching mirrors her research interests as she works to pursue social justice through linguistic equality in higher education.

Tom Do is a visiting associate professor in the Department of Public and Applied Humanities at the University of Arizona. His teaching and research explore the intersections of race, language, and heritage language speakers.

Jaclyn Hilberg is assistant professor of English at Albright College in Reading, Pennsylvania, where she teaches first-year writing and upper-level professional writing courses. Her work has previously appeared in *College English* and the edited collection *Making Future Matters*. Before joining Albright, she taught English and integrated reading and writing at Collin County Community College in Frisco, Texas. She holds a PhD in rhetoric and composition from the University of Louisville.

Bruce Horner teaches composition, composition theory and pedagogy, and literacy studies at the University of Louisville. His recent books include *Rewriting Composition: Terms of Exchange* and the co-edited collections *Teaching and Studying Translingual Composition*, co-edited with Christiane Donahue; *Economies of Writing: Revaluations in Rhetoric and Composition*, co-edited with Brice Nordquist and Susan Ryan; *Toward a Transnational University: WAC/WID across Borders of Language, Nation, and Discipline*, co-edited with Jonathan Hall; *Mobility Work in Composition*, coedited with Megan Favers Hartline, Ashanka Kumari, and Laura Sceniak Matravers; and *Crossing Divides: Exploring Translingual Writing Pedagogies and Programs*, coedited with Laura Tetreault and winner of the 2018 Modern Language Association Mina P. Shaughnessy Prize.

CONTRIBUTORS

Aja Martinez is assistant professor of English at the University of North Texas. Her scholarship, published nationally and internationally, makes a compelling case for counterstory as methodology through the well-established framework of critical race theory (CRT). Her book *Counterstory: The Rhetoric and Writing of Critical Race Theory* was named one of the 20 Best New Rhetoric Books to Read in 2021 by BookAuthority and is the recipient of the inaugural 2021 Coalition for Community Writing Vision Book Award. Her writing has appeared in *College English, Composition Studies, Peitho,* and *Rhetoric Review.*

Esther Milu is assistant professor at the University of Central Florida. Her scholarship centers on multilingual pedagogies, translingual writing, immigrant and transnational literacies, and decolonial rhetorics. Previous work has appeared in *Research in the Teaching of English, College English, Composition Studies, College Composition and Communication,* and several edited collections.

Stephanie Mosher earned her PhD in English, composition, and rhetoric from the University of South Carolina in 2017. Her work has appeared in *Pedagogy* and the *Journal of Popular Culture*, and in a former life she made a few dollars as a book and film reviewer for the *Buffalo News*. She currently teaches business writing at the University of South Carolina and works as a freelance editor and researcher. A proud native of West Virginia, she now lives in Irmo, South Carolina, with her husband, Daniel, a civil engineer, and their three demanding feline companions. She enjoys running and attempting to garden.

Yasmine Romero is associate professor of English at the University of Hawai'i, West O'ahu. Her research and teaching foreground students' lived experiences by not only bringing diversified identities and identification practices into the classroom as pedagogical resources but also by complicating and nuancing the meaning of diversity through an intersectional lens. Her work has been published in *Across the Disciplines* and *Critical Inquiry in Language Studies*. She teaches courses in applied linguistics, rhetoric and composition, gender and sexuality studies, critical race theory, and critical pedagogy. She is working on her book *Moving across Whirlpools*, which brings intersectionality into conversation with writing and language studies.

Karen Rowan is professor of English at California State University–San Bernardino. Her teaching and research attend to the intersections of writing and literacy, pedagogy, antiracism, and language. She is coeditor of *Writing Centers and the New Racism*, winner of the 2012 IWCA Outstanding Book Award.

Rachael Shapiro is associate professor of writing arts at Rowan University, where she is currently serving as the Provost's Fellow for Diversity, Equity, and Inclusion. She has taught developmental, freshman, critical research, professional, and digital writing and literacy studies classes both online and face-to-face, in addition to working for years in writing centers. She has focused her research, teaching, and service on social justice, linguistic diversity, and antiracist and decolonial pedagogy for fifteen years in areas like digital literacies, language politics, feminism, and globalization. Her work has appeared in journals like *College English, Composition Forum,* and *Literacy in Composition Studies.*

Shawanda Stewart is associate professor of English at Huston-Tillotson University. Her primary research interests include African American rhetoric, language ideology and culture, and first-year composition pedagogy.

Brian Stone is associate professor of English and director of Writing Programs at Indiana State University. He has published on critical writing pedagogies, the intersections of culture and rhetoric, and the history of vernacular and non-Western rhetorical tradition.

Victor Villanueva is Regents Professor Emeritus, a former director of comp, director of a university-wide writing program, director of an American studies program, English department chair (twice), editor of the Studies in Writing and Rhetoric monograph series of the Conference on College Composition and Communication, former head of that organization, and its Exemplar, Rhetorician of the Year, among other honors—especially the honor of having worked with so many undergraduate and graduate students. His work has always been concerned with the rhetorics of racism.

Missy Watson is associate professor of composition and rhetoric at City College of New York, CUNY. She serves as the director of the First-Year Writing Program and teaches undergraduate and graduate courses in composition, pedagogy, language, and literacy. Her research lies at the intersection of composition and second-language writing and revolves around seeking social and racial justice. Her recent publications can be found in the *Journal of Basic Writing, Basic Writing e-Journal, Composition Forum, Composition Studies,* the *Journal of Second Language Writing,* and *Pedagogy.*

www.ingramcontent.com/pod-product-compliance
Lightning Source LLC
Chambersburg PA
CBHW020521080526
44583CB00013B/682